BUSINESS COMPUTER APPLICATIONS FOR REINFORCEMENT

Wynema Anderson

Stacey Golightly
Ada High School
Ada, Oklahoma

Reviewers:

Blanca Andrade
Del Valle High School
El Paso, Texas

Karen Short
Taft High School
San Antonio, Texas

JOIN US ON THE INTERNET
WWW: http://www.thomson.com
EMAIL: findit@kiosk.thomson.com   A service of $I(T)P$®

South-Western Educational Publishing

an International Thomson Publishing company $I(T)P$®

Cincinnati • Albany, NY • Belmont, CA • Bonn • Boston • Detroit • Johannesburg • London • Madrid
Melbourne • Mexico City • New York • Paris • Singapore • Tokyo • Toronto • Washington

Managing Editor:	Janie F. Schwark
Project Manager:	Dave Lafferty
Marketing Manager:	John Wills
Production Services:	Shepherd, Inc.
Production Editor:	Rick Hecker

Copyright © 1998
by SOUTH-WESTERN EDUCATIONAL PUBLISHING/ITP
Cincinnati, Ohio

Microsoft and Windows are registered trademarks of Microsoft Corporation.

ISBN: 0-538-71737-8

4 5 6 7 8 9 H 01 00 99

Library of Congress Cataloging-in-Publication Data

Anderson, Wynema.
Business computer applications for reinforcement / Wynema Anderson & Stacey Golightly.
p. cm.
ISBN 0-538-71739-4
1. Office practice--Automation. 2. Word processing. 3. Database management. 4. Electronic spreadsheets. 5. Business presentation--Graphic methods. 6. Business--Computer simulation. I. Golightly, Stacey. II. Title.
HF5548.A5767 1997
651.8--dc21   96-37656
                                               CIP

Printed in the United States of America

I(T)P
International Thomson Publishing

South-Western Educational Publishing is a division of International Thomson Publishing, Inc. The ITP trademark is used under license.

PREFACE

Business Computer Applications for Reinforcement provides application practice for the following types of activities:

- word processing and desktop publishing
- spreadsheet
- database
- presentation graphics
- integrated activities
- simulation

It fills the need for adequate application exercises combined with easy-to-read text, all within one manual. The application material in each unit progresses from simple to complex uses and reinforces computer concepts and formatting skills. The textbook is generic and may be used with any software or computer capable of completing the types of activities listed above. Software-specific instructions are available for most popular software packages from South-Western Publishing Company. The textbook can also be used in conjunction with the manufacturer's training manual for the specific software used.

Business Computer Applications for Reinforcement is divided into six units: word processing and desktop publishing, spreadsheet, database, presentation graphics, integrated activities, and simulation. Each unit has some integrated exercises. All jobs in the textbook have instructions for completing the job, and most jobs include a document to create or revise. The 360 exercises in these six units are business/occupational oriented. The simulation at the end of the textbook contains 20 exercises that incorporate all applications. These exercises have limited job instructions and are designed for common personal applications.

Each unit has one or more reinforcement jobs to provide additional practice. Reinforcement jobs often combine practice for two or more software features in one job. These jobs can be used in combination with software reviews to reteach students who need more practice on a particular feature, or alone as enrichment or supplemental activities for students who need more challenging applications.

Business Computer Applications for Reinforcement may be used for group instruction or for self-paced, individualized instruction. The completion time for the textbook will vary depending upon the student's ability and previous computer experience. Completion time will also vary if the instructor chooses to have students print only selected jobs. Each chapter includes estimated completion times. An average completion time for the entire textbook is 150 classroom hours. The instructor should add additional time for specific job instructions, administration tests, and for classroom discussions.

Teacher's Material

A teacher's manual is available for use with *Business Computer Applications for Reinforcement*. This manual includes an overview of the textbook, teaching suggestions, student learning objectives, suggested grading procedures, over 50 application tests, test solutions, and job solutions.

A solutions disk is available for the instructor's use. It can be used to provide copies of files to students who have not completed prior jobs that must be retrieved to complete another job. Also, it can be used to replace any files lost or unusable on the student's data disk.

CONTENTS

Chapter 15   Create Presentations Using Automatic Slide Layouts   384

Chapter 16   Presentation Options   412

UNIT 5   INTEGRATED ACTIVITIES

UNIT 6   SIMULATION

Reference Guide   501

WORD PROCESSING AND DESKTOP PUBLISHING

ABBR	JOB 10	FAX2	JOB 87
ADDRESS	JOB 80	FITNESS	JOB 48
ANNOUN	JOB 15	FLEMING	JOB 68
BADGES	JOB 84	FLOWER	JOB 94
BOARD	JOB 73	FLOWER2	JOB 95
BOBBY	JOB 55	FORM	JOB 18
BUSINESS	JOB 28	FORM1	JOB 70
CHANDLER	JOB 92	FORM2	JOB 71
CHECK	JOB 1	FORM3	JOB 72
CHECK2	JOB 6	FORM4	JOB 73
CHOATE	JOB 83	FORM5	JOB 74
CITIES	JOB 49	FORM6	JOB 75
CLUB	JOB 25	GROUP	JOB 78
CLUES	JOB 17	HEADERS	JOB 31
CLUES2	JOB 39	HEALTH	JOB 34
COLUMN	JOB 43	HIGHER	JOB 89
COLUMN2	JOB 45	HISTEP	JOB 20
CONTENTS	JOB 11	HOME	JOB 54
COPY	JOB 30	HUNTER	JOB 96
CORNELL	JOB 61	INTERV	JOB 5
CORNELL2	JOB 63	ITIN	JOB 13
CRUISE	JOB 50	ITIN2	JOB 22
CRUISE2	JOB 51	JONES	JOB 26
CRUISE3	JOB 52	LABEL	JOB 69
DATA1	JOB 70	LABEL1	JOB 74
DATA2	JOB 71	LEASE	JOB 35
DATA3	JOB 72	LEASE2	JOB 37
DATA4	JOB 73	LETHEAD	JOB 101
DOC1	JOB 76	LISTEN	JOB 44
DOC2	JOB 76	LISTEN2	JOB 46
DOC3	JOB 76	MEETING	JOB 85
DOC4	JOB 76	MINOR	JOB 8
DOC5	JOB 76	MINOR2	JOB 24
DOC6	JOB 76	MONTHLY	JOB 58
ECU1	JOB 77	MOVIE	JOB 65
ECU2	JOB 77	NEW	JOB 97
ENDORSE	JOB 12	NOTE	JOB 61
ENDORSE2	JOB 14	OFFICE	JOB 87
ENVEL1	JOB 75	OPERATE	JOB 56
ERASE	JOB 87	ORDER	JOB 86
ETHICS	JOB 41	OUTLINE	JOB 29
EUROPE	JOB 79	OVERDUE	JOB 71
EUROPE2	JOB 81	PARKS	JOB 88
EXPECT	JOB 33	PASS	JOB 16
EXPECT3	JOB 38	PASS2	JOB 21
FAST	JOB 57	PICNIC	JOB 90
FAX	JOB 66	POSITION	JOB 99
		READ	JOB 62
		READERS	JOB 62
		RECAP	JOB 102
		REMINDER	JOB 98

SPREADSHEET

ACE	JOB 40	REPAIR	JOB 83
AGNEW	JOB 83	REPORT	JOB 32
ALUMNI	JOB 73	RESUME	JOB 67
ALUMNI2	JOB 73	RISK	JOB 60
ALUMNI3	JOB 73	RR	JOB 60
AMORT	JOB 79	SALARIES	JOB 53
ARBUCK	JOB 82	SALARY	JOB 82
ARBUCK2	JOB 82	SALES	JOB 9
ARBUCK3	JOB 86	SALES2	JOB 23
ARTHUR	JOB 49	SEMINAR	JOB 64
ARTHUR2	JOB 50	SERVICE	JOB 19
AUTO	JOB 4	SKI	JOB 72
AUTO2	JOB 24	STAR	JOB 4
AUTO3	JOB 94	STAT	JOB 3
BALANCE	JOB 75	STAT2	JOB 36
BALANCE2	JOB 76	STEPS	JOB 27
BALANCE3	JOB 76	TIME	JOB 2
BROKER	JOB 61	TITLE	JOB 40
BROOKL	JOB 83	TOUR	JOB 93
BUTLER	JOB 85	TRAINING	JOB 47
CAR	JOB 39	UPGRADE	JOB 42
CAR2	JOB 95	VISIT	JOB 70
		WASH	JOB 91
		WEB	JOB 59
		WRITING	JOB 100
		ZIP	JOB 7

JOB REFERENCE LIST

CARD	JOB 31	SANDERS2	JOB 28	ECUALUM	JOB 55
CHECK	JOB 43	SHIPE	JOB 18	EMPLOY	JOB 2
CHECK2	JOB 46	SOFT	JOB 6	EMPLOY2	JOB 11
CLAIM	JOB 9	SOFT2	JOB 23	EMPLOY3	JOB 26
CLASSES	JOB 83	SPORTS	JOB 29	EMPLOY4	JOB 29
COMM	JOB 13	STOCK	JOB 2	EMPLOY5	JOB 39
COMM2	JOB 37	STOCK2	JOB 35	EXPENSE	JOB 34
COMM3	JOB 60	STORE	JOB 47	EXPENSE2	JOB 57
COMM4	JOB 60	STORE2	JOB 48	FACULTY	JOB 60
COMP	JOB 36	SUNSET	JOB 67	GPALABEL	JOB 64
DANBURY	JOB 8	TAPES	JOB 42	HONOROL2	JOB 58
DEPR	JOB 77	TAPES2	JOB 44	HONOROLL	JOB 54
DEPR2	JOB 78	TAPES3	JOB 45	INCREASE	JOB 52
DEWEY	JOB 83	TAPES4	JOB 70	LABELS	JOB 59
EARN	JOB 11	TAPES5	JOB 70	LABREG	JOB 62
EARN2	JOB 25	TAPES6	JOB 86	LIBRARY	JOB 61
FIRST	JOB 12	TOM	JOB 62	LISTING	JOB 5
FIRST2	JOB 41	TRI	JOB 15	LISTING2	JOB 12
FLIGHTS	JOB 68	WALKER	JOB 74	LISTING3	JOB 14
FLOYD	JOB 16	WALKER2	JOB 74	LISTING4	JOB 17
FLOYD2	JOB 26	WALKER3	JOB 74	LISTING5	JOB 22
FOOD	JOB 10	WALKER4	JOB 99	MEADOWOOD	JOB 50
FUN	JOB 14	WATKINS	JOB 30	OAKS	JOB 56
FUTURE	JOB 88	WEEKLY	JOB 32	PAYROLL	JOB 35
GIFT	JOB 92	WEST	JOB 5	PPG	JOB 48
GRILL	JOB 34	WEST2	JOB 27	PRICE	JOB 51
GRILL2	JOB 69	WESTCOX	JOB 71	PROB	JOB 64
HART	JOB 80	WESTCOX2	JOB 71	REGIONAL	JOB 62
HART2	JOB 80	WESTCOX3	JOB 71	SILVERLEAF	JOB 50
HEIGHTS	JOB 7	WESTCOX4	JOB 72	STUDENT	JOB 1
HENSON	JOB 58	WESTCOX5	JOB 72	STUDENT2	JOB 10
HENSON2	JOB 58	WESTCOX6	JOB 87	STUDENT3	JOB 27
HENSON3	JOB 59	WESTERN	JOB 56	STUDENT4	JOB 33
HENSON4	JOB 59	WESTERN2	JOB 57	STUDENT5	JOB 49
HIGHTIME	JOB 63	WILEY	JOB 21	TEACHER	JOB 20
HOSP	JOB 19	WILSON	JOB 1	USED	JOB 4
INVOICE	JOB 81	WILSON2	JOB 38	USED2	JOB 13
KIRKPATR	JOB 100	YARDLEY	JOB 17	USED3	JOB 25
LIST	JOB 52	YOUNG	JOB 84	USED4	JOB 31
MACRO	JOB 51				
MACRO2	JOB 54				
MACOR3	JOB 54				
MACRO4	JOB 55	ACDEMIC	JOB 64		
MARINO	JOB 96	ALUMNI	JOB 30	AAA	JOB 29
MCPHEE	JOB 91	ALUMNI2	JOB 37	AAA2	JOB 32
MCPHEE2	JOB 91	APPLI	JOB 3	AAA3	JOB 37
OFFICE	JOB 53	APPLI2	JOB 16	ADVANCE	JOB 22
OUTLET	JOB 66	APPLI3	JOB 21	ADVANCE2	JOB 24
PCMED	JOB 64	APPLI4	JOB 23	ARCADE	JOB 62
PIER	JOB 93	APPLI5	JOB 28	ATTEND	JOB 40
PRICE	JOB 33	BIRTH	JOB 19	ATTEND2	JOB 45
RENO	JOB 83	BONUS	JOB 53	AUTO	JOB 39
RENTALS	JOB 20	BOOKS	JOB 36	BARTON	JOB 31
RENTALS2	JOB 22	CLASS	JOB 18	BIRTHDAY	JOB 53
RETIRE	JOB 89	COMMISS	JOB 63	BUSH	JOB 23
RETIRE2	JOB 97	COMREP	JOB 63	BUYER	JOB 56
RICHIE	JOB 90	DRAFT	JOB 6	C&L	JOB 33
RICHIE2	JOB 100	DRAFT2	JOB 15	CALL	JOB 54
SAFECD	JOB 65	DRAFT3	JOB 24	CHARITY	JOB 44
SANDERS	JOB 3	DRAFT4	JOB 38	CHARITY2	JOB 46

DATABASE

PRESENTATION GRAPHICS

COLLEGE	JOB 30	SERVICE2	JOB 35	PRICE-PV	JOB 1
COMPUT2	JOB 50	UNITED	JOB 11	QUESTION	JOB 3
COMPUTER	JOB 43	UNITED2	JOB 18	SIGN	JOB 5
CUNNING	JOB 4	UNITED3	JOB 49	SLIDEVAC	JOB 9
CUNNING2	JOB 9	VENDING	JOB 61		
CUNNING3	JOB 14	WESTERN	JOB 2		

SIMULATION

DEPOT	JOB 20	WESTERN2	JOB 7		
FIELDS	JOB 3	WESTERN3	JOB 13	BOOKS	JOB 15
FIELDS2	JOB 8	WESTERN4	JOB 19	BROINS	JOB 20
FIELDS3	JOB 15	WESTERN5	JOB 25	BROTITLE	JOB 20
FIELDS4	JOB 38	WESTERN6	JOB 60	CARD	JOB 4
FISHER	JOB 1	WRITING	JOB 48	CARLOAN	JOB 12
FISHER2	JOB 6			CHECKBK	JOB 9
FISHER3	JOB 12			CHECKBK1	JOB 9
FISHER4	JOB 26			CHECKBK2	JOB 9

INTEGRATED ACTIVITIES

GETAWAY	JOB 28			CRUISE	JOB 18
HOSP	JOB 55	BROCHURE	JOB 6	FAX	JOB 19
INSURANC	JOB 47	CASHFLOW	JOB 10	FRFORM	JOB 2
INTER	JOB 58	CHECK	JOB 1	FRLABELS	JOB 3
KIDS	JOB 57	CLASSIC	JOB 2	FRLIST	JOB 2
KIDS2	JOB 57	CLIP-AC	JOB 1	FRLIST2	JOB 7
KTEM	JOB 36	CLIP-CA	JOB 1	FRLIST3	JOB 7
LOAN	JOB 52	CLIP-MC	JOB 1	INVEN	JOB 8
MOBILE	JOB 42	CLIP-PV	JOB 1	JUNEMEET	JOB 6
NET	JOB 58	COMPARE	JOB 11	LOAN	JOB 12
NEWS	JOB 5	COST-CHA	JOB 1	LTRHEAD	JOB 1
NEWS2	JOB 10	INFOMEX	JOB 12	NEWSLTR	JOB 13
NEWS3	JOB 17	LETTERHD	JOB 1	REDSCH	JOB 5
NEWS4	JOB 59	MEMO	JOB 1	RESUME	JOB 11
ORCHARD	JOB 56	MEXICO	JOB 7	RESUME2	JOB 19
PROTECT	JOB 16	MEXLABEL	JOB 12	SAVINGS	JOB 10
PROTECT2	JOB 27	MEXLET	JOB 8	SAVINGS2	JOB 10
RATE	JOB 58	NEW-CANC	JOB 1	SIGN	JOB 16
RATE2	JOB 58	PRICE	JOB 4	STOCK	JOB 17
ROSS	JOB 41	PRICE-AC	JOB 1	TICKET	JOB 14
ROSS2	JOB 56	PRICE-CA	JOB 1	WDLOAD	JOB 12
SERVICE	JOB 34	PRICE-MC	JOB 1		

WORD PROCESSING AND DESKTOP PUBLISHING

CHAPTER 1

Jobs 1–26
Basic Formatting and Editing

Time Estimate: 12 hrs.

OBJECTIVES

In this chapter, students will:

1. Create, save, and print a document
2. Use the spell check
3. Change line spacing and text alignment
4. Use flush-right alignment
5. Change text styles
6. Open and edit a document
7. Clear and set left and centered tabs
8. Center page vertically
9. Set left and right margins and decimal tabs
10. Set right tabs with leaders
11. Set top margin
12. Set paragraph indents
13. Set temporary indent
14. Set temporary left and right margins
15. Set hanging indent
16. Format numbered items
17. Use copy and paste
18. Use cut and paste
19. Move tabular columns

3. Use the following text for the inside of the brochure:

Maybe those who joined the new Unity Chamber of Commerce in 1902 didn't realize the impact they would soon make on their community. Or maybe they did, because the chamber's momentum has never slowed. Its members continue to search for something better--more jobs, better highways, and entertainment for the family.

Maybe you haven't realized the difference you could make as a member of the Unity Chamber of Commerce. Maybe it's time you did.

For You . . .

Here are just a few of the things the chamber does for its members and its community:

- Acts as the "front door" to visitors and newcomers by supplying them with needed information

- Offers meeting rooms to members free of charge

- Provides statistical data to thousands of people each year, much of which is used by new or expanding businesses

- Maintains a close relationship with government officials so members stay informed on important issues

- Actively recruits major industries

- Sponsors major events such as the Balloon Festival

The People . . .

Chamber members are ordinary people with vision, hope, and energy. They offer financial support, yearly dues that fund completely the chamber's search for economic growth. They put hours of work into the chamber's many activities. They shape their city's future with input at board, committee, and general meetings.

There is so much you, as a member, can do for the Unity Chamber of Commerce. Your voice matters. Without fresh ideas, even the most powerful organizations grow stale.

Each new member adds strength to our organization. Strength to lure new businesses and major events to the Nashville area. Strength to make the area grow.

We Need You . . .

You can help. Your membership dues will help fund the area's progress. Your time will help make such popular events as the Balloon Festival and the Country Music Festival successful.

We need you and you need us. Success is a two-way street.

Application . . .

The chamber offers two kinds of memberships: business, which links professional operations to the chamber; and personal, which allows input on an individual basis. Please complete this form, detach and mail to the chamber office. Remember, your membership counts!

____ **Yes.** I am interested in a business membership.

____ **Yes.** I am interested in a personal membership.

____ **Maybe.** I would be interested if I had more information.

____ **No.** I am not interested because

_____

_____

Name _____

Business _____

Address _____

Telephone Number _____

4. Adjust the vertical spacing so the material is balanced on the page.

5. Save the file as BROINS.

6. Print the brochure. If your printer does not duplex print, manually feed the paper through a second time.

JOB 1

Create, Save, and Print a Document

1. Key the memo as shown below.

2. Save the document as CHECK.

3. Print the document.

TO: Students at Star Spencer High School

FROM: Citizens' National Bank

DATE: June 5, 19--

SUBJECT: Opening a checking account

Many of you have a savings account; you probably make a few withdrawals and deposits, while allowing your growing account to earn interest. A checking account does not work this way, but checks provide a convenient and relatively safe way of handling purchases. In addition, checks offer an up-to-date record of where your money is going. If you do not have a checking account, see us immediately.

JOB 20

Create a Brochure

Angie is a member of the Unity Chamber of Commerce Membership Committee. She has agreed to create a brochure for the committee.

1. Use the word processing software to create a brochure. If available with the software, use a template. Otherwise, subdivide your page into three parts. You will need two pages—one for the front and one for the inside.

2. Center the title and subtitle in the last column (far right). Format as desired. Save the file as BROTITLE.

Column 1	*Column 2*	*Column 3*	
		Title:	Unity Chamber of Commerce
		Subtitle:	We need you!

Continued on Next Page

1. Key the memo in simplified form as shown below.

2. Use the Spell Check to correct any misspelled words.

3. Save the document as TIME.

4. Print the document.

November 9, 19--

All Secretaries

MANAGING YOUR TIME

In even the busiest offices there are quiet days--often the lull before the storm. Such days present opportunities to catch up on all kinds of matters that cannot be taken care of on busy days. This precious time should not be wasted.

One of the first jobs might be some housecleaning. Start with your desk, restocking it with supplies and discarding unneeded items.

Even the best-organized files need attention from time to time. Certain sections will need arranging. Some folders will need new labels.

Records such as address lists, personal telephone lists, and special reference lists need updating from time to time.

You will be able to think of numerous other jobs that can be done during this time to make your job much easier during a busy time. Make a list and have it available for use.

Angie Hoover

kk

FINISH

JOB 19

Create and Send a Fax

Angie is working part time at the Valley Regional Hospital. She is now available for full-time employment. She contacted one of her former instructors at Nashville Junior College for information about local employment. She was given information about a position as an administrative assistant at the Timberlane Clinic. The instructor told her to fax a cover sheet and a resume to the clinic.

1. Open RESUME.

2. Change the objective section to "To obtain a position as administrative assistant at the Timberlane Clinic."

3. Change the employment section as follows:

   Add: Valley Regional Hospital, 2200 NE Front St., Nashville, TN 37008
   Office Assistant, January, 1996 to present
   Duties: assist with telephone and written communications, schedule patients for inpatient and outpatient surgery

   The date of employment with Dr. John Wallace is from August, 1992 to present.

4. Save the resume as RESUME2.

5. Create a cover sheet with the word processing software. Use a fax template if available with the software.

6. The fax number is "(305) 555-6022." The subject is "Employment as an Administrative Assistant." There will be two pages including the cover sheet. Angie gave you the information below. Include this information in the comment section of the cover sheet. Add any other appropriate material.

   Mr. Gerald Favor, my business instructor at Nashville Junior College, told me about the position available for an administrative assistant.

   My previous employment has been in the medical area. I worked for Dr. John Wallace here in Nashville and in the pharmacy department of Wilson's Drug. Currently, I am working part time as an office assistant at Valley Regional Hospital. I like this work, but I am now pursuing full-time employment.

   I would appreciate an opportunity to interview with you to discuss possible employment. Call me any weekday after 1:30 p.m.

7. Save the coversheet as FAX.

8. Ask your instructor for a fax number. Fax your coversheet and resume.

9. If a number is not available, print the fax and resume.

JOB 3

Change Line Spacing and Text Alignment

1. Change the line spacing to double space.

2. Key the report as shown below. Center align the heading and align the first and last paragraph using justification. Tab once for indents.

3. Save the document as STAT.

4. Print the document.

USE STATISTICS

One can find statistics that will prove almost anything. Questions can be framed to provide desirable or unique replies. Polls can produce humorous trivia or meaningful trends. Here are a few "facts" over which to mull.

99% of American women would change something about their looks if they could.

90% of Americans consider themselves happy people.

50% of American men are less than 5 feet 9 inches tall.

25% of American adults never exercise at all.

15% of American married men say they do most of the cooking.

10% of Americans say the automobile is the greatest invention of all time.

6% of Americans believe the single greatest element in happiness is great wealth.

5% of American violent crime occurs in schools.

The next time you wish to prove a point or draw a particular conclusion, try using statistics. However, be sure to keep your statistics current. Remember, most statistics change daily!

JOB 18

Use the Internet

Jeff and Angie are planning a vacation. They want to use the Internet to obtain information.

1. Angie and Jeff are interested in a cruise. Search the Internet for information about cruises. Look for the items listed below.

   - Cruise line
   - Date of the cruise (leave and return)
   - Embarking point
   - Destination
   - Stops along the way
   - Cost (check on discounts for off-season cruising)
   - Name and size of ship (number of passengers)
   - Recreational facilities

2. Use the word processing software to create a short information sheet about a suitable cruise.

3. Save the file as CRUISE.

4. Print the file.

JOB 4

Use Flush-Right Alignment

1. Key the information as shown below with the names at the left margin and titles flush with the right margin.

2. Center the heading in all caps bold.

3. Save the document as STAR.

4. Print the document.

STAR PUBLISHING COMPANY

Star Publishing is pleased to announce the following staff changes. All changes are effective immediately. Please keep this information for future use.

Wilson Thompson	Publisher
Don Allen	Accountant
Patty Martinez	Advertising Manager
James Mayes	Production Manager
Joe Slizewski	Managing Editor
Lela Mae Jackson	Circulation Manager

JOB 17

Use the Internet

Jeff and Angie own some stocks and are interested in purchasing other stocks. They want to use the Internet to get the latest stock quotes on their stocks and to watch for stocks they may want to purchase.

1. Jeff and Angie provide you with a list of stocks. Search for the New York Stock Exchange on the Internet to get the daily closing prices of all the stocks listed below.

   Wal-Mart (WalMart)   McDonald's (McDnlds)
   General Electric (GenElec)   Pepsi Cola (PepsiCo)
   General Motors (GnMotr)   Ford Motor Co. (FordM)
   International Business Machines (IBM)   Hewlett Packard (HewlPk)

2. Create a table with the spreadsheet software to keep a record of the closing prices. Keep this record for five consecutive days.

Date	WalMart	GenElec	GnMotr	IBM	McDnlds	PepsiCo	FordM	HewlPk
Average	*average formula*	*average formula*	*average formula*	*average formula*	*average formula*	*average formula*	*average formula*	*average formula*

3. Enter the dates and closing prices on your spreadsheet. Calculate the average closing price for each stock listing. Save the file as STOCK.

4. Print the file.

JOB 5

Change Text Styles

1. Key the text as shown below using plain, bold, underlined, and italicized text styles as shown.

2. Double space and center align text.

3. Save the document as INTERV.

4. Print the document.

INTERVIEWING TIPS

Dress appropriately.

Be on time.

Bring a pen.

Be very polite and courteous.

Fill out the application entirely and use your best handwriting.

Bring your reference list with addresses and phone numbers.

Answer questions <u>precisely</u> and <u>thoroughly</u>.

Thank the interviewer personally for his/her time.

Send a letter thanking the interviewer for his/her time.

One step at a time is all it takes to get there.

Create a Sign

Jeff and Angie have lost their dog. They want to create a sign to post around the neighborhood.

1. Create a sign with the information below. You decide which software to use. You could use a sign template that comes with some word processing software, or you could design your own sign. You may want to include a graphic image or graphic lines. Also, this is a good place to use text art or the drawing tools. Another option is to use the presentation software to create a slide that can be printed on a full sheet of paper.

> Lost Dog
> Black Miniature Schnauzer
> Answers to the name "Scrappy"
> Lost in the Warwick Addition on Sunday, July 28
> Reward $$$
> Call Jeff or Angie Stafford at 555-5255

2. Save the file as SIGN.

3. Print the sign. (They can print additional copies or use the hard copy to make photocopies.)

Open and Edit a Document

1. Open CHECK.

2. Make the changes as indicated by the editing marks shown below. The document below is double spaced to show the proofreader's marks. Leave the document single spaced.

3. Use Save As to save the document as CHECK2.

4. Print the document.

TO: Students at Star Spencer High School

FROM: Citizens' National Bank

DATE: June 5, 19--

SUBJECT: Opening a checking account

Many of you have a savings account, you probably make a few withdrawals and

deposits, while allowing your growing account to earn interest. A checking account

works differently. ~~does not work this way, but~~ checks provide a convenient and relatively safe way of *to handle*

~~handling~~ purchases. In addition, checks offer an up-to-date record of ~~where your~~ *how you spent*

your money ~~money is going.~~ If you do not have a checking account, ~~see us immediately.~~ *consider opening one*

5. Save the presentation as BOOKS.

6. Switch to the Slide Show View and review your work.

7. Print all slides of the presentation (six to a page) with a frame (if available with the software).

Note: The object of a presentation program is to help you prepare slides for display on the computer screen, for projection directly from the computer, for development of 35mm slides, or for use with overhead projectors. You may never need to print any part of your presentation.

JOB 7

Clear and Set Left and Centered Tabs

1. Clear all tabs and set a centered tab at 2.75 inches to center the heading over the columns. Key the heading in all caps bold.

2. On the next line, clear the centered tab, and set left tabs at 2.19 inches, 3.25 inches, and 5.3 inches for columns 2, 3, and 4.

3. Key the remaining information with the first column at the left margin.

4. Save the document as ZIP.

5. Print the document.

ZIP CODE ABBREVIATIONS

Alabama	AL	Montana	MT
Alaska	AK	Nebraska	NE
Arizona	AZ	Nevada	NV
Arkansas	AR	New Hampshire	NH
California	CA	New Jersey	NJ
Colorado	CO	New Mexico	NM
Connecticut	CT	New York	NY
Delaware	DE	North Carolina	NC
District of Columbia	DC	North Dakota	ND
Florida	FL	Ohio	OH
Georgia	GA	Oklahoma	OK
Guam	GU	Oregon	OR
Hawaii	HI	Pennsylvania	PA
Idaho	ID	Puerto Rico	PR
Illinois	IL	Rhode Island	RI
Indiana	IN	South Carolina	SC
Iowa	IA	South Dakota	SD
Kansas	KS	Tennessee	TN
Kentucky	KY	Texas	TX
Louisiana	LA	Utah	UT
Maine	ME	Vermont	VT
Maryland	MD	Virgin Islands	VI
Massachusetts	MA	Virginia	VA
Michigan	MI	Washington	WA
Minnesota	MN	West Virginia	WV
Mississippi	MS	Wisconsin	WI
Missouri	MO	Wyoming	WY

JOB 15

Create a Slide Presentation

Jeff needs a slide presentation on their community project, "Books for Children."

1. Use the presentation software. Create a new presentation.

2. If available with the software, create a look for the presentation by selecting a predesigned presentation template.

3. Create the following slides:

Slide 1 (title slide)
Books for Children
Community Project

Slide 2 (bulleted list)
Overall Status
- Need additional participants
- Activities have been planned
- Concession vendors have been contacted

Slide 3 (bulleted list)
Participants
- 14 merchants involved
- 11 restaurants involved
- 12 clubs and civic organizations involved
- Community residents

Slide 4 (bulleted list)
Activities
- 3 musical groups will perform
- 288 raffle tickets sold (maximum 1,500)
- 12 amusement rides available
- Hot air balloon rides available

Slide 5 (bulleted list)
Concessions
- 15 food stands with drinks
- 5 snack stands
- 5 dessert stands

Slide 6 (bulleted list)
What do we do next?
- Contact additional participants
- Sell raffle tickets
- Make suggestions for additional activities
- Make suggestions for additional concessions
- Next planning meeting will be August 15, 7:00 p.m.

4. If available with the software, add transitions for each slide, and use build slide text on slides 2 and 6.

Continued on Next Page

JOB 8

Center Page Vertically

1. Center the page vertically.

2. Clear all tabs and set a centered tab at 3.2 inches. Center and key the main heading and the subheading in the text styles as shown below.

3. For the remaining lines, clear the centered tab and set left tabs at 0.7 inches, 3.2 inches, 4.2 inches, and 5.4 inches.

4. Key the remaining information. Underline the column headings.

5. Save the document as MINOR.

6. Print the document.

MINOR LEAGUE BASEBALL

First-Year Team Records

Team	Year	W - L	Pct.
Los Angeles Broncos	1981	70-91	.435
Kansas City Giants	1982	69-93	.426
Houston Comets	1983	64-96	.400
Seattle Bears	1984	64-98	.395
Dallas Stars	1985	64-98	.395
Washington Generals	1986	70-91	.435
Toronto Wildcats	1987	62-98	.344
Montreal Rams	1988	81-81	.500
San Diego Chiefs	1989	68-93	.422
New York Raiders	1990	78-83	.484

FINISH

JOB 14

Create a Ticket

Jeff is chairman of a local civic organization. He needs to prepare tickets for a raffle the organization is sponsoring. The proceeds will go to their community project, "Books for Children."

1. Create a ticket with the information below. There are several options for creating the ticket. For example,

   - You could use the word processing software and create a text box, you could key the information and put a border around it, or you could use the drawing tools.
   - Another option is to use the presentation software and create a slide. Copy the slide so you have six slides, and print six to the page.

Line 1: One Chance	$2.00
Line 2: Multimedia Computer	
Line 3: Proceeds go to "Books for Children"	
Line 4: Drawing	Community Center
Line 5: Sept. 1, 19--	
Line 6: Need not be present to win.	

2. Copy this ticket so you fill a page.

3. Save the file as TICKET.

4. Print the page so it can be duplicated on heavier paper.

JOB 9

Set Left and Right Margins and Decimal Tabs

1. Center the page vertically.

2. Set the left and right margins at 2 inches.

3. Clear all tabs. Set decimal tabs at 2.3 inches and 4.2 inches.

4. Center align the heading in all caps.

5. Key the information as shown below with the first column at the left margin. Use the decimal tabs for columns 2 and 3.

6. Save the document as SALES.

7. Print the document.

SALES--SUMMER SEASON, 19--

Month	Tapes	Books
June	$ 15,525.40	$ 22,431.90
July	110,521.80	35,432.00
August	112,221.00	101,889.20

Results of the Fishing Contest

Alice caught the most fish with a total of 31 for the three days. Tommy caught the largest fish, a 12-pound catfish.

Recipe

Aunt Wanda's Mexican Fruit Cake was delicious. Everyone asked for the recipe. Here it is!

> 2 eggs, beaten
> 2 c. sugar
> 2 c. self rising flour
> 20 oz. can pineapple, juice also
> pecans
> small pkg. cream cheese
> powdered sugar
>
> Combine eggs, sugar, flour, pineapple and pecans. Pour into a 9 by 13 inch prepared cake pan. Bake at 350° for 35 to 40 minutes. Top with cream cheese and powdered sugar.

Next Reunion

The vote is in for the time and place for our next reunion.

Date: . . . . September 7, 8, and 9, 19--
Place: . . . . Felix Resort
Pagosa Springs, Colorado

2. Save the file as NEWSLTR.

3. You will need 25 copies. However, you will print only one copy.

4. You will need mailing labels for out-of-town family members. Merge FRLIST2 with FRLABELS.

5. Print the labels.

JOB 10

Set Right Tab with Leaders

1. Change the left and right margins to 2 inches, and set a right tab with dot leaders at 4.5 inches.

2. Center the heading in all caps bold, and key the information as shown below.

3. Save the document as ABBR.

4. Print the document.

COMMONLY USED ABBREVIATIONS

c/o	care of
COD	cash on delivery
dept	department
FOB	free on board
doz	dozen
gro	gross
pkg	package
pcs	pieces
amt	amount
min	minimum
max	maximum
qty	quantity
wt	weight

JOB 13

Create a Newsletter

Angie wants to create a newsletter for the family reunion. She wants to send it to all family members.

1. If available with the word processing software, use a newsletter template. Otherwise, format for two columns. Use the following information to create the newsletter:

   - Title: Family Reunion
   - Subtitle: Mountain State Resort Park
   - Volume Number   I
   - Issue Number   2
   - Date of Newsletter   September 15, 19--

Our Special Time Together

Everyone agreed that the family reunion was a success. We had 64 family members and 11 guests attend. The oldest family member was Aunt Tommie. She is proud to say she is 91 years old. She came with Wilma and John. The youngest was six-week-old baby Devon. She came with her proud parents, Charles and Lynn, and her brother Tanner. Everyone had a great time.

Favorite Activities

Rachel and Sue. . . . . Tennis
John, Hershel, Kevin, and Mike. . . . . Golf
Debbie, Mike, and Jim . . . . Hiking
Alice, Dan, Christy, and Tommy. . . . . Fishing
Susan . . . . Horseback riding

Results of the Golf Tournament

Name	Friday	Saturday	Sunday	Total
Hershel	83	79	84	246
Debbie	81	80	90	251
John	78	81	85	244
Christy	102	100	106	308
Sue	**74**	**79**	**86**	**239**
Harold	99	110	104	313
Charles	89	91	99	279
Kevin	**79**	**79**	**81**	**239**

Congratulations, Sue and Kevin!

Continued on Next Page

JOB 11

Set Top Margin

1. Set the top margin at 1.5 inches.

2. Key the table of contents as shown below. Center the main heading, and use flush-right alignment for "Page."

3. Clear all tabs. Set a left tab at 0.5 inches, and set a right tab with dot leaders at 6.4 inches.

4. Save the document as CONTENTS.

5. Print the document.

CONTENTS

JOB 12

Loan Amortization

Jeff and Angie would like some type of form that they could use to determine payments on a loan. They want to use it to determine the payments on a car, on furniture or appliances, or on a vacation.

1. Use the spreadsheet software and the payment formula to determine the amount of the payments on a loan.

2. Use the information below.

Loan Amortization	
Loan Principal	
Annual Interest Rate	
Loan Period in Months	
Payment per Month	*payment formula*

3. Save the file as LOAN.

4. Use LOAN and insert the following information. Jeff and Angie want to know the payments if they decide to buy a new car and borrow $20,000. They could get this loan for 9% interest and would have three years (36 months) to repay the loan.

5. Add an appropriate title at the top of the spreadsheet, and save the file as CARLOAN.

6. Print the file.

7. Open the file LOAN and add the following information. Jeff and Angie want to know the payments for a new washer and dryer. They will need $850. The appliance store will charge 7% interest, and they will have two years (24 months) to repay the loan.

8. Add an appropriate title at the top of the spreadsheet, and save the file as WDLOAN.

9. Print the file.

FINISH

JOB 12

Set Paragraph Indents

1. Key the document below with bold text as shown.

2. Center the heading in all caps bold. Quadruple space after the heading.

3. Set 0.5-inch paragraph indents using the Format menu (do not use tabs).

4. Save the document as ENDORSE.

5. Print the document.

ENDORSEMENTS

A check cannot be cashed until it is endorsed. An **endorsement** usually includes the signature of the party to whom the check is made payable (some companies use rubber stamps for depositing checks). All **endorsements** are made on the back of the check at the left end. There are three types of **endorsements: blank endorsements, restrictive endorsements,** and **special endorsements.**

A **blank endorsement** is the signature of the person to whom the check is made payable and shoud be written on the back of the check exactly as it appears on the front. A lost or stolen check with a **blank endorsement** can be cashed by anyone who has the check. **Blank endorsements** should be used only when the depositor is ready to deposit or cash the check.

A **restrictive endorsement** limits the way in which a check may be handled; it allows the check to be deposited only. The **endorsement** can be either written or stamped on the back. By using such an **endorsement,** an individual may safely mail a signed check to his or her bank without fear of anyone else cashing it.

A **special endorsement** makes a check payable to a third party. Only the individual or business named in a **special endorsement** can cash or transfer a check.

When using a **blank,** a **restrictive,** or a **special endorsement,** the endorser guarantees payment of the check. If a bank does not receive payment, the endorser must pay the bank.

Angela R. Stafford
4421 SW Freeman Street
Nashville, TN 37212
(305) 555-5255

Objective:

   To obtain a part-time job as an office assistant at Valley Regional Hospital

Employment:

   Dr. John Wallace, 4436 NW Highland Street, Nashville, TN 37007
   Office Assistant, August, 1992, to present
   Duties: make all patient appointments, assist with telephone
   communications, inventory, order office and medical supplies, and keep all
   office files current

   Wilson's Drug, 8821 SW Grant Street, Nashville, TN 36019
   Cashier/Sales, September, 1987 to August, 1992
   Duties: assist in the pharmacy department

Education:

   Andrew Jackson High School   Nashville, Tennessee
   Graduated, May, 1982   September, 1978 until May, 1982

   Nashville Junior College   Nashville, Tennessee
   Graduated, May, 1984   September, 1982 until May, 1984
   Associate Degree in Business
   Minor - Communications

Skills:

   - Key 50 wpm
   - Computer System Operations: experience with word processing and
     spreadsheet software
   - Excellent verbal and written communication skills
   - Organization skills

JOB 13

Set Temporary Indent

1. Key the following itinerary. Use temporary indents to arrange it attractively on the page as shown below.

2. Save the document as ITIN.

3. Print the document.

AN ITINERARY PREPARED FOR

Mrs. Olivia Castillo

May 22

10:15 a.m.	Leave Will Rogers Airport on United Flight 743.
12:15 p.m.	Arrive Fresno International Airport. Patricia Jackson of Fresno office will meet you and drive you to Skyline Hotel.
1:30 p.m.	Meet with Daryl Reininger and the property owners at the Skyline Hotel in the Chadwick Room.
3:00 p.m.	See properties with Ms. Jackson.
7:00 p.m.	Presentation with the Fresno Realtors in the Gold Room at the Fresno Convention Center.

May 23

7:00 a.m.	Breakfast at hotel with Patricia Jackson before drive to Kingsburg office to discuss acquisition of properties.
12:30 p.m.	Lunch with property owners.
2:00 p.m.	Meet with Chad Baltimore and the Zoning Commission Board at the Skyline Hotel in Room 133.
5:30 p.m.	Leave Fresno International Airport on Pacific Western Flight 759.
6:05 p.m.	Arrive Will Rogers Airport.

JOB 11

Create a Resume

Angie is applying for a part-time job at the local hospital. She needs a resume.

1. If available with the word processing software, use a template for a resume. If not, key the information as shown on the next page and use an appropriate format.

2. Save the file as RESUME.

3. Print the resume.

Continued on Next Page

JOB 14

Set Temporary Left and Right Margins

1. Open ENDORSE.

2. Set temporary left and right margins to indent the three paragraphs 0.5 inches inside the normal margin as shown below.

3. Use Save As to save the document as ENDORSE2.

4. Print the document.

ENDORSEMENTS

A check cannot be cashed until it is endorsed. An **endorsement** usually includes the signature of the party to whom the check is made payable (some companies use rubber stamps for depositing checks). All **endorsements** are made on the back of the check at the left end. There are three types of **endorsements: blank endorsements, restrictive endorsements,** and **special endorsements.**

A **blank endorsement** is the signature of the person to whom the check is made payable and should be written on the back of the check exactly as it appears on the front. A lost or stolen check with a **blank endorsement** can be cashed by anyone who has the check. **Blank endorsements** should be used only when the depositor is ready to deposit or cash the check.

A **restrictive endorsement** limits the way in which a check may be handled; it allows the check to be deposited only. The **endorsement** can be either written or stamped on the back. By using such an **endorsement,** an individual may safely mail a signed check to his or her bank without fear of anyone else cashing it.

A **special endorsement** makes a check payable to a third party. Only the individual or business named in a **special endorsement** can cash or transfer a check.

When using a **blank,** a **restrictive,** or a **special endorsement,** the endorser guarantees payment of the check. If a bank does not receive payment, the endorser must pay the bank.

JOB 10

Find the Future Value of a Savings Plan

Angie and Jeff want to start a savings plan. They would like to save approximately $30,000 within the next five years. They want to know how much a month they need to save if they can invest at 6% interest with Security State Bank.

1. Use the spreadsheet software and the future value formula to determine the amount of savings needed per month. Create a form like the one shown below.

Monthly Savings	Rate of Interest	No. of Payments	Future Value
	6%	60	*future value formula*

2. Enter an estimated amount in the "Monthly Savings" column. Adjust the amount (up or down) until the "Future Value" column is approximately $30,000.

3. Save the spreadsheet as SAVINGS.

4. Create an appropriate heading with the word processing software.

5. Insert the spreadsheet into the word processing document under the heading.

6. Save the file as SAVINGS2.

7. Print the file.

JOB 15

Set Hanging Indent

1. Key the announcement as shown below.

2. Use the Hanging Indent function for paragraphs 2, 3, and 4.

3. Set temporary left and right margins for paragraph 5.

4. Save the document as ANNOUN.

5. Print the document.

ANNOUNCEMENT

I am pleased to announce that we have several new employees to fill new positions created by growth in the firm. Please join me in welcoming them to the company.

Kunio Akita, Director of Marketing, West Coast region. Kunio joins us from the Fox Corporation where he was Assistant Marketing Director.

Julia Anderson, Office Manager, Indianapolis office. Julia joins us from a local firm where she was in charge of office administration and payroll.

Greg Patton, Director of Security, Midwest region. Greg joins us from a local security firm where he was in charge of the security for numerous events.

A reception will be held for our new people in the employee dining room, Tuesday, January 8, 19--. All employees are invited.

Katie Stephens
Director of Personnel

4. Format the appropriate columns for commas with two decimal places. Center the check numbers and dates.

5. Save the file as CHECKBK2.

6. Insert the spreadsheet file (CHECKBK2) into the word processing document (CHECKBK1) under the heading. Make any desired changes in formatting.

7. Save the file as CHECKBK.

8. Print the register.

JOB 16

Format Numbered Items

1. Key the report in unbound report format as shown below. (See Reference Guide, page 501.)

2. Set tabs at 0.5 and 0.8 inches for the numbered items. Single space and use the Indent feature.

3. Save the document as PASS.

4. Print the document.

THE UNITED STATES PASSPORT

Millions of U.S. citizens travel to other countries every year. If you, too, decide to travel to a foreign country, you may need a passport. To apply for a passport, you must appear in person at one of the passport agencies. These agencies are often located in local federal buildings. A passport is an official document issued by the U.S. Department of State that includes a photograph of you and identifies you as a U.S. citizen.

When applying for a passport, you will need to bring the following:

1. Some identification that shows your signature and description. A driver's license could be used.

2. Proof of U.S. citizenship. Most people use a birth certificate or a certificate of naturalization.

3. The completed passport application.

4. The required fee for the passport.

A passport is good for ten years from the date it is issued. After receiving your passport, sign your name on the inside cover. When traveling in a foreign country, always carry your passport with you. NEVER leave it in a hotel room.

JOB 9

Create a Checkbook Register

Jeff and Angie want you to create a file to keep a running balance of their checking account.

1. Use the word processing software to create a heading. Use the information below. Change the font and point size as desired. Save the file as CHECKBK1.

Checkbook Register
Jeffrey and Angela Stafford
First Security National Bank
Opened 6/22/--, Account No. 22-333-4444

2. Use the spreadsheet software to create a checkbook register file. Use the information below.

Ck. No.	Date	Payee	Check	Deposit	Balance
	6/15/--				2,000.00
101	6/28/--	Food Mart	86.40		*formula*

3. If available with the software, use the Fill function for the check numbers. Show Jeff and Angie how to enter the transactions for the first week. Use the following information:

Ck. No.				
	101	6/28/--	Food Mart	86.40
	102	6/28/--	City Utilities	72.80
	103	6/28/--	Sports Club	31.00
	104	6/28/--	Discount World	106.40
	105	6/29/--	Dr. David Lott	46.00
	106	6/29/--	Central University	722.00
	107	6/30/--	Thompson's Books	86.00
		7/01/--	Deposit	2600.00
	108	7/01/--	Garden Terrace	550.00
	109	7/01/--	Sparkle Cleaners	18.00
	110	7/01/--	Trade Mart Gasoline	22.40
	111	7/02/--	B & B Telephone	44.11
	112	7/02/--	Tax Commission	22.80
	113	7/03/--	Evening Tribune	55.00
	114	7/06/--	AC Computers	72.40
	115	7/06/--	Food Mart	77.92

Continued on Next Page

JOB 17

Format Numbered Items

1. Key the report below in unbound format as shown. (See Reference Guide, page 501.)
2. Set tabs at 0.5 and 0.7 inches for the numbered items. Single space and use the Indent feature.

CLUES FOR INTERVIEWS

The interview has been compared by adults and students alike to a final exam or a talent competition. Some college students call interviews "civilized torture." However, the interview is a crucial step in your job search. How you conduct yourself in an interview can make or break your chances of getting the job you want. A job interview gives you an opportunity to display your intelligence, talent, and enthusiasm.

The employment interview is the only chance the company has to make a first hand evaluation of a prospective employee. The suggestions for a successful interview are the same whether you interview for a full-time or part-time job. A successful interview can make the difference between receiving and not receiving a job offer.

The objectives for any job interview are the same as well. A few suggestions to help you prepare for a job interview are as follows:

1. Gather enough accurate information about the job to help you make a decision about it.

2. Introduce yourself to the receptionist. State your name, why you are there, and who you want to see.

3. Tell the interviewer what you are like, what qualifications you have, and that you are interested in the job.

4. Use good eye contact and speak loudly and clearly. Maintain good posture.

JOB 8

Create a Database

The insurance company told Angie that she needed an inventory of items that are covered under her insurance policy. Create a database and use a table to create the list.

1. Create a database. Name it INVEN.

2. Create the categories as shown below.

3. Print the database in List View.

4. Close the database.

ITEM	PURCHASE DATE	CATEGORY
Sofa	June, 1995	Furniture
Computer	July, 1997	Furniture
Speedy Lawn Mower	May, 1994	Yard
Speedy Gas Trimmer	May, 1994	Yard
Dining Room Table with 6 Chairs	April, 1990	Furniture
Occasional Chair	June, 1995	Furniture
4 Living Room Tables	June, 1995	Furniture
Diamond Necklace	September, 1990	Jewelry
Pearl Necklace	Over 10 years old	Jewelry
36" Television	September, 1995	Electronics
4-Piece Bedroom Suite	Over 10 years old	Furniture

3. Save the document as CLUES.

4. Print the Document.

JOB 7

Edit a Mail Merge List

The family reunion letter to Sue Anderson was returned. Jeff called Sue and got the correct address. Also, he received addresses for two additional family members.

1. Open FRLIST and change Sue Anderson's address to 7204 Mill Brook Road.

2. Add two new records to the end of the file.

   Carol and Keith Broadrick
   6825 Doubletree Rd.
   Prescott, AZ 86301
   Carol and Keith
   Leisure Hotel

   Kay and John Broadrick
   2247 Santa Florencia
   Salona Beach, CA 92075
   Kay and John
   Leisure Hotel

3. Sort the records in ascending order. The primary sort is the last name. The secondary sort will be the first name.

4. Save the file as FRLIST2.

5. Use the Select function to select the three records mentioned above. Change the date to August 5, 19--.

6. Save the three records with the name FRLIST3.

7. Merge FRLIST3 with FRFORM.

8. Print the letters.

9. Merge FRLIST3 with FRLABELS.

10. Print the labels.

JOB 18

Use Copy and Paste

1. Prepare one copy of the form below using your own judgment for line length and word placement.

2. Use the Copy and Paste function to create a second and third copy of the form on the page. Adjust the spacing as necessary.

3. When you have three copies of the form on one page, save the document as FORM.

4. Print the document.

ORANGE COUNTY SKILL DEVELOPMENT CENTER
Short-Term Enrollment Form

Name_____
      First   Middle   Last

Social Security No._____

Address_____
      Street   City   State   Zip

Home Phone_____ Work Phone_____

JOB 6

Use a Form

1. Use the form (REDSCH) created in the previous job, for the current minutes of the School House Restoration Committee.

2. Angie supplied the information as shown below.

3. Save the file as JUNEMEET.

4. Print the minutes.

The Little Red Schoolhouse Committee met on June 8, 19--, 4:00 p.m., at the Chamber of Commerce Building.

Sue Moranetz, chairperson, called the meeting to order.

Minutes were read by Cassy Logue. The minutes were approved.

Members present: Sue Moranetz, Cassy Logue, Lindsey Floyd, Sara Clinton, Eddy Ballard, Carol Daniels, Alice Fitzgerald, Glen Wilson, and Bill Landrith.

Members absent: Randy Abbott, Nan Kaebnick, and Susan Todd.

Eddy Ballard reported that all repairs discussed at the last meeting have been made including replacing the facings and door jams. Also, the leak in the roof has been sealed.

At the last meeting, the need for restroom facilities was discussed. Carol Daniels reported on the expenses of attaching a facility to the building. Each member received copies of three bids for the project. Sara Clinton made a motion that Carol contact the low bidder and go forth with the attachment. The motion was seconded by Bill Landrith and approved by the committee.

Lindsey Floyd said she had been contacted by the Davey School Group asking permission to present a program for the July 4th celebration. Nan Kaebnick made a motion that Lindsey contact the group and accept their offer. Eddy Ballard seconded the motion, and it was approved by the committee.

Sue told the members that she would be making a work schedule for summer cleanup and for July 4th activities. She asked any member who will not be available to contact her before June 20.

The next meeting will be August 2 at 4:00.

A motion was made by Alice Fitzgerald to adjourn the meeting. The motion was seconded and approved. The meeting adjourned at 4:40.

JOB 19

Use Copy and Paste

1. Create an announcement similar to the one shown below.

2. Use the Copy and Paste function to create a second form on the same page.

3. Save the document as SERVICE.

4. Print the document.

IMPORTANT ANNOUNCEMENT

You and a friend can receive a free copy of our new brochure, *Planning for the Future,* by simply filling in the form below and mailing it to University Counseling Service, P.O. Box 11289, Des Moines, IA 50340-1289.

Please send me the brochure, *Planning for the Future.* There is no obligation on my part.

Name_____

Street_____

City_____ State_____ Zip_____

Please check one:
I plan to attend   a university   _____

                           a vocational school   _____

                           work   _____

                           other   _____

FINISH

JOB 5

Create and Use a Form

Angie is secretary for a community organization, "The School House Restoration Committee," that maintains an old school building. This building is located in the park and is open to the public for viewing. She wants to use her word processing program to create a form to use for the minutes of the meetings.

1. With the word processing software, create the form as shown below to be used for each meeting.

2. Save the file as REDSCH.

THE SCHOOL HOUSE RESTORATION COMMITTEE

===

Date:
Time:
Place:

===

Members Present:

Members Absent:

1. The meeting was called to order by **insert name**, chairperson.

2. The minutes were read by **insert name**, secretary. The minutes were **approved or changed**.

3. **Unfinished business**

4. **New business**

5. **Announcements and miscellaneous items**

6. A motion was made by **insert name** to adjourn the meeting. The motion was seconded and approved. The meeting was adjourned at **time**.

JOB 20

Use Copy and Paste

1. Key the memo as shown below.

2. Use the Copy and Paste function to copy the guarantee and paste as indicated.

3. Save the document as HISTEP.

4. Print the document.

TO: John England

FROM: Darren Ford

DATE: June 19, 19--

SUBJECT: Advertising Campaign

Please develop advertising material for the fitness equipment below. Include all of the information listed.

1. HiStep Stair Climber Stepper, $50 down and $25 per month.

guarantee {

Unconditional 90-Day Money-Back Guarantee

If you are not completely satisfied for any reason during the first 90 days of ownership, simply return the product and you'll receive a 100% refund, no questions asked.

2. HiStep Treadmill, $100 down and $40 per month.

[COPY AND PASTE GUARANTEE]

3. HiStep Tracker Ski Machine, $100 down and $50 per month.

[PASTE GUARANTEE]

4. HiStep Breeze Bike, $30 down and $25 per month.

[PASTE GUARANTEE]

JOB 4

Design a Greeting Card

Angie wants you to show her how to create a greeting card. She decided to create a birthday card for her mother.

1. If available with the word processing software, use a greeting card template. Angie supplied you with the content for the cover and the inside message. Key the content in the appropriate location. Change the font and size as desired. Add appropriate pieces of clip art.

2. If a template is not available, follow the steps below.

   - Subdivide your page into two columns and two rows.
   - Fold a sheet of paper as you would a greeting card. Sketch the content of each section. Unfold the sheet and use it as a guide. As you can see, two of the four sections will have to be rotated so the content will be upside down.
   - Key the content for the cover and the inside message. Add appropriate pieces of clip art.
   - Rotate the text and/or graphics as needed.

3. Save the file as CARD.

4. Print the card.

Happy Birthday *Mother*	*The family ties that keep us close hold so many memories of a loving family. This message comes with joy in sharing family ties with you.* *Happy Birthday*
(cover)	(inside message)

JOB 21

Use Cut and Paste

1. Open PASS.

2. Cut and paste and renumber the information as shown by the editing marks below.

THE UNITED STATES PASSPORT

Millions of U.S. citizens travel to other countries every year. If you, too, decide to travel to a foreign country, you may need a passport. To apply for a passport, you must appear in person at one of the passport agencies. These agencies are often located in local federal buildings. A passport is an official document issued by the U.S. Department of State that includes a photograph of you and identifies you as a U.S. citizen.

When applying for a passport, you will need to bring the following:

3 1.   Some identification that shows your signature and description. A driver's license could be used.

2.   Proof of U.S. citizenship. Most people use a birth certificate or a certificate of naturalization.

1 3.   The completed passport application.

4.   The required fee for the passport.

A passport is good for ten years from the date it is issued. After receiving your passport, sign your name on the inside cover. When traveling in a foreign country, always carry your passport with you. NEVER leave it in a hotel room.

Continued on Next Page

JOB 3

Create and Print Labels

Create labels for the family reunion letter.

1. With the word processing software, create a label form. Consider the brand, size of label, and number of labels per page.

2. Insert merge codes on the label for the name; street address; and city, state, and zip code.

3. Center the text on the page (label). If needed, change the left margin.

4. Save the file as FRLABELS.

5. Merge FRLIST and FRLABELS.

6. Print the labels.

> *Name Code*
> *Street Address Code*
> *City, State, Zip Code*

3. Use Save As to save the document as PASS2.

4. Print the document.

5. Open the letterhead file (LTRHEAD) created in Job 1. Angie wrote the letter shown below to use with the mail merge. Key the letter using merge codes for the name; street address; city, state, and zip code; salutation; and overnight.

6. Save the file as FRFORM.

7. Merge FRLIST with FRFORM.

8. Print the letters.

August 1, 19--

(Name Code)
(Street Address Code)
(City, State, and Zip Code)

Dear **(Salutation Code)**,

We finally have a date, time, and place for the big family reunion. The date is Friday, Saturday, and Sunday, September 2, 3, and 4. The time is <u>as early as you can come</u>. The place is the main lodge at the beautiful Mountain State Resort Park located ten miles east of Willis, Tennessee. We have arranged for overnight lodging for each family. Your family will stay at **(Overnight Code)**. A brochure giving details about your accommodations is enclosed.

If the arrangements are not satisfactory with you, please let us know. We look forward to seeing you.

Sincerely,

Angie and Jeff

Enclosure

Use Cut and Paste

1. Open ITIN.

2. Cut and paste information as shown below.

AN ITINERARY PREPARED FOR

Mrs. Olivia Castillo

__May 22__

10:15 a.m.	Leave Will Rogers Airport on United Flight 743.
12:15 p.m.	Arrive Fresno International Airport. Patricia Jackson of Fresno office will meet you and drive you to Skyline Hotel.
1:30 p.m.	Meet with Daryl Reininger and the property owners at the Skyline Hotel in the Chadwick Room.
3:00 p.m.	See properties with Ms. Jackson.
7:00 p.m.	Presentation with the Fresno Realtors in the Gold Room at the Fresno Convention Center.

__May 23__

7:00 a.m.	Breakfast at hotel with Patricia Jackson before drive to Kingsburg office to discuss acquisition of properties.
12:30 p.m.	Lunch with property owners.
2:00 p.m.	Meet with Chad Baltimore and the Zoning Commission Board at the Skyline Hotel in Room 133.
5:30 p.m.	Leave Fresno International Airport on Pacific Western Flight 759.
6:05 p.m.	Arrive Will Rogers Airport.

Continued on Next Page

JOB 2

Use Mail Merge

1. The Staffords are in charge of notifying all out-of-town family members of the upcoming family reunion. With the word processing software, use mail merge to create a letter for each family. Angie supplied you with the information in the table as shown below.

2. Create categories for the mail merge as follows:

   Name
   Street Address
   City, State, Zip Code
   Salutation
   Overnight

3. Use the table for your records. The salutation should be first names such as "Rachel and Hershel."

4. Save the file as FRLIST.

Name	Street Address	City, State, ZIP	Overnight
Rachel and Hershel Anderson	P.O. Box 7723	Lathrop, CA 95330	St. John Inn
Sue Anderson	1272 Rivershore Lane	Granite Falls, WA 98252	St. John Inn
Jean and Clyde Buckelew	111 Oak Forrest Circle	Upland, CA 51786	Leisure Hotel
Wilma and John Craig	1048 Rempas NW	Albuquerque, NM 87114	Leisure Hotel
Jim Craig	901 Villa Dr.	Euless, TX 76039	Leisure Hotel
Debbie and Mike Fox	1807 Wayne Ave.	South Pasadena, CA 91030	Leisure Hotel
Wanda and Harold Anderson	No. 11, Rd. 3400	Aztec, NM 87410	St. John Inn
Charles and Lynn Lankow	1527 Rubenstein Ave.	Cardiff by Sea, CA 92007	Georgetown Inn
Alice and Dan Richardson	1422 Foster Ave.	Seminole, OK 74868	Georgetown Inn
Christy and Tommy Vance	1029 Headingly NW	Albuquerque, NM 87107	Leisure Hotel
Susan and Kevin Buckelew	4458 Foster Rd.	Upland, CA 51784	Leisure Hotel

Continued on Next Page

JOB 22

Continued

3. Use Save As to save the document as ITIN2.

4. Print the document.

JOB 1

Create a Letterhead

1. Using the word processing software, create a letterhead similar to the one shown below. You may make desired changes, but make it attractive by using special effects such as graphics, text art, or graphic lines.

2. Save the letterhead as LTRHEAD.

3. Print the letterhead.

THE STAFFORDS

Angie & Jeff
4421 SW Freeman Street
Nashville, TN 37212

JOB 23

Move Tabular Columns

1. Open SALES.

2. Change the order of columns 2 and 3 as shown below. (Some applications may require that you convert the data to a table and then cut and paste the columns.)

3. Make the title bold.

4. Use Save As to save the document as SALES2.

5. Print the document.

SALES--SUMMER SEASON, 19--

Month	Tapes	Books
June	$ 15,525.40	$ 22,431.90
July	110,521.80	35,432.00
August	112,221.00	101,889.20

CHAPTER 18

Jobs 1–20
Simulation

Time Estimate: 10 hrs.

OBJECTIVES

Jeff and Angie Stafford are a married couple living in Nashville, Tennessee. They have purchased a new multimedia computer with an integrated software package. Neither of them has experience with this program, so they have asked you to show them how to use some of the features and to create some files that they can use with their computer.

Some of the things they want to do with their computer are listed below.

1. Create a letterhead
2. Use mail merge
3. Create and print labels
4. Design a greeting card
5. Create and use a form
6. Edit a mail merge list
7. Create a database
8. Create a checkbook register
9. Find the future value of a savings plan
10. Create a resume
11. Loan amortization
12. Create a newsletter
13. Create a ticket
14. Create a slide presentation
15. Create a sign
16. Use the Internet
17. Create and send a fax
18. Create a brochure

JOB 24

Move Tabular Columns

1. Open MINOR.

2. Move the columns as shown below. (Some applications may require that you convert the data to a table and then cut and paste the columns.)

3. Adjust the tabs settings if necessary.

4. Use Save As to save the document as MINOR2.

5. Print the document.

MINOR LEAGUE BASEBALL

First-Year Team Records

Team	Year	W - L	Pct.
Los Angeles Broncos	1981	70-91	.435
Kansas City Giants	1982	69-93	.426
Houston Comets	1983	64-96	.400
Seattle Bears	1984	64-98	.395
Dallas Stars	1985	64-98	.395
Washington Generals	1986	70-91	.435
Toronto Wildcats	1987	62-98	.344
Montreal Rams	1988	81-81	.500
San Diego Chiefs	1989	68-93	.422
New York Raiders	1990	78-83	.484

FINISH

SIMULATION

Challenge Reinforcement

Create the memo as shown below. Use the Copy and Paste function to copy the membership information three times.

TO: Alberto Perez, Chairperson

FROM: Lisa Staller, Membership Committee

DATE: January 4, 19--

SUBJECT: New Members

I am enclosing a list of members who joined our club during December. They are all employed by the Business Hardware and Software Association.

Please add this information to our new membership brochure.

Membership Information

Membership:
Children:
Home Address:
Telephone:
Employment: Business Hardware and Software Association
                          9307 Lee Highway, 6th Floor
                          Phoenix, AZ 85026-9300
                          Tele: 602-555-0140, Fax: 602-555-0144

Key the data below to complete the membership information. Save the document as CLUB. Print the document.

Jackie and David Dole
Larry, 12; Jack, 10
1107 Williams Avenue
Phoenix, AZ 85008-1817
602-555-0100

Cecilia and Daniel Ames
Amy, 4; Brook and Brian, 2
P.O. Box 6624
Phoenix, AZ 85018-6624
602-555-0105

Angela and Jeffrey Yandle
None
4862 Casterline Avenue
Phoenix, AZ 85008-4811
602-555-0198

Jessica and Jackson Reese
Jack, 18
Highway 402 North
Phoenix, AZ 85066-0402
602-555-0151

2. The title of the brochure will be "CROSSING THE BORDER."

3. The subtitle will be "Just Enough Spanish to Get By." Include in the brochure the name of the company, the address, city, state, zip code, telephone number, and fax number.

4. Save the document as INFOMEX.

5. Print the brochure. If your printer does not duplex print, manually feed the sheet through a second time.

6. Create a report to print labels. Use the database CLIENT2 and the query MEXICO to create a report that will print labels for the people interested in going to Mexico. Select a label size of your choice.

7. Save the report as MEXLABEL.

8. Print the labels. Assemble the brochure with the mailing labels.

9. Close the database and query.

You are working as the word processing supervisor for Jones Trucking. Compose a memo to the department heads instructing them to use the abbreviations composed in Job 10 for all invoices, purchase orders, letters, and packing slips. Use the Copy and Paste function to include the table in the memo. Inform them that they are to be using the metric system to express units of length, weight, and volume. Also, remind the department heads that all correspondence should be free of spelling errors and that all workers should proofread all correspondence carefully and run the Spell Check on all documents before the correspondence is sent. Save the document as JONES. Print the document.

Create a Brochure and Mailing Labels

Several of the clients of the Classic Travel Agency have requested a brochure listing some information they will need when traveling to Spanish-speaking countries. Prepare a brochure using a predesigned template or create your own.

1. Create the inside of the brochure using the information as shown below. You may use a predesigned template or create your own.

Essential Information

Do not waste time practicing what you're going to say to the border officials—the chances are that you won't have to say anything at all, especially if you travel by air. It's important to check that you have your documents handy for the journey. Before traveling, check to see if you have the following documents:

- ▶ **Passport**
- ▶ **Tickets**
- ▶ **Travelers' checks**
- ▶ **Insurance documents**
- ▶ **Driver's license**

Some common signs that you will need to be familiar with are:

- ▶ **ADUANA** (customs)
- ▶ **FRONTERA** (border)
- ▶ **FUNCIONARIOS DE ADUANAS** (frontier police)
- ▶ **CONTROL DE EQUIPAJES** (baggage control)

Most towns and even some villages in Spanish-speaking countries have a tourist information office. Look for these words:

- ▶ **OFICINA DE INFORMACION Y TURISMO**
- ▶ **DELEGACION PROVINCIAL DE INFORMACION Y TURISMO**

Everyday Expressions

The following are everyday expressions and words to help you get by while you are traveling in a Spanish-speaking country. Practice makes perfect, so it is a good idea to speak aloud the phrases you think you might use. This will give you a greater confidence.

▶ Hello	**Hola**
▶ Good morning	**Buenos días**
▶ Good afternoon	**Buenas tardes**
▶ Goodnight	**Buenas noches**
▶ Good-bye	**Adiós**
▶ See you later	**Hasta luego**
▶ Yes	**Sí**
▶ Thank you	**Gracias**
▶ That's right	**Exacto**
▶ No	**No**
▶ No, thank you	**No, gracias**
▶ Excuse me	**Perdone**
▶ It doesn't matter	**No importa**
▶ I'm sorry	**Lo siento**
▶ I don't speak Spanish	**No hablo español**
▶ Repeat that	**Repetir eso**
▶ Pleased to meet you	**Mucho gusto**
▶ My name is	**Me llamo**
▶ I don't understand	**No comprendo**
▶ I'd like that	**Quiero eso**
▶ I am American	**Soy Americano**
▶ The telephone	**El telefono**
▶ The toilet	**El servicio**
▶ I'm staying	**Estoy en**
▶ Dollar	**El dolar**

Eating and Ordering

By law, menus must be displayed outside or in the window, and that is the best way to determine if a place is right for your needs. The place to ask for is **un restaurante,** but you can eat at any of these places: restaurante, cafeteria, hosteria, meson, parador, posada, albergue de carreter (roadside inn), fonda (cheap simple food), merendero (meals or snacks during the early evening), or a casa de comidas (a simple restaurant).

When eating out in a restaurant, you might want to be familiar with the following key words:

▶ A table for one	**Un mesa para uno**
▶ A glass	**Un vaso**
▶ Some water	**Agua**
▶ I'd like…please	**Quiero…por favor**
a tea	**un te**
a glass of milk	**un vaso de leche**
a mineral water	**un agua mineral**
a Coca Cola	**una Coca Cola**
▶ The bill, please	**La cuenta, por favor**
▶ Soup	**Sopa**
▶ Egg dishes	**Huevos**
▶ Fish	**Pescado**
▶ Meat	**Carne**
▶ Game	**Caza**
▶ Fowl	**Ave**
▶ Vegetables	**Verduras/Legumbres**
▶ Cheeses	**Quesos**
▶ Fruits	**Frutas**
▶ Ice Creams	**Helados**
▶ Desserts	**Postres**

Continued on Next Page

CHAPTER 2

Jobs 27–42
Document Formatting

Time Estimate: 10 hrs.

OBJECTIVES

In this chapter, students will:

1. Use the Outline function
2. Use the Thesaurus
3. Create headers and footers
4. Set the Widow/Orphan Protect function
5. Create page numbers
6. Create an endnote
7. Change the font and font size
8. Use the Find and Replace function

Create a Memorandum with Integrated Spreadsheets

The accountant in the home office needs a report comparing the cost and charges for the resort and airfare rates for the vacations in Mexico.

1. Open MEMO.

2. Use your memo heading and the information as shown below to create a memorandum with the information requested.

3. Save the memo as COMPARE.

4. Print the memo.

TO:	William J. Garcia, Classic Travel, Home Office
FROM:	Greta Jewels, Chicago Branch Office
DATE:	March 17, 19--
SUBJECT:	Vacations in Mexico

Below is the comparison you asked for between our current (1/1 to 3/31) expenditures and charges for our resort and airfare rates to Mexico.

Insert the spreadsheet file COST-CHA.

JOB 27

Use the Outline Function

1. Change the top margin to 1.5 inches.

2. Use the Outline function to create the outline as shown below.

STEPS IN THE WRITING PROCESS

I.   PREWRITING

    A.   Clustering
    B.   Freewriting
    C.   Brainstorming
    D.   Charting

II. WRITING THE FIRST DRAFT

    A.   Purpose
    B.   Audience
    C.   Main Idea Development
        1.   Facts
        2.   Concrete detail
        3.   Examples
        4.   Reasons

III. REVISING

    A.   Purpose
    B.   Audience
    C.   Main Idea
    D.   Supporting Sentences

IV. EDITING AND PROOFREADING

    A.   Sentence Structure
    B.   Wording
    C.   Spelling
    D.   Capitalization
    E.   Punctuation

Continued on Next Page

JOB 10

Create a Memorandum with Integrated Spreadsheets

The accountant in the home office needs a report on the cash flow for January.

1. Open MEMO.

2. Use your memo heading and the information as shown below to create a memorandum with the information requested.

3. Save the memo as CASHFLOW.

4. Print the memo on one page.

TO: William J. Garcia, Classic Travel, Home Office

FROM: Greta Jewels, Chicago Branch Office

DATE: February 10, 19--

SUBJECT: January Cash Flow Chart

Below is the information you need for the January cash flow report. If you need any other information, please let me know.

| Insert the spreadsheet file CHECK. |

V.   PUBLISHING

   A.   Standard-Size Paper
   B.   Double Space
   C.   One-Inch Margins
   D.   Typewritten or Written in Ink

---

3. Save the document as STEPS.

4. Print the document.

JOB 9

Create a Memorandum with Integrated Spreadsheets

The marketing manager in the home office needs a price sheet for the vacations in Mexico.

1. Open MEMO.

2. Use your memo heading and the information as shown below to create a memorandum with the information requested.

3. Save the memo as PRICE.

4. Print the memo.

TO: Phil Ware, Classic Travel, Home Office

FROM: Greta Jewels, Chicago Branch Office

DATE: February 17, 19--

SUBJECT: Vacations in Mexico

Below is our Mexico price lists for hotels and airfares. These prices are expected to be good through the current year.

| Round-Trip Airfare: | $189.00 | Round-Trip Airfare: | $199.00 |
| Hotel: | Paradise Club | Hotel: | Krystal Plaza |

Insert the spreadsheet file PRICE-AC

Insert the spreadsheet file PRICE-CA

| Round-Trip Airfare: | $209.00 | Round-Trip Airfare: | $214.00 |
| Hotel: | Casa Maya | Hotel: | Fiesta Galleria Plaza |

Insert the spreadsheet file PRICE-PV

Insert the spreadsheet file PRICE-MC

FINISH

JOB 28

Use the Outline Function

1. Change the top margin to 1.5 inches.

2. Use the Outline function to create the outline as shown below.

3. Save the document as BUSINESS.

4. Print the document.

BUSINESS REPORTS

I.   INTRODUCTION

II.   OUTLINES

    A.   Purpose
    B.   Types
        1.   Topic
        2.   Sentence
    C.   Structure
        1.   Parallel
        2.   Nonparallel

III.   ROUGH DRAFT

    A.   Purpose
    B.   Body
    C.   Recommendation

IV.   FINAL DRAFT

    A.   Form
        1.   Letter format
            a.   Styles
            b.   Special features
        2.   Memorandum format
        3.   Manuscript format
            a.   Introductory pages
            b.   Body
            c.   Supplementary pages
    B.   Proofreading

V.   SUMMARY

FINISH

Slide 9 (bulleted list)
- **Sights include:**
- The great pyramids at Chichen Itza
- The ancient Mayan ruins in Tulum
- The natural aquarium at Xel-Ha
- Isla Mujeres

Slide 10 (bulleted list)
Krystal Plaza, Cancun
- Beautiful beachfront location
- Watersports facilities
- 2-, 3-, or 4-bedroom suites
- Year-round kids program
- Nearby shopping mall
- Tennis court

Slide 11 (slide with one title)
Rates for the Krystal Plaza
in Cancun

Insert file PRICE-CA

Slide 12 (title slide)
PUERTO VALLARTA

Slide 13 (bulleted list)
- Cobblestone streets wind among bleached white houses with red-tiled roofs.
- Puerto Vallarta has managed to keep the essence of Old Mexico at its core.

Slide 14 (bulleted list)
- If you prefer the beaches, you won't be disappointed.
- The northern shore of the Bahia de Banderas offers long stretches of golden sand.
- To the south, one finds many private coves warmed by the Mexican sun.

Slide 15 (bulleted list)
Casa Maya
Puerto Vallarta
- Beachfront location
- 1,200 ft. beach
- 2 Olympic-size freshwater pools
- Fitness/health center
- 10,000 sq. ft. casino
- Boutiques
- Watersports

Slide 16 (slide with one title)
Rates for the Casa Maya
in Puerto Vallarta

Insert file PRICE-PV

4. Add a transition of your choice for each slide.

5. Use build slide text on slides 1, 3, 4, 5, 8, 9, 10, 13, 14, and 15.

6. Switch to the Slide Show View and review your work.

7. Save your presentation as SLIDEVAC.

8. Print all slides of your presentation.

JOB 29

Use the Outline Function—Bullet Style

1. Key the title and the first paragraph of the unbound report as shown below. (See Reference Guide, page 501.)

2. Change the left and right margins to 1.5 inches and the line spacing to 1.0 for the bulleted items.

3. Select the bullet style outline if available with the software. Otherwise use bullets to create the list.

OUTLINES

Outlines have several uses, mainly as summaries for something we have read or something we plan to develop into a paper or speech. Below are some characteristics of a good outline.

- An outline has a title.

- It can be topics or sentences, but not both.

- In topic outlines, only the first word of each topic is capitalized, and periods are omitted after topics. In sentence outlines, the first word of each sentence is capitalized, and periods are included at the ends of sentences.

- There are at least two divisions at any level so that an item designated *1* will be followed by *2*, and an item designated *a* will be followed by *b*.

- A combination of Roman numerals, uppercase and lowercase letters, and Arabic numbers are used to show relationships. Number-letter designations are followed by a period and use the pattern below:

  ○ Roman numerals
  ○ Capital letters
  ○ Arabic numbers
  ○ Lowercase letters
  ○ Arabic numbers followed by parentheses
  ○ Lowercase letters followed by parentheses

JOB 8

Create a Presentation

The Classic Travel Agency needs a slide show of vacations in Mexico to show to prospective clients.

1. Use your presentations software to create a slide show for vacations in Mexico.

2. If available with your software, create a look for the presentation by selecting a predesigned presentation template.

3. Create the 16 slides below.

Slide 1 (title slide)
VACATION IN MEXICO
Luxurious Beachfront Resorts

Slide 2 (title slide)
ACAPULCO

Slide 3 (bulleted list)
- Acapulco is the world's capital of resorts.
- There are excellent shops and boutiques selling authentic Mexican goods.
- Enjoy coffee at the zocalo— a popular pedestrian plaza located in the center of town.

Slide 4 (bulleted list)
- Acapulco's beaches offer everything from rolling waves to spectacular sunsets.
- No trip to Acapulco would be complete without seeing the cliff divers of La Quebrada.

Slide 5 (bulleted list)
Paradise Club Resort
Acapulco
- Beachfront location
- 3 restaurants
- All oceanview suites
- 4 swimming pools
- 12 tennis courts
- 18-hole golf course
- 24-hour room service

Slide 6 (slide with one title)
Rates for the Paradise Club
in Acapulco

Insert file PRICE-AC

Slide 7 (title slide)
CANCUN

Slide 8 (bulleted list)
- Cancun is on Mexico's Yucatan Peninsula.
- The native language is Spanish, but English is widely spoken.
- The warm year-round temperature is 75 to 90 degrees.
- The currency is the Mexican peso.

- Roman numerals have a ragged left margin so that the periods after them align vertically.

- Each level has equal indentation. For example, all items designated by a capital letter are at the same left margin.

---

4. Save the document as OUTLINE.

5. Print the document.

2. Save the letter as MEXLET. Close the file.

3. Open the database CLIENT2 and the query MEXICO. Merge the query MEXICO with the letter MEXLET. Insert merge fields where appropriate.

4. Print the merged documents.

5. Do not save the merged document.

6. Close the query and the database.

FINISH

JOB 30

Use the Thesaurus

1. Key the unbound report as shown below. (See Reference Guide, page 501.)

2. Use the Thesaurus to replace the underlined words with words of your choice.

3. Save the document as COPY.

4. Print the document.

THE COPYRIGHT LAW

The problem of software theft can <u>threaten</u> all new development of software products. The illegal copying of software is popularly called "piracy."

Software development is a team <u>effort</u> that combines the talents of writers, programmers, and graphic artists. Those who copy software without permission are stealing from an entire team. They should understand the results of their actions. Making illegal copies robs all members of the team of a <u>just</u> compensation for their work.

Laws are made to protect the rights of the copyright holder. No <u>variation</u> is made between copying and <u>distributing</u> the software for free distribution or for sale. **The only exception is the right of the owner to make a backup copy.**

Copying of copyrighted software for any purpose other than stated above is a federal offense. The copyright law is very clear. The law states that it is illegal to make or circulate copies of copyrighted material without permission. Penalties include fines of up to $50,000 and jail terms of up to five years.

JOB 7

Merge a Query with a Letter

The Classic Travel Agency would like to send a letter with the *Vacation in Mexico* brochure to the clients that plan to travel to Mexico. Create a letter similar to the one shown below, and merge it with the query MEXICO.

1. Create a letter similar to the one shown below.

March 1, 19--

(First and Last)
(Address)
(City, State Zip Code)

Dear (First):

Even before the new world was discovered, the people of Mexico had discovered the delights of sunny shores and laid-back living. Now you can discover it all for yourself with the comfort and convenience of Classic Travel's *Vacation in Mexico.*

You'll see ruins of ancient civilizations and picturesque villages where work is done the same way it has been for centuries. You'll enjoy beautiful beaches, extraordinary shopping, lively music, and the warmth of the Mexican people. Dine in elegant restaurants, or find a cozy cantina where the flavor of the country can be experienced.

Classic Travel's *Vacation in Mexico* has a package that's great for you. Refer to the enclosed brochure for detailed information, round-trip air fare, and a hotel package that's right for any budget.

Classic Travel's *Vacation in Mexico* is waiting for you. For more information and reservations, call Classic Travel at 555-509-5525 today!

Sincerely,

Greta Jewels
Travel Agent

Enclosure

JOB 31

Create Headers and Footers

1. Key the unbound report as shown below. (See Reference Guide, page 501.)

HEADERS AND FOOTERS

The Header and Footer options are used for a multi-page document when the writer wants to have the same header or footer information placed on several pages of a document.

A header is usually one or two lines of type that will appear at the top of every page or every other page of a document. A footer is one or two lines of text that will appear at the bottom of a page or pages of a document. You can have one header or footer printed on every even-numbered page and a different header printed on every odd-numbered page.

Two headers and two footers may be defined in one document. A total of four lines can be used for the headers and footers on a page. Headers use one or two lines of space plus one blank line at the top of the text area. Headers print just below the top margin. Footers use one or two lines plus one blank line at the bottom of the text area. Footers print just above the bottom margin.

When headers and footers are used, the amount of space available for text will adjust automatically. Do not expect to be able to use the full 54 lines for text when you are using headers and/or footers.

Continued on Next Page

JOB 6

Continued

Name:	Carrell Falsarella	**Name:**	Bryan Harwell
Destination:	Mexico	**Destination:**	The Caribbean
Month and Year:	August, 1998	**Month and Year:**	July, 1999
Traveled Overseas:	No	**Traveled Overseas:**	No
Short Notice:	Yes	**Short Notice:**	No
Interests:	Sailing	**Interests:**	Golfing
Name:	June Hughes	**Name:**	Rosa Perez
Destination:	Europe	**Destination:**	Mexico
Month and Year:	June, 1999	**Month and Year:**	July, 1998
Traveled Overseas:	No	**Traveled Overseas:**	Yes
Short Notice:	No	**Short Notice:**	Yes
Interests:	Arts and Culture	**Interests:**	Hiking
Name:	Roy Vasquez	**Name:**	Susan Willoughby
Destination:	The Far East	**Destination:**	Mexico
Month and Year:	June, 1999	**Month and Year:**	May, 1998
Traveled Overseas:	Yes	**Traveled Overseas:**	Yes
Short Notice:	No	**Short Notice:**	Yes
Interests:	Arts and Culture	**Interests:**	Sailing

3. Save the database as CLIENT2.

4. Prepare a query of the clients that are interested in traveling to Mexico. List each client's first name, last name, address, city, state, zip code, and destination.

5. Save the query as MEXICO.

6. Print the query on one page.

7. Close the query and the database.

JOB 31

Continued

The appearance of the text in the header or footer can be varied in any manner that you can vary ordinary text. You can change the pitch and font or use boldface or underline. The text in headers and footers may be positioned using the space bar or tab stops or by using the center or flush right commands. If desired, you can also include a graphic for the header or footer. Date Text or Date Code may be used as part of a header or footer to insert the current date. Remember to use Date Code rather than Date Text if you wish the date to always be current.

To view headers and footers on the edit screen, change to Page Mode. The Page Mode is slower, but you have the advantage of seeing what the document will look like when it is printed.

---

2. Use the Page Header function to place "HEADERS AND FOOTERS" at the top of every page except page 1.

3. Use the Page Footer function to place "WordPerfect Functions" at the bottom right-hand corner of every page.

4. Save the document as HEADERS.

5. Print the document.

The following people responded to the survey mailed out by the Classic Travel Agency. Add the following information to the database CLASSIC.

1. Open the database CLASSIC.

2. Add the following fields and information to the database.

Name:	Danny Barnett	**Name:**	Carroll Brendle
Destination:	Mexico	**Destination:**	The Caribbean
Month and Year:	December, 1998	**Month and Year:**	January, 1998
Traveled Overseas:	No	**Traveled Overseas:**	Yes
Short Notice:	Yes	**Short Notice:**	No
Interests:	Golfing	**Interests:**	Sailing
Name:	Nancy Cobb	**Name:**	Jim Cooper
Destination:	Europe	**Destination:**	Mexico
Month and Year:	September, 1998	**Month and Year:**	February, 1999
Traveled Overseas:	No	**Traveled Overseas:**	Yes
Short Notice:	Yes	**Short Notice:**	Yes
Interests:	Arts and Culture	**Interests:**	Fishing
Name:	Sharon Dean	**Name:**	Wade Evans
Destination:	Mexico	**Destination:**	The Caribbean
Month and Year:	November, 1998	**Month and Year:**	January, 1999
Traveled Overseas:	No	**Traveled Overseas:**	Yes
Short Notice:	No	**Short Notice:**	No
Interests:	Hiking	**Interests:**	Sailing

Continued on Next Page

JOB 32

Set the Widow/Orphan Protect Function

1. Key the report as shown below in leftbound report format. (See Reference Guide, page 501.)

2. Set the Widow/Orphan Protect function.

PARTS OF A BUSINESS REPORT

Before writing a business report, the writer must study the subject of the report. Material should be gathered from several sources and arranged in a logical order. The paragraphs below describe the parts of a business report.

Cover Letter. The cover letter is usually one page long. It shows the name of the person requesting the report and the reason for the report.

Title Page. The title page shows the report title, the writer's name and title, and the date. The information should be attractively centered on the page.

Contents Page. The contents page outlines the major parts of the report. The report should be divided into fewer than a dozen parts. This gives the reader a quick reference to the main parts and saves the reader time.

Summary. If a report is long, a separate summary may be used. The summary gives the important suggestions of the report. It is helpful to those who do not have time to read the full report.

Continued on Next Page

JOB 5

Create a Brochure with Integrated Files

The Classic Travel Agency needs a brochure promoting the three resort locations in Mexico. Prepare a brochure using the information shown below.

1. The title of the brochure will be "VACATION IN MEXICO."

2. The subtitle will be "Acapulco • Cancun • Puerto Vallarta." Include in the brochure the name of the company, the address, city, state, zip code, telephone number, and fax number.

3. Follow the form as shown below for the inside of the brochure. Your brochure does not have to look exactly like the example as long as you include all of the material. The drawing tool was used for the airfare fees.

4. Save the file as BROCHURE.

5. Print the brochure. If your printer does not support duplex printing, manually feed the sheet through a second time.

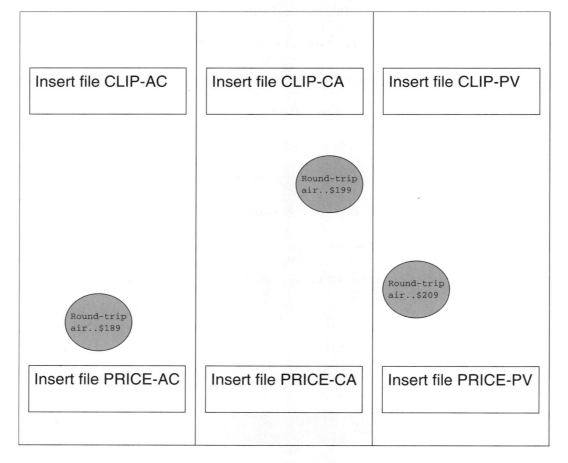

<u>Body</u>. The body has as many pages as needed to support the report's final findings and suggestions. All the information that the writer wants the reader to have about the subject of the report is placed in the body.

<u>Appendix</u>. Extra reading material that supports the ideas of the report is listed in the appendix. Information should be placed in the appendix when its length distracts from the understanding of the report. Additional references, graphs, or tables are examples of material that might be included in the appendix.

---

3. Place the header "PARTS OF A BUSINESS REPORT" in the upper left-hand corner of page 2 only.

4. Save the document as REPORT.

5. Print the document.

JOB 4

Create an Advertisement

1. Use your word processing or presentations software to create a sign for the local newspapers.

2. You can be creative, but use all of the information as shown in the slide below. This slide was created with presentations software, a predesigned template, and a bulleted list slide layout.

3. Save the advertisement as SIGN.

4. Print the sign.

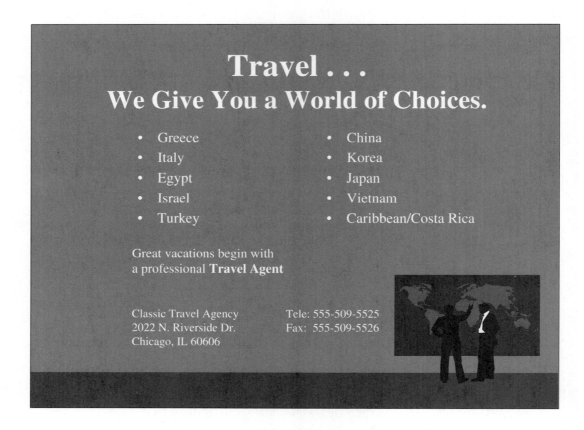

JOB 33

Create Page Numbers

1. Key the topbound report as shown below. (See Reference Guide, page 501.)

2. Set the Widow/Orphan Protect function.

WHAT A BUSINESS EXPECTS FROM PROSPECTIVE EMPLOYEES

Recommended Skills

Computer Skills. Today almost all companies use computers in one form or another. Employees must be computer literate. Any computer experience you have will be helpful to your future.

Accounting Skills. A day seldom goes by in most companies when basic accounting skills are not used. Debits, credits, depreciation, and the general ledger are common business terms. If you have at least a basic understanding of accounting, you have the edge on many of your fellow employees.

Keyboarding and 10-Key Skills. For many years, these two areas were marked as "secretarial" skills. Since the computer is a tool used by everyone from clerical workers to top management, keyboarding is considered a basic skill by many employers. You are strongly urged to have, at the very least, one year of keyboarding.

Communication Skills (Speaking and Writing). Businesses today require employees to possess both strong speaking and writing skills. Though often overlooked, listening is also an important communication skill.

Continued on Next Page

Current date

(First and Last)
(Address)
(City, State Zip Code)

Dear (First):

Thank you for expressing an interest in traveling with us. To receive more information, please fill out the information below and return it to us. A prepaid envelope is enclosed.

1. Which destinations are you planning to visit?
   ☐ The Caribbean   ☐ The Far East   ☐ Europe   ☐ Mexico

2. When do you intend to travel? _____ Month _____ Year

3. Have you taken an overseas vacation trip within the past three years?
   ☐ Yes   ☐ No

4. Can you travel on short notice to take advantage of special travel offers?
   ☐ Yes   ☐ No

5. Check all areas that interest you.
   ☐ Arts and Culture
   ☐ Cycling
   ☐ Diving
   ☐ Fishing
   ☐ Golfing
   ☐ Hiking
   ☐ Sailing
   ☐ Skiing

Thank you for taking the time to fill out the questionnaire. Remember that the Classic Travel Agency is here to make all of your travel arrangements. If we can be of assistance to you, contact our office at 555-509-5525 or fax us at 555-509-5526.

Sincerely,

Greta Jewels
Travel Agent

You are encouraged to take as many "speech" classes as your schedule will allow. These classes help remove the natural fear of standing before a group and teach you to write and speak clearly and to listen carefully.

Your ability to communicate well will differentiate you from other job applicants or employees. The more you develop your communication skills, the more efficient and productive you will be as an employee.

Leadership/Involvement Skills. Every business needs people who are natural leaders. When interviewing for a job, be sure to tell the interviewer about leadership positions you have held. Being a club or class officer or serving on the student council or other student organizations is a good way to develop leadership skills.

Applying or Interviewing for Employment

Dress Appropriately. Do not wear jeans or tennis shoes! Men are encouraged to wear a suit or slacks with a dress shirt. Women are encouraged to wear a business suit with hose and shoes with low heels.

Be Prepared. Bring a pen and any other material you will need to complete the job application. Bring a list of questions you wish to ask the interviewer about the job. In many places of business, the way you apply for a job is "graded" and is very influential in your getting the job.

Be Polite and Courteous. The impression you make may have as much to do with whether you get the job as your skills do.

Continued on Next Page

JOB 3

Merge a Table with a Letter

Classic Travel wants to send out a letter to its clients requesting information about their travel plans. Create a letter similar to the one shown on the next page and merge it with the database table to perform a mail merge.

1. Create a letter with a questionnaire similar to the one on the next page.

2. Save the file as QUESTION.

3. Open the database CLASSIC. Merge the database CLASSIC with the letter QUESTION. Insert merge fields where appropriate.

4. Print the merged documents.

5. Do not save the merged document.

6. Close the database.

Continued on Next Page

JOB 33

Continued

Fill Out the Application Completely. Filling out a job application is a very long and tedious process. It is important to fill out each section of the job application completely. Write "N/A" in areas of the application which do not apply to you. Double check names, addresses, and dates to be sure all the information is correct; never lie on an application.

Bring Your Reference List. Nearly every job application will have a place for you to list references. Prepare a list of personal references before you go to apply for the job. The list should include a full name, address, and both a home and business phone number of the reference. Good references include teachers, former employers, community leaders, and business leaders. Do not use relatives as references.

Know Your Employment History. Most job applications will have a space for you to list your employment history. For each job you have held, you should know your employer's name, address, and phone number. Also, be prepared to list your job title, your supervisor's name, and your dates of employment for each job. You may be asked to give a short description of your job duties. Gather all your employment history information before you go to apply for the job. This will help you complete the job application quickly and correctly.

---

3. Place page numbers at the bottom center of each page using the Page Number function.

4. Save the document as EXPECT.

5. Print the document.

JOB 2

Create a Database

The Classic Travel Agency would like a database that includes a list of clients. Prepare a database that includes the information shown below.

1. Use the list as shown below to create a database of the clients for the Classic Travel Agency. Save the database as CLASSIC.

2. Print the database in List View.

3. Close the database.

LAST	FIRST	NUMBER	ADDRESS	CITY	STATE	ZIP
Barnett	Danny	603-555-1286	930 W. 22nd	Chicago	IL	60606
Brendle	Carroll	603-555-2954	2002 Crossgate	Chicago	IL	60606
Cobb	Nancy	708-555-6935	343 Timber Ridge	Chicago	IL	60606
Cooper	Jim	312-555-6679	1833 Santa Fe	Chicago	IL	60606
Dean	Sharon	312-555-2948	1312 Market Place	Chicago	IL	60606
Evans	Wade	708-555-2802	13401 Northwood Blvd.	Chicago	IL	60606
Falsarella	Carrell	603-555-6789	515 Garvin	Chicago	IL	60606
Harwell	Bryan	603-555-1290	727 Oak Harbor	Chicago	IL	60606
Hughes	June	708-555-1223	326 W. 17th	Chicago	IL	60606
Perez	Rosa	312-555-2828	525 N. Rockwell	Chicago	IL	60606
Vasquez	Roy	708-555-1799	1316 Whispering Hills	Chicago	IL	60606
Willoughby	Susan	312-555-5802	2256 Kerr Lab Drive	Chicago	IL	60606

FINISH

1. Key the topbound report as shown below without the endnote reference numbers. (See Reference Guide, page 501.)

MAINTAINING GOOD HEALTH

by Susan Miller

Citizens of the United States eat too much, sleep too little, take on too much stress, and avoid exercise when possible. Maintaining good health, or wellness, could be defined as efforts to combine physical, emotional, social, and educational components of life in a balance that results in feeling well.

Adolescents need to learn about behavior, attitudes, and activities that will improve the quality of life. The stresses of modern life influence our health and often contribute to the leading causes of death in this country.[1] Even though the three leading causes of death for adolescents, according to the U.S. Department of Commerce's Statistical Abstract of the United States (1989), are accidents, homicides, and suicides, it is important to note that the major causes of death among all age groups are heart disease, cancer, and stroke.

These diseases have their origin in the lifestyle choices established during the early years of life and result from poor habits practiced over many years. The lack of accurate nutrition knowledge among adolescents and the poor dietary practices of many adolescents have been topics of concern for several decades.

Continued on Next Page

JOB 1

Continued

Name: CLIP-MC

MEXICO CITY

A few words hardly describe the exciting things you can do in the world's largest city. But you can start at La Zona Rosa. It's Mexico City's most chic area, and it's filled with restaurants, stores, and nightclubs.

Try not to miss Chapultepec Castle, either. It not only serves as the National Museum of History, but it also offers a sensational view of Paseo de la Reforma, the main street in Mexico City.

Adolescents are identified as a group in critical need of accurate nutrition information, but they have been resistant to many nutrition education efforts.[2] The need continues to grow for assessing the impact of nutrition among adolescents and its relationship to major health threats.

---

2. Use the Page Header function to place the following at the top of every page except page 1.

   MAINTAINING GOOD HEALTH   Current Date

3. Place page numbers at the bottom center of each page.

4. Set the Widow/Orphan Protect function.

5. Create the following endnote references using the endnote function. The endnote function will automatically place the reference in the text and will compile the list of endnotes at the end of the document. If you prefer to have the endnotes on a separate page, create a new page, center the heading "ENDNOTES" on line 1.5 inches and quadruple space.

---

[1]J. Marshall, Applied Biology/Chemistry: Disease and Wellness (Waco: Center for Occupational Research and Development, 1990), 60.

[2]J. Skinner, "Nutrition Knowledge of Teen-Agers," Journal of School Health, 54, No. 2, (1984): 71-73.

---

6. Save the document as HEALTH.

7. Print the document.

5. Use your word processing software to create the following short documents.

Name: CLIP-AC

ACAPULCO

Acapulco is the world's capital of resorts. Excellent shops and boutiques selling authentic Mexican goods are always easy to find.

Enjoy a morning coffee at the zocalo--a popular pedestrian plaza located in the center of town.

Acapulco's beaches offer everything from rolling waves to spectacular sunsets. No trip to Acapulco would be complete without seeing the cliff divers of La Quebrada.

Name: CLIP-CA

CANCUN

Cancun is on Mexico's Yucatan Peninsula. The native language is Spanish, but English is widely spoken.

The warm year-round temperature is 75 to 90 degrees. The currency is the Mexican peso.

Sights include the great pyramids at Chichen Itza, the ancient Mayan ruins in Tulum, the natural aquarium at Xel-Ha, and Isla Mujeres.

Name: CLIP-PV

PUERTO VALLARTA

In spite of its rapid development, Puerto Vallarta has managed to keep the essence of Old Mexico at its core. Cobblestone streets wind among bleached white houses with red-tiled roofs.

If you prefer the beaches, you won't be disappointed. The northern shore of the Bahia de Banderas offers long stretches of golden sand. To the south, one finds many private coves warmed by the Mexican sun. In town, numerous shops and restaurants maintain a quaint and authentic quality, still unspoiled by commercial development.

Continued on Next Page

1. Key the lease as shown below using a 1.5-inch top margin. Center the heading using 24 point Courier New all caps bold. Use 12 point Courier New for the remainder of the document. (If Courier is not available on your computer, choose a comparable font.)

2. Single space the paragraphs. Double space between paragraphs, and tab twice for the paragraph indents. Use the Underline key to create the signature lines. Use your own judgment for the line length.

LEASE AGREEMENT

CHARLES B. HARRISON and CATHERINE HARRISON, the LANDLORD, and GLEN C. KOPCZYNSKI and PAULA W. KOPCZYNSKI, the TENANT, agree to lease Apartment 5F, 222 South Parkway Avenue, Albany, New York 12205-3049, for a period of two (2) years.

Rent in the amount of Five Hundred Dollars ($500.00) per month is to be paid on the 1st day of each month for the period of this Lease either in person or by mail to CHARLES B. HARRISON and CATHERINE HARRISON at the address given in this Lease. Failure to pay the rent due each month on time for the period of this Lease will give cause to cancel this Lease by giving GLEN C. KOPCZYNSKI and PAULA W. KOPCZYNSKI a written five- (5) day notice.

The security of Five Hundred Dollars ($500.00) given by GLEN C. KOPCZYNSKI and PAULA W. KOPCZYNSKI to CHARLES B. HARRISON and CATHERINE HARRISON will be returned to GLEN C. KOPCZYNSKI and PAULA W. KOPCZYNSKI at the end of the period of this Lease.

GLEN C. KOPCZYNSKI and PAULA W. KOPCZYNSKI may not transfer this Lease or sublet the Apartment to any other person.

Continued on Next Page

3. Use your word processing software to create a letterhead. You should be creative and use many of the special tools and functions available to you through your word processing software. You may change the design of the letterhead, but use all of the information. The example was created with word art, clip art, and graphic lines.

   Name: LETTERHD

CLASSIC TRAVEL AGENCY

2022 N. Riverside Dr.
Chicago, IL 60606
Telephone: 555-509-5525
Fax: 555-509-5526

4. Use your word processing software to create a memo form. You may create a new heading or use your letterhead and add the following data.

   Name: MEMO

TO:

FROM:

DATE:

SUBJECT:

Continued on Next Page

IN AGREEMENT OF THESE TERMS, GLEN C. KOPCZYNSKI and PAULA W. KOPCZYNSKI and CHARLES B. HARRISON and CATHERINE HARRISON have hereunto recorded their signatures this third day of November, 19--.

————————————		————————————	
GLEN C. KOPCZYNSKI	Date	CHARLES B. HARRISON	Date
————————————		————————————	
PAULA W. KOPCZYNSKI	Date	CATHERINE HARRISON	Date

3. Save the document as LEASE.

4. Print the document.

2. Create the spreadsheet as shown below. Enter a formula under the balance to add the balance to the deposit column and to subtract the check column. Copy and paste the formula to complete the balance column.

Name: CHECK

CLASSIC TRAVEL AGENCY					
CASH FLOW FOR JANUARY, 19--					
Ck. No.	Date	Payee	Check	Deposit	Balance
	12/31/96				5,000.00
	1/1/97	Deposit		27,577.24	*formula*
101	1/1/97	Mexicana Air	11,900.56		
102	1/1/97	Travel Airlines	9,005.55		
103	1/1/97	City Utilities	188.44		
104	1/1/97	Krystal Plaza	1,459.88		
105	1/8/97	Paradise Club Resort	2,989.14		
106	1/8/97	OG&G Electric Co.	125.25		
107	1/15/97	Federal Printing	90.00		
108	1/16/97	Postmaster	96.31		
109	1/20/97	Tax Commission	65.00		
110	1/25/97	B & B Telephone	475.25		
111	1/25/97	Daily Tribune	13.40		
112	1/25/97	Treet's Cleaning Service	200.00		
113	1/25/97	Global Insurance	155.00		
114	1/31/97	PC Computers	150.00		
115	1/31/97	Ehrlich Rentals	1,260.00		
	1/31/97	Deposit		28,604.88	
116	1/31/97	Salary Expense	6,300.00		
117	2/1/97	Tax Commission	63.00		
118	2/2/97	Internal Revenue	1,417.50		
119	2/4/97	FICA Tax Expense	422.50		
120	2/5/97	Casa Maya	7,721.76		
121	2/8/97	Transfer of Funds	5,000.00		

Continued on Next Page

JOB 36

Use the Find and Replace Function

1. Open STAT.

2. Move the cursor to the top of the document.

3. Use the Find and Replace function to replace "American" with "all." Do not replace "Americans."

4. Use Save As to save the document as STAT2.

5. Print the document.

Name: PRICE-PV

Puerto Vallarta			
	3 Nights	7 Nights	Extra Night
19--	DBL	DBL	DBL
6/1 to 9/30	320	451	33
10/1 to 12/31	379	588	53
1/1 to 3/31	421	687	67
4/1 to 5/31	332	488	33

Name: PRICE-MC

Mexico City			
	3 Nights	7 Nights	Extra Night
19--	DBL	DBL	DBL
6/1 to 9/30	442	779	109
10/1 to 12/31	472	799	112
1/1 to 3/31	482	809	114
4/1 to 5/31	462	789	109

Name: COST-CHA

City	Resort	Cost/Charges 3 Nights		Cost/Charges 7 Nights		Cost/Charges Airfare	
Acapulco	Paradise Club	266	346	655	809	113	188
Cancun	Krystal Plaza	266	346	655	809	119	199
Mexico City	Fiesta Galleria	371	482	655	809	128	214
Puerto Vallarta	Casa Maya	324	421	556	687	125	209

Continued on Next Page

JOB 37

Use the Find and Replace Function

1. Open LEASE.

2. Use the Find and Replace function to replace "GLEN C. KOPCZYNSKI" with "DONALD R. BOWERS" and "PAULA W. KOPCZYNSKI" with "KATHERINE BOWERS."

3. Replace "Five Hundred Dollars ($500.00)" with "Six Hundred Dollars ($600.00)."

4. Use Save As to save the document as LEASE2.

5. Print the document.

JOB 1

Create Files for Integration

The files created in the activity will be used to create letters, memos, and brochures for the Classic Travel Agency.

1. Use your spreadsheet software to create the following files. Save the files using the name indicated to the left of or above each spreadsheet.

Name: PRICE-AC

Acapulco			
	3 Nights	7 Nights	Extra Night
19--	DBL	DBL	DBL
6/1 to 9/30	247	553	77
10/1 to 12/31	338	766	107
1/1 to 3/31	346	809	114
4/1 to 5/31	342	778	109

Name: PRICE-CA

Cancun			
	3 Nights	7 Nights	Extra Night
19--	DBL	DBL	DBL
6/1 to 9/30	327	743	104
10/1 to 12/31	337	788	111
1/1 to 3/31	346	809	114
4/1 to 5/31	342	778	109

Name: NEW-CANC

Cancun			
	3 Nights	7 Nights	Extra Night
19--	DBL	DBL	DBL
6/1 to 9/30	337	756	107
10/1 to 12/31	340	800	113
1/1 to 3/31	352	820	115
4/1 to 5/31	360	810	113

Continued on Next Page

1. Open EXPECT.

2. Make the changes as indicated by the editing marks shown below.

WHAT A BUSINESS EXPECTS FROM PROSPECTIVE EMPLOYEES

Recommended Skills

Computer Skills. Today almost all companies use computers in one form or another. Employees must be computer literate, *to find a place in the business world* Any computer experience you have will be helpful to ~~your future.~~ *you when you apply for a job*

Accounting Skills. A day seldom goes by in most companies when basic accounting skills are not used. Debits, credits, depreciation, and the general ledger are common business terms. If you have at least a basic understanding of accounting, you have the edge on many of your fellow employees.

Keyboarding and 10-Key Skills. For many years, these two areas were marked as "secretarial" skills. Since the computer is a tool used by everyone from clerical workers to top management, keyboarding is considered a basic skill by many employers. You are strongly urged to have, at the very least, one year of keyboarding.

Continued on Next Page

CHAPTER 17

Jobs 1–12
Integrated Activities

Time Estimate: 10 hrs.

OBJECTIVES

In this chapter, students will:

1. Create files for integration
2. Create a database
3. Merge a table with a letter
4. Create a memorandum with integrated spreadsheets
5. Create an advertisement
6. Create a brochure with integrated files
7. Create a query
8. Merge a query with a letter
9. Create a presentation
10. Create a brochure and mailing labels

Communication Skills (~~Speaking and Writing~~). Businesses today require employees to possess both strong speaking and writing skills. Though often overlooked, listening is also an important communication skill.

You are encouraged to take as many "speech" classes as your schedule will allow. These classes help remove the natural fear of standing before a group and teach you to write and speak clearly and to listen carefully.

Your ability to communicate well will ~~differentiate you~~ *set you apart* from other job applicants or employees. The more you develop your communication skills, the more efficient and productive you will be as an employee.

Leadership/Involvement Skills. Every business needs people who are natural leaders. When interviewing for a job, be sure to tell the interviewer about leadership positions you have held. Being a club or class officer or serving on the student council or other student organizations is a good way to develop leadership skills.

Applying or Interviewing for Employment

Dress Appropriately. Do not wear jeans or tennis shoes! *See that your clothes are neat, clean, and freshly pressed. Wear conservative colors— blues, grays, and browns are preferred.* Men are encouraged to wear a suit or slacks with a dress shirt. Women are encouraged to wear a business suit with hose and shoes with low heels. *Avoid flashy colors, loud fashions, and excessive jewelry.*

Continued on Next Page

INTEGRATED ACTIVITIES

Be Prepared. Bring a pen and any other material you will need to complete the

job application. Bring a list of questions you wish to ask the interviewer about the

job. In many places of business, the way you apply for a job is "graded" and is very

influential in your getting the job.

Be on time and check in with the receptionist or secretary. Be polite and

Be Polite and Courteous. ʌThe impression you make may have as much to do *pleasant.*

with whether you get the job as your skills do.

Fill Out the Application Completely. Filling out a job application is a very long

but don't let it scare you.

and tedious process, ʌIt is important to fill out each section of the job application

completely. Write "N/A" in areas of the application which do not apply to you.

Although it

Double check names, addresses, and dates to be sure all the information is correct; ʌ *might be tempting*

to stretch the truth in order to look

never lie on an application. *more qualified, don't do it.*

job

Bring Your Reference List. Nearly every job application will have a place for

you to list references. Prepare a list of personal references before you go to apply for

and always ask permission to use a person as a job reference.

the job ʌ The list should include a full name, address, and both a home and business

phone number of the reference. Good references include teachers, former employers,

community leaders, and business leaders. Do not use relatives as references.

Continued on Next Page

<u>Slide 3 (blank slide)</u>

3. Switch to the Slide Show View and review your work.

4. Save your presentation as ARCADE.

5. Print all slides of your presentation.

JOB 38

Continued

Move this section to follow the section <u>Fill-out the Application Completely</u> on the previous page

<u>Know Your Employment History</u>. Most job applications will have a space for you to list your employment history. For each job you have held, you should know your employer's name, address and phone number. Also, be prepared to list your job title, your supervisor's name and your dates of employment for each job. You may be asked to give a short description of your job duties. Gather all your employment history information before you go to apply for the job. This will help you complete the job application quickly and correctly.

<u>Follow-up after the Interview</u>. A simple thank you note could help you stand out from the competition. Thank the interviewer and state that you are definitely interested in the job. A few days later, follow-up with a telephone call to see if they have made a decision.

If you have gaps of employment between jobs, offer some explanation. Since it sometimes takes time to find a job, "job-hunting" is a legitimate reason, as are continuing education and retraining.

3. Add a header "WHAT A BUSINESS EXPECTS" on each page except page 1.

4. Use Save As to save the document as EXPECT2.

5. Print the document.

6. Create an outline for the report.

7. Use Save As to save the document as EXPECT3.

8. Print the outline.

Challenge Reinforcement

Prepare slides for John Frigg to introduce his maintenance classes.

1. Create the slides below.

2. If your software does not have all of these capabilities, substitute where necessary.

<u>Slide 1 (blank slide)</u>

<u>Slide 2 (blank slide)</u>

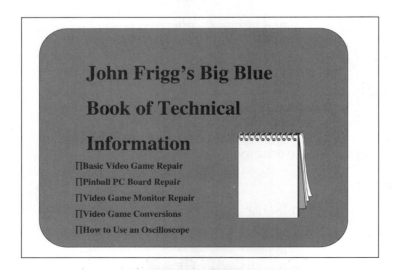

Continued on Next Page

JOB 39

Challenge Reinforcement

1. Open CLUES.

2. Make the changes as indicated by the editing marks as shown below.

CLUES FOR INTERVIEWS

The interview has been compared by adults and students alike to a final exam or a talent competition. Some college students call interviews "civilized torture." However, the interview is a crucial step in your job search. How you conduct yourself in an interview can make or break your chances of getting the job you want. A job interview gives you an opportunity to display *show* your intelligence, talent, and enthusiasm.

The employment interview is the only chance the company has to make a first *learn about you* hand evaluation of a prospective employee. The suggestions for a successful interview are the same whether you interview for a full-time or part-time job. A successful interview can make the difference between receiving and not receiving a job offer.

The objectives for any job interview are the same as well. A few suggestions to help you prepare for a job interview are as follows:

1. Gather enough accurate information about the job to help you make a decision about it.

Continued on Next Page

Slide 3 (blank slide)

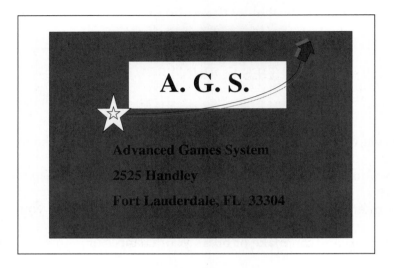

3. Switch to the Slide Show View and review your work.

4. Save your presentation as VENDING.

5. Print all slides of your presentation.

2. Introduce yourself to the receptionist. State your name, why you are there, and who you want to see.

3. Tell the interviewer what you are like, what qualifications you have, and that you are interested in the job.

4. Use good eye contact and speak loudly and clearly. Maintain good posture.

5. *Take with you a list of important facts about the company and a list of questions you would like answered.*

6. *Ask when a decision on the job will be made if the interviewer has not told you.*

7. *Thank the interviewer and express a positive interest in the job.*

8. *Send a brief letter to the interviewer thanking him or her for the chance to meet and discuss the job opening.*

After the interview, think about how you handled the interview and what went right or wrong during the interview. Make a list of DOs and DON'Ts that may be helpful to you in another interview. The more prepared you are for the interview, the better your chances will be of getting the job.

---

3. Place page numbers at the bottom center of each page.

4. Place the header "CLUES FOR INTERVIEWS" at the left on page 2 only.

5. Protect the document against widows and orphans.

6. Use Save As to save the document as CLUES2.

7. Print the document.

Challenge Reinforcement

Prepare the slides below to encourage vending machine operators to use games from Advanced Games System.

1. Create the slides below.

2. If your software does not have all of these capabilities, substitute where necessary.

Slide 1 (blank slide)

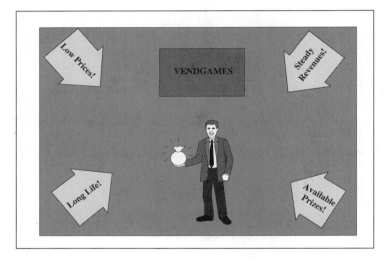

Slide 2 (blank slide)

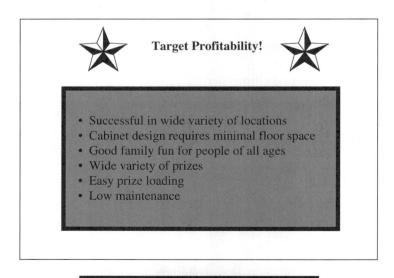

Continued on Next Page

JOB 40

Challenge Reinforcement

Create a title page for the report created in Job 33. The title page should include the title of the report, your name, and the date. Arrange the data attractively on the page. Change the font, font size, and attributes as desired. Save the document as TITLE, and print the document.

JOB 60

Run a Presentation

Prepare your slide show for presentation.

1. Open WESTERN5.

2. Switch to the Slide Show View and review your work.

3. Switch to Edit View and make any desired changes in the text.

4. If available with your software, create a look for the presentation by selecting a predesigned presentation template. Use a light background for overheads and a dark background for on-screen presentations and 35mm slides.

5. Add a transition of your choice to all slides.

6. If available with your software, add build effects of your choice to slides 2 and 3.

7. Dim after the build effects on slides 2 and 3.

8. Add sound effects to all slides.

9. Switch to the Slide Show View and review your work.

10. Switch to Sorter View and add timing effects for builds and transitions.

11. Switch to the Slide Show View and review your work.

12. Make any needed changes in the transitions, builds, or timings.

13. Use Save As to save your presentation as WESTERN6.

JOB 41

Challenge Reinforcement

If you go to a store and purchase software, you pay for it, but you do not own it. You have only purchased a license to use that software under the terms of the agreement. There are also several other kinds of software not sold in typical commercial institutions. The way software is sold or distributed places the ethical responsibility on the user. Write a short report covering the different kinds of software (commercial, shareware, public domain, freeware, etc.). Discuss the copyright laws and the ethics of making illegal copies of a copyrighted program or using software that you have not purchased. Save the document as ETHICS, and print the document.

JOB 59

Run a Presentation

Prepare your slide show for presentation.

1. Open NEWS2.

2. Switch to the Slide Show View and review your work.

3. Switch to Edit View and make any desired changes in the text.

4. If available with your software, create a look for the presentation by selecting a predesigned presentation template. Use a light background for overheads and a dark background for on-screen presentations and 35mm slides.

5. Add a transition of your choice to all slides.

6. If available with your software, add build effects of your choice to slides 2, 3, and 4.

7. Dim after the build effects on slides 2, 3, and 4.

8. Add sound effects to slides 2, 3, and 4.

9. Switch to the Slide Show View and review your work.

10. Switch to Sorter View and add timing effects for builds and transitions.

11. Switch to the Slide Show View and review your work.

12. Make any needed changes in the transitions, builds, or timings.

13. Use Save As to save your presentation as NEWS4.

JOB 42

Challenge Reinforcement

Go to a business in your area such as a doctor's office, attorney's office, or the school secretary's office. Write a brief report on the type of system they have and the software they are currently using. State whether they are using a stand-alone application or an integrated software package. Assuming cost is not a variable, offer suggestions for improving the operation of the office by upgrading the system or purchasing new software. Save the document as UPGRADE, and print the document.

Slide 2 (blank slide)
- *Link the spreadsheet NET.*
- *Key the title and the footnote.*
- *Use the cross and the thick down arrow drawing tools for the title background.*
- *Use the rectangle tool for the background behind the spreadsheet.*
- *Move and size as needed.*
- *Fill these items with a color of your choice.*

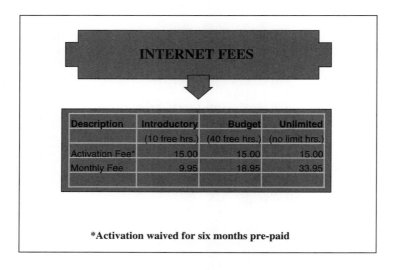

5. Switch to the Slide Show View and review your work.

6. Save your presentation as RATE.

7. Print all slides of your presentation.

8. Open your spreadsheet NET, and change the price of the monthly fees to "9.95," "18.95," and "33.95."

9. Open your word processing document INTER. Delete the last sentence.

10. Update your presentation.

11. Use Save As to save your presentation as RATE2.

12. Print all slides of your presentation.

CHAPTER 3

Jobs 43–59
Format Columns and Tables

Time Estimate: 8 hrs.

OBJECTIVES

In this chapter, students will:

1. Create text columns—newspaper style
2. Create text columns—balanced newspaper style
3. Change the column type
4. Create a column border
5. Create a table
6. Format numbers in a table
7. Join cells
8. Adjust column widths
9. Insert rows
10. Delete rows and columns
11. Create a table with addition
12. Set the table position
13. Create a memo with a table
14. Create a letter with a table

JOB 58

Link Data from Another Application

Create a presentation for a local internet company.

1. Using word processing software, create the text on slide 1. Save the document as INTER.

2. Using spreadsheet software, create the spreadsheet located in the middle section of slide 2. Save the spreadsheet as NET.

3. Create a new presentation.

4. Create slides similar to the ones below.

Slide 1 (blank slide)
- *Use the seal drawing tool.*
- *Fill with a color of your choice.*
- *Link the word processing document INTER.*

Get on the
INTERNET

Take advantage of low
introductory rates when you sign
up for the Oklahoma Online and
internet access! Much of the
Oklahoma Online's content is free,
including the Oklahoma City
bombing archives. A subscription is required
to read full text of news and feature articles,
to join in live chats, and for other services.

Continued on Next Page

JOB 43

Create Text Columns—Newspaper Style

1. Set the Widow/Orphan Protect function.

2. Set a 1.5-inch top margin.

3. Key the article as shown below. Center the title, and quadruple space below.

CREATING MULTICOLUMN DOCUMENTS

WordPerfect's Columns function makes it easy to create multicolumn documents. You can create newsletters, glossaries, scripts, inventory lists, or any other documents in which you want to divide text vertically on the page. You can create as many as 24 side-by-side columns.

There are four types of columns: newspaper, balanced newspaper, parallel, and parallel with block protect. Text in a newspaper column flows from the bottom of one column to the top of the next column, as it does in a newspaper article. If desired, you can select balanced newspaper columns with each column adjusted on the page so that they are equal in length. With parallel columns, related text can be grouped across the page in rows. Parallel columns can be used for scripts, charts, or inventory lists. Block Protect keeps each row of columns together. If a row in one column is so long that it moves across a page break, the entire row moves to the next page.

Columns are easy to create if you have a few simple guidelines to follow. Use the following suggestions when creating your columns:

WordPerfect's Columns function can be defined before or after the material has been keyed.

To prevent a ragged right margin, change the justification setting to full justification and turn hyphenation on.

Select balanced newspaper if the text ends up uneven and you prefer the length of each column to be approximately the same. Because of certain fonts selected, or the number of lines in the text, it may be impossible for the last lines of each column to end on the baseline. However, it is a better method than trying to do it manually.

To make the text look more attractive, change the tabs to repeat every .25 inch. This will indent the tab setting only a quarter of an inch instead of a half inch.

Continued on Next Page

Slide 2 (blank slide)
- *Link the spreadsheet CDROM.*
- *Size and move as shown.*
- *Add text as shown.*
- *Rotate and size the text.*

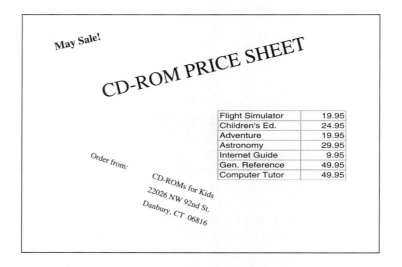

4. Add a transition of your choice to all slides.

5. If available with your software, use a build slide text of your choice.

6. Switch to the Slide Show View and review your work.

7. Save your presentation as KIDS.

8. Print all slides of your presentation.

9. Open your spreadsheet CDROM, and change the price of Gen. Reference to "39.95."

10. Sort your spreadsheet so the titles are in alphabetical order.

11. Update your presentation.

12. Change the first line of slide 2 to "August Sale!"

13. Use Save As to save your presentation as KIDS2.

14. Print all slides of your presentation.

JOB 43

Continued

If you want to force text from one column to the next, press Ctrl+Enter. Use the Ctrl+arrow keys to move from one column to another.

Remember you can add any kind of graphic to a column by putting it in a graphics box. When you are creating a graphics box for a table that spans several columns, attach it to the page. If your columns are formatted with several graphics or tables, change to Page Mode to display the document as it will look when it is printed.

---

4. Set the Columns function after the title. Use newspaper style with two columns and .5 inch between columns.

5. Save the document as COLUMN.

6. Print the document.

JOB 57

Link Data from Another Application

Create a presentation for a software company to introduce software for kids.

1. Using spreadsheet software, create the spreadsheet located on slide 2 as shown below. Save the spreadsheet as CDROM.

2. Create a new presentation.

3. Create the slides similar to the ones below.
   Slide 1 (title slide)
   - *Use the seal drawing tool.*
   - *Add text as shown.*

Continued on Next Page

Create Text Columns—Balanced Newspaper Style

1. Set the Widow/Orphan Protect function.

2. Set a 1.5-inch top margin.

3. Key the article as shown below. Center the title, and quadruple space below.

4. Set the Columns function after the title. Use the balanced newspaper style with 3 columns and .5 inch between columns. Turn on hyphenation, and use full justification.

5. Save the document as LISTEN.

6. Print the document.

LISTENING SKILLS

Too often we have trouble understanding what has been said because we are not really tuned in to the person talking to us. You can avoid some everyday misunderstandings by being a better listener. Here are helpful ideas to improve your listening skills.

Think about your reasons for being in a conversation. Ask yourself, "Am I here to learn something?" "Am I here to defend my position?" "Am I here to give support to the speaker?" It is important to understand the purpose of the conversation. This will help you become a better listener.

If someone gives you instructions, listen carefully and then repeat the instructions. If you're not sure you understand what someone has said, repeat what you think is meant, and ask if you've understood correctly.

Look often at those speaking to you. Make eye contact and smile if appropriate. Looking down might make them think you're not interested in what they have to say.

Take notes during phone conversations. Be sure to write down the purpose of the phone call. Also, write down the facts, the date, and the time of day. You're more likely to pay close attention if you are jotting down key words and phrases. Ask questions to be sure you understand important points.

When someone wants to argue with you, don't interrupt; let them talk. When they are finally done, simply repeat their position as you understand it. This lets them know you've been listening and are interested in what they have to say.

Slide 3 (slide with one title)
POSSIBLE INTERESTED PARTIES

Embed the spreadsheet BUYER into your presentation.

Name	Company	Phone No.	Fax No.
Bill Vandiver	Ames Services	(918) 555-1234	(918) 555-5802
Treva Gurley	Evans Realty	(918) 555-2684	(918) 555-2221
Mary Cummings	Martin, Wass & Co.	(918) 555-2991	(918) 555-5109
Jeff Hobbs	Hobbs' Catering	(918) 555-3287	(918) 555-9988

Slide 4 (slide with one title)
CONTACT RANDY VARA WITH OFFERS

Add an appropriate piece of clip art.
Add the text "Remember Open House, 1:00 to 5:00 Daily!"

5. Add a transition of your choice to all slides.

6. If available with your software, use a build slide text of your choice.

7. Switch to the Slide Show View and review your work.

8 Save your presentation as ROSS2.

9. Print all slides of your presentation.

JOB 45

Change the Column Type

1. Open COLUMN.

2. Change the column type to balanced newspaper style with 3 columns, and add a column border between the columns. Use .5 inch between columns.

3. Change the justification to full, and turn on hyphenation.

4. Change the tab settings to repeat every .25 inch.

5. Use Save As to save the document as COLUMN2.

6. Print the document.

Embed Data from Another Application

Create a presentation for use at the May sales meeting of Ross Real Estate Agency.

1. Using spreadsheet software, create the spreadsheets as shown below and on the following page. Save the first spreadsheet as ORCHARD and the second as BUYER.

2. Create a new presentation.

3. If available with your software, create a look for the presentation by selecting a predesigned presentation template.

4. Create the following slides:

   Slide 1 (title slide)
   ROSS REAL ESTATE AGENCY
   May Sales Meeting

   Slide 2 (slide with one title)
   CONTRACT EXPIRES JUNE 1, 19--

   Embed the spreadsheet ORCHARD into your presentation.
   Use the drawing tool to create the arrow.

Location:	410 West Orchard
	414 West Orchard
Price:	$210,000 each
Price Reduction:	15% for quick sale
Open House:	1:00 to 5:00 daily

Continued on Next Page

JOB 46

Create a Column Border

1. Open LISTEN.

2. Add a column border between the columns in the document.

3. Use Save As to save the document as LISTEN2.

4. Print the document.

JOB 55

Embed Data from Another Application

Create a slide for the National Hospital Association to use at the fall conference.

1. Using spreadsheet software, create the spreadsheet as shown below. Save the spreadsheet as HOSPITAL.

2. Create a new presentation.

3. Create the following slides:

   Slide 1 (title slide)
   NATIONAL HOSPITAL ASSOCIATION
   Report for First Quarter, 19--

   Slide 2 (slide with one title)
   Admissions, Occupancy, Length of Stay

   Embed the spreadsheet HOSPITAL into your presentation.

Type of Hospital	Patients Admitted	Average Occupancy	Average Stay
A-1	2682	72%	6.2
A-2	1824	81%	6.9
A-3	1498	88%	5.9
A-4	986	79%	4.7
A-5	494	62%	6.1
A-6	201	91%	6.2

4. Switch to the Slide Show View and review your work.

5. Save your presentation as HOSP.

6. Print all slides of your presentation.

JOB 47

Create a Table

1. Set the page to center vertically.

2. Use the Table function to create and format the table as shown below.

3. Center and underline the column headings.

4. Save the document as TRAINING.

5. Print the document.

COMPUTER TRAINING CLASS

Spring Roster

Name	Age	Social Security No.
Mary Alice Roberts	22	409-88-9047
Benson Carlson	18	304-90-2389
Maria Sanchez	30	204-78-7892
Jack Chung	16	309-89-0459
Elmer Crosset	15	209-89-8765
Carol Ostendorf	28	309-67-9026

4. Create a new slide similar to the third example as shown below. Use the slide layout with one title.
   - Key the title. Format as shown.
   - Use the rounded rectangle tool to create the background box for the text. Key the text as shown. Format as shown.
   - Group the text with the rectangle and rotate as shown.
   - Use the thick left arrow tool to create an arrow. Position and rotate as shown.
   - Add an appropriate piece of clip art.

5. Save your presentation as CALL.

6. Print all slides of your presentation.

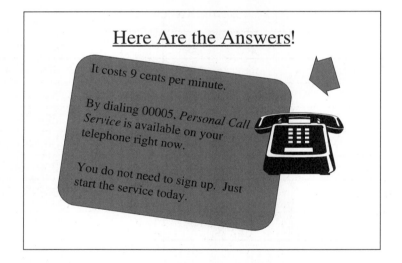

JOB 48

Format Numbers in a Table

1. Set the page to center vertically.

2. Use the Table function to create and format the table as shown below.

3. Center and underline the column headings. Right align the number columns.

4. Remove all lines and borders from the table.

5. Save the document as FITNESS.

6. Print the document.

PHYSICAL FITNESS CONNECTION

Income Comparison Report

<u>Income</u>	<u>1991</u>	<u>1992</u>	<u>1993</u>
Membership Fees	$52,968.25	$64,986.75	$68,201.04
Vending Machines	6,882.50	9,882.50	8,542.00
Equipment Sales	8,289.41	7,006.56	3,072.78
Private Classes	4,827.50	9,882.50	11,005.64
Clothing Sales	3,905.45	4,216.79	5,111.04
Shoe Sales	6,894.11	6,996.12	7,021.25

3. Create a new slide similar to the second example as shown below. Use the title and two-column slide layout.
   - Add the title. Use bold italic print as shown.
   - Key the bulleted items.
   - On the right side, draw a seal with the seal tool. Size as shown. Make the seal green.
   - Key the text inside the seal. Format as shown.
   - Put a heavy border around the text. The color inside the border should be a lighter shade of green.

Continued on Next Page

1. Set the page to center vertically. Center the heading of the article, and key the first paragraph.

2. Use the Table function to create and format the table as shown below. Join the cells as necessary.

3. Set the position of the table to center horizontally.

MEGACITIES IN THE YEAR 2000

At the start of the next century, 40% of the world's people will be living in cities, according to a new report from the United Nations Population Fund. The report predicts that at least 83% of the population growth through the end of the 1990s will be in urban areas, as a result of industrialization in Asia, Africa, and Latin America.

No.	City	Population
1	Mexico City	25.6 million
2	Sao Paulo	22.1 million
3	Tokyo	19 million
4	Shanghai	17 million
5	New York	16.8 million
6	Calcutta	15.7 million
7	Bombay	15.4 million
8	Beijing	14 million
9	Los Angeles	13.9 million
10	Jakarta	13.7 million

Source: United Nations Population Fund

Continued on Next Page

Work with Graphics

Create slides to introduce a new calling service.

1. Create a new presentation. Use a blank slide layout.

2. Create a slide similar to the first example as shown below.
   - Draw a diamond with the diamond tool and fill the diamond with green.
   - Draw a rectangle with the rectangle tool and fill the rectangle with light blue.
   - Add text to the rectangle. Increase the point size and use bold print as shown in the example.
   - Put a border around the text.
   - Use the star tool to create the star at the end of the text. Make the star green.
   - Position the diamond, the rectangle, the text, and the star similar to the example below.
   - Add a suitable piece of clip art and position it as shown below.

Continued on Next Page

4. Remove all lines and borders from the table.

5. Save the document as CITIES.

6. Print the document.

4. Create a new slide similar to the third example as shown below. Use a blank slide layout.
   - Draw a rectangle for the first line of text. Add a heavy border around it and turn the shadow on.
   - Add text to the rectangle and group the text with the rectangle.
   - Increase the point size of the text and change to bold italic print.
   - Move and rotate as shown.
   - Use the drawing tools to create the letter, the mailbox, and the flower.
   - Add text as shown.
   - Rotate the letter.
   - Add an appropriate piece of clip art.

5. Save your presentation as BIRTHDAY.

6. Print all slides of your presentation.

Adjust Column Widths

1. Set the page to center vertically.

2. Key the first three lines as shown below.

3. Use the Table function to create and format the table as shown below. Adjust the column widths as necessary.

4. Save the document as CRUISE.

5. Print the document.

WESTERDAM CRUISE TO ALASKA

Friday, June 7, 19--   Sunrise: 5:11 a.m.
                                                                      Sunset: 9:32 p.m.

7:00 a.m.		Pools are open.
8:30 a.m.	Walk-a-Mile	Cruise Staff Carol will stamp your "passport" on the Upper Promenade Deck.
9:15 a.m.	Fitness Workout	Meet Cruise Staff Greg in the Ocean Spa Fitness Center for a supervised morning workout.
9:30 a.m.	Aerobics	Meet Cruise Staff Jamie for the last battle in the War on the Waistline in the Queen's Lounge.
10:00 a.m.	Visit to the Bookchest	Books and indoor games are available from Cruise Staff Gayle in the Bookchest.

3. Create a new slide similar to the second example as shown below. Use a blank slide layout.
   - Add a piece of clip art representing a notebook, page, or book.
   - Add text inside the notebook. Use bold italic print.
   - Add a suitable piece of clip art on the left side.

Continued on Next Page

JOB 51

Insert Rows

1. Open CRUISE.

2. Insert rows and add the information as shown below in the proper place. Use the time of day as your guide.

3. Use Save As to save the document as CRUISE2.

4. Print the document.

7:30 a.m.	Paddle Tennis	Mixed doubles paddle tennis tournament begins with Cruise Staff Catherine on the sports deck.
7:45 a.m.	Golf	Mixed golf chipping tournament begins with Cruise Staff Richard and Greg at the lobby outside the Admiral's Lounge.
11:00 a.m.	Mileage Pool	Enter your best estimate with Cruise Staff Brian in the Ocean Lounge for how many miles you think the ship might have sailed since leaving Sitka yesterday until noon today.
12:00 p.m.	Lunch	The Lido and Verandah Restaurants will serve an Indonesian lunch. The Amsterdam Dining Room will have a Smorgasbord Buffet and Ice Cream Parlor.

JOB 53

Work with Graphics

Create a presentation for the sales representatives of Perfect Protection.

1. Create a new presentation. Use a blank slide layout.

2. Create a slide similar to the first example as shown below.
   - Draw a rectangle and fill the rectangle with green.
   - Add text to the rectangle and group the text with the rectangle.
   - Increase the point size of the text and change to bold italic print.
   - Rotate the rectangle as shown.
   - Add a suitable piece of clip art.

Continued on Next Page

Delete Rows and Columns

1. Open CRUISE2.

2. Delete row 3 (the 7:45 a.m. golf outing).

3. Delete column 2 (the activity).

4. Change the width of column 1 to approximately 2 inches and column 2 to approximately 4.5 inches.

5. Use Save As to save the document as CRUISE3.

6. Print the document.

Create a slide for the loan department of First Security Bank.

1. Create a new presentation.

2. Create a slide similar to the example as shown below. Choose the slide with clip art on the right.
   - If needed, increase the point size of the title and the bulleted items.
   - Insert clip art that includes people and a board. You may need to use the drawing tool to draw a board.
   - Add the message as shown below to the board. Make this message bold print.

3. Save your presentation as LOAN.

4. Print the slide.

JOB 53

Create a Table with Addition

1. Set the page to center vertically.

2. Use the Table function to create and format the table as shown below.

3. Use the Calculation or Table formula function to total the December salaries.

4. Save the document as SALARIES.

5. Print the document.

DECEMBER SALARIES	
Abramson, Stanley	$3,750.00
Chiang, Kuang-fu	1,950.00
Delgado, Dolores	2,740.00
Guzman, Eduardo	990.00
Jackson, Rosie	2,000.00
McClain, Malcom	1,545.00
O'Malley, Johnny	3,655.00
Total	$

JOB 51

Use the Print Options

In this exercise, you will use some of the presentation print options. If your software does not accommodate a particular option, substitute an option of your choice.

1. Print INSURANC in Outline View.

2. Print WRITING in Outline View.

3. Print handouts (3 slides per page) of UNITED3. Add frames to the printouts if possible. This has an area for notes.

4. Print handouts (3 slides per page) of COMPUT2. Add frames to the printouts if possible.

JOB 54

Create a Table with Addition

1. Set the page to center vertically.

2. Use the Table function to create and format the table as shown below.

3. Use the Calculation or Table formula function to total each quarter.

4. Save the document as HOME.

5. Print the document.

ELSTON'S REAL ESTATE	
First Quarter	
New Homes	$ 21,300,000
Existing Homes	10,500,000
First Quarter Total	$
Second Quarter	
New Homes	$ 30,500,000
Existing Homes	11,500,000
Second Quarter Total	$
Third Quarter	
New Homes	$ 31,350,000
Existing Homes	6,550,000
Third Quarter Total	$
Fourth Quarter	
New Homes	$ 25,500,000
Existing Homes	11,775,000
Fourth Quarter Total	$

JOB 50

Add Notes to a Presentation

Joe Mainelli asked you to add his notes to the presentation he will be giving on building a computer.

1. Open COMPUTER.

2. Switch to Notes View.

3. Add notes to the slides listed below. You may need to zoom in for a larger view.

Slide 2

- You don't have to pay for features you don't need.

- You can make your own repairs. It is not only less expensive, but it is also faster. You can usually do it within a day.

- You have more flexibility when it is time to upgrade.

- Unfortunately, many computer makers' idea of upgrade is "buy a new computer."

Slide 5

- Don't skimp on your CPU and motherboard. If they fail, you are out of luck.

- The more memory you have, the better. You need at least 16MB.

- When you purchase a hard drive, size is important. The bigger the better. We recommend at least a one gigabyte (GB) hard drive. Don't be cheap with the hard drive. Stick with the big names.

- Make sure the monitor and video card are compatible. A good monitor is a 15-inch, noninterlaced, SVGA monitor with a dot pitch of .28mm or less.

- Desktop or tower cases are available. Most come with a power supply already installed. Be sure to buy one with enough bays to let you expand your system in the future.

- You can spend a lot or a little on your keyboard and mouse. Keep down your initial cost by buying cheap and replacing with better quality later.

4. Use Save As to save your presentation as COMPUT2.

5. Print note pages of slides 2 and 5.

JOB 55

Set the Table Position

1. Set the page to center vertically. Change the left and right margins to 2.5 inches.

2. Use the Table function to create and format the table as shown below.

3. Use the Calculation or Table formula function to total the "Total Accounts Receivable."

4. Set the table position to center horizontally.

5. Save the document as BOBBY.

6. Print the document.

BOBBY Z SPORTS CENTER
Schedule of Accounts Receivable
December 31, 19--

James Clark	$65.00
Jim McCharen	73.14
Frank Martinez	206.85
Gary McNutt	241.80
James Waters	25.00
Paula Jones	93.88
Tommie Meharg	25.00
Total Accounts Receivable	$

Slide 4

- Capture the attention. You could use a poem, a current event, statistics, rhetorical questions, historical references, quotes, humor, or startling facts.

- Develop your transitions to move smoothly between subjects by using stories, illustrations, anecdotes, or jokes.

- The body is the main point of the presentation. Remember to summarize your content often.

- The call to action is what you want your audience to do after hearing your presentation. Move your audience.

4. Use Save As to save your presentation as UNITED3.

5. Print note pages of slides 2, 3, and 4.

JOB 56

Create a Memo with a Table

1. Set the top margin at 1.5 inches, and key the memo as shown below.

2. Use the Table function to create and format a table for the financial information.

3. Use the Calculation or Table formula function to total the columns.

4. Remove all lines and borders.

5. Save the document as OPERATE.

6. Print the document.

TO: All Department Heads

FROM: Jason O'Neal

DATE: October 1, 19--

SUBJECT: Operation Expenses for September

Please review the list of budgeted and actual operating expenses listed in the table below.

	Budget	Actual
Salary Expense	$77,300.00	$77,363.00
Advertising	1,990.52	3,015.21
Delivery	4,589.85	5,604.50
Depreciation	5,450.15	5,655.15
Supplies	4,460.00	5,469.00
Total	$	$

I need your suggestions for improvement at our regular Friday meeting.

kg

JOB 49

Add Notes to a Presentation

Add your notes to the presentation you will give to the Public Relations Department of United Tire Company.

1. Open UNITED2.

2. Switch to Notes View.

3. Add notes to the slides listed below. You may need to zoom in for a larger view.

<u>Slide 2</u>

- The size of the group affects your content, logistics, and presentation style.
- Fewer than 30 people can be relatively informal.
- With 30 to 50 people, you have less flexibility.
- More than 50 people is considered formal. If you need a microphone, try a lapel microphone.

- Your Superiors. Suggest—don't lecture or dictate. Be sure you have the facts.
- Your Peers. Relate or share information. Include them in the presentation.
- Special Interest Groups. Build the presentation around the concerns of the group.
- Mixed Groups. Use a combination of presentation techniques in order to reach everyone.

- The audience's expertise will set the stage for the presentation.
- If they are interested, you can teach them.
- If they don't want to be there, try to involve them.
- If they are uninterested, you must entertain them.

<u>Slide 3</u>

- Be sure you know exactly what the topic is for your presentation. If you are doing this for someone else, double check with him or her.

- The theme must be short and clear--only a few words.

- Research by talking to customers, talking to users, reviewing annual reports, reviewing any available company information, and reading current magazine articles.

- Consider using graphs, charts, and maps. Also, consider using slides or a videotape.

Continued on Next Page

JOB 57

Create a Letter with a Table

1. Set the page to center vertically. Key the letter as shown below in block style. (See Reference Guide, page 501.)

2. Use the Table function to create and format a table for the list of charges.

3. Use the Calculation or Table formula function to total the charges.

4. Remove all lines and borders.

Current Date

Fast and Easy Print
205 Chubb Avenue
Lyndhurst, NJ 07071-2050

Ladies and Gentlemen:

Thank you for your order No. 32985 for laser printer paper.

Below is a list of your charges. You have 30 days to make payment with no interest.

5 reams of 8 1/2 by 11, 24 lb., white	$23.00
3 reams of 11 by 17, 24 lb., white	18.90
2 reams of 8 1/2 by 11, 24 lb., blue	10.15
1 ream of 11 by 17, 24 lb., blue	7.02
Total Charges	$

Remember, we have all colors and weights of laser paper and the best prices in town. Please call us again when you need to order more paper.

Sincerely,

PAPER DIRECT

Lee Holmes
Sales Representative

jt

Slide 5
Editing and Proofreading
- Sentence structure
- Wording
- Spelling
- Capitalization
- Punctuation

Slide 6
Publishing
- Standard-size paper
- Double-spaced lines
- One-inch margins

4. If available with your software, use build slide text on slides 2 through 6. Have the text fly from the left.

5. Switch to the Slide Show View and review your work.

6. Save your presentation as WRITING.

7. Print all slides of your presentation.

5. Save the document as FAST.

6. Print the document.

JOB 48

Use Outline View

Prepare a slide presentation for PC Publishing House.

1. Create a new presentation.

2. If available with your software, create a look for the presentation by selecting a predesigned presentation template.

3. Switch to the Outline View, and enter the text below for slides 1 through 6.

Slide 1 (title slide)
PC PUBLISHING HOUSE
Steps in the Writing Process

Slide 2
Prewriting
- Clustering
- Freewriting
- Brainstorming
- Charting

Slide 3
Writing the First Draft
- Purpose
- Audience
- Main idea development
  - facts
  - concrete details
  - examples
  - reasons

Slide 4
Revising
- Purpose
- Audience
- Main idea
- Supporting sentences

Continued on Next Page

1. Key the memo in simplified form as shown below.

2. Use the Table function to create and format a table for the marketing report.

3. Use the Calculation or Table formula function to total the sales.

4. Save the document as MONTHLY.

5. Print the document.

October 4, 19--

Ralph Santiago

MONTHLY MARKETING REPORT

Below is our monthly marketing report for the East and Southeast. As you compare this with last month's report, you will see that changes have occurred in our Sporting Goods Department. Sales indicate a growing trend for physical fitness products and a demand for sports clothing and accessories.

Department	September
Household Goods	$102,222.25
Furniture and Fixtures	241,104.40
Auto Accessories	89,415.32
Sporting Goods	106,255.82
Total	$

If you have any questions, please contact me.

Martha Bray

ys

JOB 47

Use Outline View

Create a presentation for the sales representatives of Midwest Star Life Insurance.

1. Create a new presentation.

2. If available with your software, create a look for the presentation by selecting a predesigned presentation template.

3. Switch to the Outline View, and enter the text below for slides 1 through 5.

Slide 1 (title slide)
MIDWEST STAR LIFE INSURANCE
Birthday Benefit

Slide 2
Act Now, Before Your Next Birthday!
- $5,000 birthday life insurance policy
- Financial protection for the family
- Applying for coverage is easy
- Money-back guarantee

Slide 3
Customer Guarantees
- Lifetime coverage
- No medical exam required
- Renewable for life
- You cannot be turned down
- You can consider this exclusive offer in your home

Slide 4
Low Birthday Premium
- $1.00 premium for the first month
- Starting with the second month, premiums based on age
- Coverage begins with application approval

Slide 5
Our Strengths
- Over 2.5 million policies in force
- $23 billion of life insurance in force
- Over $724 million in assets

4. Switch to the Slide Show View and review your work.

5. Save your presentation as INSURANC.

6. Print all slides of your presentation.

JOB 59

Challenge Reinforcement

You have been assigned to write an article about the World Wide Web for your company's upcoming newsletter. Include in the article the difference between the Internet and the World Wide Web, some characteristics of hypertext, and what a Web navigator can find. Explain what a home page is and how you can create one. Format the article for 2 columns with balanced newspaper style. Save the document as WEB, and print the document.

JOB 46

Work with Color

1. Open CHARITY.

2. Delete the background color.

3. Change the text color for all titles to red.

4. Change the other text color to blue.

5. Add a clip art *heart* to the bottom right-hand corner of the first slide. Change the color to red. If this piece of clip art is not available, add an appropriate one.

6. Change all bullets to a heart (♥). If this bullet is not available, add an appropriate one.

7. Add an appropriate clip art to the bottom right-hand corner of the fourth slide. If available, use a group of buildings.

8. Use Save As to save your presentation with the name CHARITY2.

9. Print slides 1 and 4 as a representation of the changes. If you do not have a color printer, print as directed by your instructor.

CHAPTER 4

Jobs 60–89
Advanced Document Formatting

Time Estimate: 12 hrs.

OBJECTIVES

In this chapter, students will:
1. Record a macro
2. Edit a macro
3. Use a memo template or wizard
4. Use a letter template or wizard
5. Create a fax transmittal
6. Create a resume
7. Create an envelope
8. Create mailing labels
9. Use the Merge function
10. Merge from the keyboard
11. Create mailing labels using merge
12. Create envelopes using merge
13. Create documents using document assembly
14. Use line sort
15. Use numeric sort
16. Use merge sort
17. Use sort and select

JOB 45

Work with Color

1. Open ATTEND.

2. Make the following changes to the first slide:
   - change the background to blue
   - change the title text to red
   - add shadows to the title text

3. Make the following changes to the second slide:
   - change the background to purple
   - change the title text to green
   - add shadows to the title text
   - change the bullets and bulleted items to green, and increase the size of the bullets

4. Change the color of one group of bars on the third slide to yellow.

5. Use Save As to save your presentation as ATTEND2.

6. If you have a color printer, print all slides of your presentation. Otherwise, print as directed by your instructor.

JOB 60

Record a Macro

1. Record a macro for "RISK AND REWARDS OF OWNING A SMALL BUSINESS." Name the macro RR.

2. Set the page to center vertically. Set the left and right margins at 1.5 inches.

3. Key the letter in modified block style as shown on the next page. Use the macro as needed. (See Reference Guide, page 501.)

4. Save the document as RISK.

5. Print the document.

Continued on Next Page

Slide 11
Next Steps

Next Steps
- Contact additional groups from East Central University
- Collect all fees
- Suggestions for additional activities
- Suggestions for additional concessions
- Planning Committee meeting July 8, 7:00 p.m.

6. Add transitions for each slide and, if available with your software, use build slide text on all slides.

7. Save your presentation as CHARITY.

8. Print all slides of your presentation.

Current Date

Word Processing Instructors
Pontotoc County Skill Development Center
P.O. Box 228
Ada, OK 74820-2288

Dear Business Instructor:

If you're looking for materials for your marketing program, you'll be interested in the RISK AND REWARDS OF OWNING A SMALL BUSINESS.

This outstanding program covers the important questions that small business owners face daily. RISK AND REWARDS OF OWNING A SMALL BUSINESS is designed to introduce students to the world of self-employment.

RISK AND REWARDS OF OWNING A SMALL BUSINESS offers an interesting variety of practical activities and exercises to help students understand what it takes to start a business of their own. Students will get a chance to see the real-life problems of running a small business.

RISK AND REWARDS OF OWNING A SMALL BUSINESS is a complete program. It includes a student workbook, a teacher's guide, enrichment activities, and a set of colorful posters.

Order a copy of RISK AND REWARDS OF OWNING A SMALL BUSINESS today. Return the enclosed postage-paid reply card. We will mail a copy of RISK AND REWARDS OF OWNING A SMALL BUSINESS to you within ten days.

Sincerely,

Yvonna Stephens
Sales Manager

sg

Slide 5
Component One: Status

Participants: Status
- 62 merchants involved, all fees paid
- 14 groups from East Central University, fees paid by 12 groups

Slide 6
Component Two:
Background

Activities: Background
- Concerts
- Car raffle
- 5K run
- Amusement rides

Slide 7
Component Two: Status

Activities: Status
- Four groups will perform
- 755 raffle tickets sold (maximum 1,000)
- 5K run, 81 entrants
- Contracted with Felix Amusement Rides (12 rides)

Slide 8
Add a Slide

Concessions: Background
- 16 food stands with drinks (complete meals)
- 8 stands with drinks and snacks
- 8 dessert stands

Slide 9
Add a Slide

Concessions: Status
- All have been contacted and agreed to participate
- All setup expenses are owner expenses
- No minimum guarantee

Slide 10
Key Issues

Delete this slide

Continued on Next Page

JOB 61

Record a Macro

1. Record a macro for "NoteWrite by Cornell Publishing Company." Name the macro NOTE.

2. Key the advertisement in unbound report style as shown below. Use the macro as needed. (See Reference Guide, page 501.)

3. Save the document as CORNELL.

4. Print the document.

NOTEWRITE BY CORNELL PUBLISHING COMPANY

NoteWrite by Cornell Publishing Company is easier to teach, easier to learn, and easier to read and transcribe than symbol shorthand. Whether you have taught a symbol system or are new to shorthand instruction, NoteWrite by Cornell Publishing Company will meet your needs.

NoteWrite by Cornell Publishing Company can be used for personal, educational, and business use. In classrooms across the United States, students and instructors are finding that NoteWrite by Cornell Publishing Company is easy to learn and easy to teach.

NoteWrite by Cornell Publishing Company can increase your students' success in the study and use of shorthand. Examine NoteWrite by Cornell Publishing Company today!

JOB 44

Create a Quick Presentation

Sara Winfield of the North Hills Association needs slides for a presentation on its community project "Fun for Charity."

(Note: Some software does not include quick presentations. If yours does not, create the presentation in the usual way.)

1. Create a new presentation.

2. Select the quick presentation option.

3. Follow the on-screen instructions.

4. Choose the quick presentation for "Reporting Progress" or a similar title.

5. When you have completed the on-screen instructions, you will see slides to edit. Some programs show an outline to help you organize your presentation. Edit the slides or outline using the following information:

Sample Outline

Slide 1
Status Report

Fun for Charity
North Hills Association

Slide 2
Define the Subject

Fun for Charity
• Participants
• Activities
• Concessions

Slide 3
Overall Status

Overall Status
• Need additional participants
• Activities are planned
• Concession vendors have been contracted

Slide 4
Component One:
Background

Participants: Background
• All merchants in the North Hills Association
• Groups from East Central University

Continued on Next Page

JOB 62

Record a Macro

1. Record a macro for *"Reader's Guide to Periodical Literature."* Name the macro READ.

2. Key the unbound report as shown below. Use the macro as needed.

3. Save the document as READERS.

4. Print the document.

READER'S GUIDE TO PERIODICAL LITERATURE

Libraries provide a variety of materials that can help with the research and writing of reports. To find newspaper or periodical articles on a specific topic, consult one or more indexes or reference books. Indexes usually are found in the reference section of the library. One of the most frequently used indexes is the *Reader's Guide to Periodical Literature.*

The *Reader's Guide to Periodical Literature* is a cumulative author and subject index to periodicals. The guide lists, in alphabetical order by subject and author, all articles published in over 100 magazines. *Reader's Guide to Periodical Literature* coverage includes computers, business, health, fashion, politics, education, science, sports, arts, and literature.

The *Reader's Guide to Periodical Literature* was first published in 1900. It is published semimonthly in September, October, December, March, April, and June; and monthly in January, February, May, July, August, and November. The *Reader's Guide to Periodical Literature* is also available on CD-ROM. A free pamphlet, How to use the *Reader's Guide to Periodical Literature* is also available upon request.

<u>Slide 10</u>
Where to Get More
Information

Where to Get More Information
- A+ Computer Craft, Inc.
  (800) 555-5555
- Best Buy Computer Supplies
  (800) 555-0005
- *Build It Yourself*
  By David Laidlow
  McBride and Logue Publishing Co.

6. Add transitions for each slide and, if available with your software, use build slide text on all slides.

7. Save your presentation as COMPUTER.

8. Print all slides of your presentation.

JOB 63

Edit a Macro

1. Edit the macro created in Job 61 (NOTE). Change "NoteWrite by Cornell Publishing Company" to "NoteWrite by Cornell and Mason Publishing."

2. Set the page to center vertically. Set the left and right margins at 2 inches.

3. Key the block style letter as shown below. Use the edited macro where appropriate.

4. Use Save As to save the document as CORNELL2.

Current Date

Ms. Betty Townsend
Cornell and Mason Publishing
2202 Fullview Drive
Cincinnati, OH 45201-2201

Dear Ms. Townsend:

Subject: NoteWrite by Cornell and Mason Publishing

Thank you for sending me the information on NoteWrite by Cornell and Mason Publishing. Would you please send me 25 copies of this text as soon as possible? I am looking forward to using NoteWrite by Cornell and Mason Publishing in my classes.

Sincerely,

Charlene Bowers
Business Instructor

jt

Slide 5
Vocabulary

Delete this slide

Slide 6
Topic One

Shop Around
- Local computer stores
  - higher prices
  - more personal service and greater accountability
- Mail-order company
  - substantial savings
  - a reputable company will take care of a problem

Slide 7
Topic Two

What to Purchase
- List the components you need
  - CPU and motherboard
  - memory
  - hard drive and disk drive
  - monitor and video card
  - case and power supply
  - keyboard and mouse
- Set a budget

Slide 8
Add a slide

Put It Together
- Assemble tools needed
- If needed, get assistance
  - someone with assembling experience
  - read manuals
  - read directions that come with components

Slide 9
Summary

Summary
- Decide what components you need
- Do comparison shopping
- Put it together

Continued on Next Page

1. Create the memo shown below. Use a memo template or wizard if your software has this feature.

2. Save the document as SEMINAR.

3. Print the document.

To: Donna Cranford
From: [Name]
Re: Time Management Seminar
Date: September 10, 1996

The time management seminar is scheduled for September 21, 19-- through October 14, 19--. The class will meet Tuesday and Thursday nights from 7:00-9:00 p.m. in the White Conference Room.

Please notify all personnel in your department of these dates. This is the only time the seminar will be offered this year.

JOB 43

Create a Quick Presentation

Joe Mainelli of the South Booker Computer Group needs slides for a presentation on building your own computer.

(Note: Some software does not include quick presentations. If yours does not, create the presentation in the usual way.)

1. Create a new presentation.

2. Select the quick presentation option.

3. Follow the on-screen instructions.

4. Choose the quick presentation for "Training" or a similar title.

5. When you have completed the on-screen instructions, you will see slides to edit. Some programs show an outline to help you organize your presentation. Edit the slides or outline using the following information:

Sample Outline

Slide 1
Training

How to Build a PC
By Joe Mainelli

Slide 2
Introduction

But . . . Why?
- Put together exactly as you want it
- It will be easier to repair
- Future upgrades will be a breeze

Slide 3
Agenda

Agenda
- Where to purchase parts and supplies
- What you need to purchase
- How to put it together

Slide 4
Overview

Delete this slide.

Continued on Next Page

JOB 65

Use a Letter Template or Wizard

1. Create the letter as shown below. Use a letter template or wizard if your software has this feature. (Use the following information for the return address: Vernon Company, 1400 Hatfield Drive, Girard, OH 44420, 216-555-5555, Fax: 216-555-5554.)

2. Save the document as MOVIE.

3. Print the document.

(Current Date)

Mrs. Mary McGuire
Western Publishing Co.
4450 Delmar Avenue
Long Beach, CA 90801-8762

Dear Movie Enthusiast:

Have you ever found yourself looking for the perfect video to rent? Do you wish you knew who starred in a movie? Let Best Selection take you to the movies by providing personalized video recommendations plus all the facts about the movies and the stars.

Best Selection uses artificial intelligence to list recommendations that are a perfect fit for every mood. Check out a summary of thousands of movies, complete with directors and a list of actors. You can choose from more than 20 film types or styles to refine your list of recommendations. Print out your list, and take it to the video store so you'll enjoy the movie you rent!

This intelligent guide to over 50,000 videos is all on just one CD-ROM. To order, simply fill out the enclosed card and return it in the enclosed envelope. Allow ten working days to receive your order. You will be billed $59.95 plus $2.00 shipping. Don't delay; the quantity is limited.

Sincerely,

Vernon Fitzgerald
Advertising Manager

CHAPTER 16

Jobs 43–62
Presentation Options

Time Estimate: 10 hrs.

OBJECTIVES

In this chapter, students will:

1. Create a quick presentation
2. Work with color
3. Use Outline View
4. Add notes to a presentation
5. Use the print options
6. Work with graphics
7. Embed data from another application
8. Link data from another application
9. Run a presentation

JOB 66

Create a Fax Transmittal

1. Create the fax transmittal sheet as shown below. Use a fax template or wizard if your software has this feature.

2. Save the document as FAX.

3. Print the document.

FAX TRANSMISSION
CHILDERS AND SON
1318 North Broadway
St. Louis, MO
555-0100
Fax: 555-0101

To: Mike Anderson   **Date:**   Current Date

Fax #:   555-0102   **Pages:**   5

From: Preston O'Brien

Subject: Construction Bid

COMMENTS: If you have any questions regarding the bid, contact the office and we will be glad to answer your questions.

C. H. O. Canada
Vice President
Human Resources

   1. Kimberly Stout
Director
Employee Benefits

   2. Devon Anderson
Director
Recruitment

4. Save your chart as MOBILE.

5. Print the organization chart.

Create a Resume

1. Create a resume similar to the one shown below. Use a resume template or wizard if your software has this feature.

MIKELLA MAYS

1325 Willowbrook • Ponca City, OK 73501 • 555-0104

OBJECTIVE

To obtain a part-time job as an office assistant while attending college.

EXPERIENCE

THE HEARTLAND COMPANY
Clerk/Typist, May, 1994 to present
Perform general office duties: telephone communications, ordering, inventory, and filing. Assist management with special projects and assignments.

ABBOTT'S DAY CARE CENTER
Child Care Worker, May, 1993 to May, 1994
Assisted in the care of children. Planned and assisted with recreational activities.

EDUCATION

PONCA CITY HIGH SCHOOL
Graduate, May 1995

National Honor Society, 1993-95
National Business Society Award, 1995
Student Council President, 1995
Student Council Member, 1993-95
Spanish Club President, 1995
Spanish Club Member, 1993-95
Keywanette Member, 1993-95
SADD Member, 1993-95
Cheerleader, 1993-95

SKILLS

- Type 50 wpm
- Computer System Operations: WordPerfect, Lotus 1-2-3, and dBASE IV
- 10-key Skills
- Effective Communication Skills; written and verbal
- Office Procedures

Create a Presentation with an Organization Chart

Create an organization chart for the Lincoln Office of Southwest Mobile System.

1. Create a new presentation.

2. If available with your software, create a look for the presentation by selecting a predesigned presentation template.

3. Create an organization chart with the following information:

Slide 1 (organization chart)
Southwest Mobile System
Lincoln Office

I. Craig Rogers
    President

    A. Stanley Sanders
        Vice President
        Marketing

        1. Andrew Thetford
            Assistant VP
            Domestic Sales

        2. Meredith Floyd
            Assistant VP
            International Sales

    B. Murel Walker
        Vice President
        Finance

        1. Cynthia Shaw
            Assistant VP
            Finance

Continued on Next Page

2. Save the document as RESUME.

3. Print the document.

JOB 41

Create a Presentation with an Organization Chart

Create an organization chart for the home office of Ross Real Estate Agency.

1. Create a new presentation.

2. If available with your software, create a look for the presentation by selecting a predesigned presentation template.

3. Create an organization chart with the information as shown below.

<u>Slide 1 (organization chart)</u>
ROSS REAL ESTATE AGENCY
Home Office Staff

I. David Ross, President
   A. Loren Agler, Finance Manager
      1. Calvin Agee
      2. Jack Wiggin
      3. Dale Zachary
   B. Leonard Wofford, Marketing Manager
      1. Alma Shaw
      2. Randy Vara
      3. C. D. Rieger

4. Save your chart as ROSS.

5. Print the organization chart.

JOB 68

Create an Envelope

1. Set the page to center vertically, and set the left and right margins at 1.5 inches.

2. Create the letter as shown below in modified block style. (See Reference Guide, page 501.)

April 6, 19--

Mr. Larry Cranford
Douglas Business College
4409 Mississippi Avenue
El Cajon, CA 92021-2623

Dear Mr. Cranford:

Subject: Word Processing Positions

I am happy to answer your request for information about the skills we require for word processing positions.

Future applicants need the following skills: (1) the ability to type at least 50 words a minute; (2) the ability to proofread accurately; (3) the ability to spell, punctuate, divide words, and recognize proper sentence structure; and (4) the ability to key from handwritten rough drafts and edited typewritten copy.

The best people for the jobs will be those who have excellent typing skills and who have experience in working with word processing equipment.

I am enclosing an information sheet with skills needed for other positions with our company. If you have any further questions, please call me. My telephone number is 406-555-0189.

Sincerely,

FLEMING CORP.

Jerry Fleming
Personnel Manager

kk

Enclosure

---

6. Format the x-axis for vertical alignment. If necessary, change the point size in order to display all of the text (days).

7. If a legend is displayed, remove it.

8. Add a new slide.

Slide 3 (slide with a chart)
Fall Performances
Attendance

	Friday	Saturday	Sunday
"Charlie"	1,071	1,303	624
"Say Goodbye"	761	1,063	404

9. Switch to the Slide Show View and review your work.

10. Save your presentation as ATTEND.

11. Print all slides of your presentation.

3. Create an envelope with the USPS POSTNET bar code, and append the envelope information to the current document if this feature is available with your software. Use the envelope size 9.5 inches wide and 4.13 inches deep unless otherwise instructed by your teacher. Use the following return address:

   Jerry Fleming
   Fleming Corporation
   3303 Gateway Boulevard
   El Cajon, CA 92021-2623

4. Save the document as FLEMING.

5. Print the letter and the envelope.

Create a Presentation with Text and a Chart

The business manager of Act III Theater provided information for slides to show the attendance at the fall performances.

1. Create a new presentation.

2. Create the following slide:

   Slide 1 (slide with text on the left and a chart on the right)
   "Charlie"
   Attendance

   - Friday
     - Matinee, 465
     - Evening, 606

   - Saturday
     - Matinee, 428
     - Evening, 875

   - Sunday
     - Matinee, 624

	Friday	Saturday	Sunday
"Charlie"	1,071	1,303	624

3. Format the x-axis for vertical alignment. If necessary, change the point size in order to display all of the text (days).

4. If a legend is displayed, remove it.

5. Add a new slide.

   Slide 2 (slide with text on the left and a chart on the right)
   "Say Goodbye"
   Attendance

   - Friday
     - Matinee, 255
     - Evening, 506

   - Saturday
     - Matinee, 308
     - Evening, 655

   - Sunday
     - Matinee, 404

	Friday	Saturday	Sunday
"Say Goodbye"	761	963	404

Continued on Next Page

JOB 69

Create Mailing Labels

1. Open CLUB. Create mailing labels for the list of names who joined the club. Include the name, street address, city, state, and zip code on the label. Consult with your instructor to determine the label type and sheet size.

2. Use Save As to save the information as LABEL.

3. Print the labels.

JOB 39

Create a Presentation with Text and a Chart

The accountant for Auto Security, Inc. needs a slide to report the expenses for the last quarter of 19--. This will be used at the board meeting.

1. Create a new presentation.

2. Create the following slide. Increase the point size of the title and text as desired.

   Slide 1 (slide with a chart on the left and text on the right)
   Expenses -- 4th Quarter, 19--

	4th Qtr
Repairs	3,000
Auto	4,500
Supplies	1,800
Rent	4,800
Taxes	2,500
Office	1,200

- Repairs $3,000
- Auto $4,500
- Supplies $1,800
- Rent $4,800
- Taxes $2,500
- Office $1,200

3. Change to a pie chart. Center the pie on the left-hand side of the slide.

4. Add labels to show the percentage each slice represents.

5. Move the legend to the bottom of the chart.

6. Switch to the Slide Show View and review your work.

7. Save your presentation as AUTO.

8. Print all slides of your presentation.

Use the Merge Function

1. Create a data file for the list of names as shown below.

2. Save the document as DATA1.

3. Open a new word processing document. Set the page to center vertically, and set the left and right margins at 2 inches.

Mr. Leon B. Jackson
Jackson's Furnishings
23 Main Street
Oklahoma City, OK 73101-2301
Mr. Jackson
Tuesday, August 15

Ms. Martha Ehrlich
Shipe's Shoe Store
3536 Johnson Avenue
Midwest City, OK 73110-3536
Ms. Ehrlich
Thursday, August 17

Ms. Yvonna Stephens
Stephens & Shane
65 Midway Street
Norman, OK 73069-6511
Ms. Stephens
Friday, August 18

Mr. Stuart Holloway
Central University
1000 East Main
Norman, OK 73069-1001
Mr. Holloway
Monday, August 21

Continued on Next Page

6. Create a third slide.

   <u>Slide 3 (slide with text on the left and a chart on the right)</u>
   4th Quarter Projection
   - Men's clothing to increase by 8%
   - Women's clothing to increase by 10%
   - Children's clothing to increase by 10%

	4th Qtr
Men	151,280
Women	357,500
Children	284,500

7. Format the y-axis for commas with zero decimal places.

8. Remove the x-axis.

9. Move the legend to the upper right-hand corner of the chart section.

10. Switch to the Slide Show View and review your work.

11. Save your presentation as FIELDS4.

12. Print all slides of your presentation.

4. Create a form file by keying the letter as shown below in block style. The information shown in bold needs to be replaced with the correct merge codes for the application you are using.

5. Save the letter as FORM1.

6. Merge DATA1 with FORM1.

7. Use Save As to save the letters as VISIT.

8. Print the letters.

August 2, 19--

(name)
(company name)
(street)
(city, state, zip)

Dear **(salutation):**

May I visit you at your office on **(date)?** There is an important matter I would like to discuss with you. It concerns a decision that must be made about your office staff.

I will call your secretary on Friday, August 11. Please let your secretary know what time will be convenient for me to see you.

Cordially,

Joel Stafford
Senior Office Manager

wa

JOB 38

Create a Presentation with Text and a Chart

The sales manager for Field's Department Store needs a presentation for a sales meeting. He provided information for actual sales for the first three quarters and a projection for the fourth quarter.

1. Create a new presentation.

2. Create the following slides. Increase the point size of the title and text as desired.

Slide 1 (title with text)
Congratulations!
Sales have increased for the first three quarters of 19--. This is due to our outstanding sales force. Thanks to everyone involved in the selling of our fine products.

3. Create a new slide.

Slide 2 (slide with a chart)
Actual Sales

	lst Qtr	2nd Qtr	3rd Qtr
Men	122,000	132,000	145,000
Women	275,000	296,500	328,000
Children	202,000	231,000	259,000

4. Change to a 3-D column chart.

5. Format the y-axis for commas with zero decimal places.

Continued on Next Page

JOB 71

Use the Merge Function

1. Create a data file for the list of names as shown below.

2. Save the document as DATA2.

3. Open a new word processing document. Set the page to center vertically, and set the left and right margins at 2 inches.

Mr. Jim Sanders (name)
(leave company name blank)
87 Jacks Avenue (street)
Forest Hills, NY 11375-8721 (city, state, and zip)
Mr. Sanders (salutation)
10937 (number)
5,200 (amount)
May 8, 19-- (date)

Mr. Howell Hill
Star Insurance Agency
1500 Broadway
New York, NY 10001-1500
Mr. Hill
11936
4,275
May 12, 19--

Mr. Ronnie Brendle
(leave company name blank)
876 Garden Lane
Long Beach, CA 90801-8762
Mr. Brendle
10886
6,330
May 15, 19--

Ms. Pat Sutton
The Gift House
982 Shady Lane
Miami, FL 33101-9820
Ms. Sutton
10989
1,428
May 13, 19--

Continued on Next Page

JOB 37

Create a Presentation with a Pie Chart

The sales manager of AAA Manufacturing wants a slide with a pie chart for the June sales. He provided you with the information below. Prepare a two-slide presentation.

1. Open AAA2.

2. If available with your software, create a look for the presentation by selecting a predesigned presentation template.

3. Change the subtitle on the first slide and the title on the second slide to "June Sales, 19--."

4. Select the data entry sheet and delete the columns for April and May. Move June into the April position.

5. Change to a pie chart. Make sure it shows all parts. If it does not, change to column series instead of row series.

6. Add labels to show the value of each piece of the pie. Format the numbers for currency with zero decimal places.

7. Add a legend if it is not included.

8. Add transitions to your slides.

9. Switch to the Slide Show View and review your work.

10. Use Save As to save your presentation as AAA3.

11. Print all slides of your presentation.

4. Create a form file by keying the letter as shown below in modified block style. The information shown in bold needs to be replaced with the correct merge codes for the application you are using.

5. Save the letter as FORM2.

6. Merge DATA2 with FORM2.

7. Use Save As to save the letters as OVERDUE.

8. Print the letters.

September 8, 19--

(name)
(company)
(street)
(city, state, zip)

Dear **(salutation):**

Your payment for Invoice No. **(number)** in the amount of $**(amount)** for purchases made on **(date),** is past due. This is your third reminder that this invoice is past due.

Please send us your payment for $**(amount)** in the enclosed envelope to arrive before the first of next month. If you do not, we plan to take legal action immediately.

Please give this matter your prompt attention.

Sincerely,

Jonathan Meharg
Collection Manager

wa

Enclosure

JOB 36

Create a Presentation with a Pie Chart

The CEO of KTEM Television Station wants a chart that shows a comparison of each salary category to the total salary.

1. Create a new presentation.

2. Create the following slides:

   <u>Slide 1 (title slide)</u>
   KTEM Television Station
   Salary Comparison Chart

   <u>Slide 2 (slide with a chart)</u>
   Salaries for First Quarter, 19--

Department	Salary
Advertising	30,500
Administration	51,000
Public Relations	6,500
Maintenance	6,000
Sales	39,000
Office	25,000

3. Change to a pie chart. Make sure it shows all parts. If it does not, change to column series instead of row series.

4. Add labels to show the percentage of each piece of the pie.

5. Add a legend if it is not included.

6. Explode the largest slice.

7. Add a transition to your slides.

8. Switch to the Slide Show View and review your work.

9. Save your presentation as KTEM.

10. Print all slides of your presentation.

1. Set the page to center vertically, and set the left and right margins at 2 inches.

2. If the keyboard merge is available with your software, create the following form file for a keyboard merge. Otherwise, go to instruction 6. The information shown in bold needs to be replaced with the correct merge codes for the application you are using.

3. Save the letter as FORM3.

(date)

(name)
(address)
(city), (state) (zip)

Dear **(salutation):**

Thank you for responding to our television commercial advertising SKI THE WEST.

The trip to **(place)** will cost **(price),** which includes airfare and lodging. The price is for **(length of stay)** in ski country. You and your family will stay in the beautiful **(lodge),** which is close to the ski area and has a wonderful restaurant. There are also other restaurants and shopping close by.

Please let us know if we can make reservations for you.

Sincerely yours,

FUNWAY HOLIDAYS FUNJET, INC.

Paula Kedy, Travel Agent

Continued on Next Page

JOB 35

Create a Presentation with a Line Chart

The sales manager for Service Auto Supplier also wants a chart showing the units sold each month.

1. Create a new presentation.

2. Create the following slides:

   Slide 1 (title slide)
   Service Auto Supplier
   Sales Data, 19--

   Slide 2 (slide with a chart)
   Units sold in 19--

	Jan	Feb	Mar	Apr	May	June	July	Aug	Sept	Oct	Nov	Dec
New Cars	82	85	90	88	91	82	99	85	84	92	91	86
Used Cars	186	191	191	184	185	149	179	122	103	151	186	102

3. Change to a line chart.

4. Align the x-axis vertically.

5. Add a piece of clip art representing cars to the bottom right-hand corner of the first slide.

6. Switch to the Slide Show View and review your work.

7. Save your presentation as SERVICE2.

8. Print all slides of your presentation.

4. Use the keyboard merge to merge the information as shown below with FORM3.

5. Save the letters as SKI. Print the letters.

6. Create a data file for the list of names as shown below. Save the data file as DATA3. Create a form file by keying the letter shown on the previous page. The information shown in bold needs to be replaced with the correct merge codes for the application you are using. Save the letter as FORM3. Merge DATA3 with FORM3. Save the file as SKI. Print the letters.

Mr. Robert Mason
198 Brianwood Ct.
Monroe, OH 45019-1982
Mr. Mason
Winter Park
936
four days and three nights
Hi Country Condos

Mrs. Ann Hamblin
2515 St. Joseph Street
Moore, OK 73160-2515
Mrs. Hamblin
Copper Mountain
976
five days and four nights
Copper Mountain Haus

Mr. Tim Hibbard
5521 West Oakview
Norman, OK 73069-5521
Mr. Hibbard
Lake Tahoe
1,401
four days and three nights
Lakeland Crestview

JOB 34

Create a Presentation with a Line Chart

The sales manager for Service Auto Supplier wants a chart showing the sales by quarter for 19--.

1. Create a new presentation.

2. Create the following slides:

   Slide 1 (title slide)
   Service Auto Supplier
   Sales Data, 19--

   Slide 2 (slide with a chart)
   Sales for 19--

	1st Qtr	2nd Qtr	3rd Qtr	4th Qtr
New Cars	5,200,000	5,400,000	5,900,000	5,700,000
Used Cars	2,500,000	2,100,000	2,400,000	2,000,000

3. Change to a line chart.

4. Change the format of the y-axis to currency with zero decimal places.

5. Switch to the Slide Show View and review your work.

6. Save your presentation as SERVICE.

7. Print all slides of your presentation.

Merge from the Keyboard

1. Set the top margin at 1.5 inches.

2. If the keyboard merge is available with your software, create the following form file to create a keyboard merge. Otherwise, go to instruction 6. The information shown in bold needs to be replaced with the correct keyboard merge codes for the application you are using.

3. Save the memo as FORM4.

To: **(receiver)**

From: **(sender)**

Date: **(date)**

Subject: Board Meeting

The annual meeting of the Board of Directors will be held **(time and place).** Please notify me by **(date)** if you will be able to attend.

cb

Continued on Next Page

JOB 33

Create a Presentation with a Bar Chart

The manager of C & L Overhead Door Company needs a bar chart to show a comparison of the actual and estimated sales for each quarter.

1. Create a new presentation.

2. Create a look for the presentation by selecting a predesigned presentation template.

3 Create the following slides:

Slide 1 (title slide)
C & L Overhead Door Company
Sales Comparison Report
19--

Slide 2 (slide with a chart)
C & L Overhead Door Company
19--

	Sales Estimate	Actual Sales
1st Qtr	300,000	296,800
2nd Qtr	300,000	302,600
3rd Qtr	325,000	382,200
4th Qtr	325,000	380,600

4. Change the chart type to a 2-D bar chart.

5. Switch to the Slide Show View and review your work.

6. Save your presentation as C&L.

7. Print all slides of your presentation.

4. Use the keyboard merge to merge the information as shown below with FORM4.

5. Save the memos as BOARD. Print the memos.

6. Create a data file for the list of names as shown below. Save the data file as DATA4. Create a form file by keying the memo shown on the previous page. The information shown in bold needs to be replaced with the correct merge codes for the application you are using. Save the memo as FORM4. Merge DATA4 with FORM4. Use Save As to save the file as BOARD. Print the memos.

Mr. Gary Fischer
Mr. Jack Cooper
January 1, 19--
at 6:30 p.m. on Tuesday, January 19, at the Sheraton Hotel
January 10

Ms. Peggy Taylor
Ms. Ruth Sauer
April 15, 19--
at 7:00 p.m. on Tuesday, May 19, in Room 18, City Hall Building
May 1

Create a Presentation with a Column Chart

The sales manager of AAA Manufacturing wants a slide with a bar chart for the second-quarter sales meeting. He provided you with the information as shown below. Prepare a two-slide presentation.

1. Create a new presentation.

2. Create the following slides:

   Slide 1 (title slide)
   AAA Manufacturing Co.
   Second-Quarter Sales

   Slide 2 (slide with a chart)
   Second-Quarter Sales

Month	April	May	June
Belts	20,229	26,444	27,022
Shoes	44,820	49,599	51,081
Purses	32,420	41,281	44,110

3. Change the chart type to a 2-D column chart.

4. Check your work using the Spell Check function.

5. Add a transition to each slide.

6. Switch to the Slide Show View and review your work.

7. Save your presentation as AAA2.

8. Print all slides of your presentation.

1. Create a form file for mailing labels for the list of names created in DATA1. Include the name, company name, street address, city, state, and zip. Check with the instructor to determine the type of label you will be using. Save the file as FORM5.

2. Merge the mailing labels (FORM5) with the data document (DATA1).

3. Use Save As to save the document as LABEL1.

4. Print the labels.

<u>Slide 4 (slide with a table)</u>
Open House - September 12

Address	Sq. Ft.	Bedrooms	Baths	Price
829 Motiff	2,680	4	3	150,000
4445 45th St.	3,650	4	4	225,000
249 Reed Blvd.	1,800	3	2	115,500
1133 Bank St.	2,410	3	2	129,500

<u>Slide 5 (slide with a table)</u>
Open House - September 14

Address	Sq. Ft.	Price
300 Walnut Dr.	7,500	1,119,200

All agents should attend this open house.

<u>Slide 6 (title slide)</u>
Thanks for Coming!
Next Meeting - October 1, 19--

3. Add a piece of clip art to the bottom of the last slide. The clip art should represent real estate.

4. Check your work using the Spell Check function.

5. Switch to the Slide Show View and review your work.

6. Save your presentation as BARTON.

7. Print all slides of your presentation.

JOB 75

Create Envelopes Using Merge

1. Create a form file for envelopes for the list of names created in DATA2. Include the name, company name, street address, city, state, and zip. Check with the instructor to determine the type of envelope you will be using. Save the file as FORM6.

2. Merge the envelope (FORM6) with the data document (DATA2).

3. Use Save As to save the document as ENVEL1.

4. Print the envelopes.

Create a Presentation with a Table

Create a presentation for Barton Real Estate for the September meeting.

1. Create a new presentation.

2. Create the following slides. Add tables and format the tables as shown by changing the point size, centering text, changing the line height, etc.

Slide 1 (title slide)
BARTON REAL ESTATE
September Meeting, 19--

Slide 2 (slide with a table)
Open House - September 7

Address	Sq. Ft.	Bedrooms	Baths	Price
723 Motiff	2,449	4	3	170,500
251 18th St.	2,550	3	2	162,500
98 Collis Blvd. B	2,931	3	2	190,500
4233 First St.	2,440	3	2	150,500

Slide 3 (slide with a table)
Open House - September 8

Address	Sq. Ft.	Bedrooms	Baths	Price
725 Kings Rd.	2,370	4	3	175,500
250 Kings Rd.	3,550	5	4	200,500
244 Fox Dr.	2,100	3	2	119,500
533 Bank St.	2,210	4	2	123,500

Continued on Next Page

JOB 76

Create Documents Using Document Assembly

1. Use the preset margins and tabs and key the paragraphs as shown below.

2. Save each paragraph with the name indicated.

3. Do not print the documents. They will be used in the next activity.

Thank you for your recent letter inquiring about a scholarship to East Central University.

Save the file as DOC1.

Thank you for taking the time to complete our application for a scholarship to East Central University.

Save the file as DOC2.

Please complete the enclosed application and return it to us promptly. After we have had an opportunity to review your transcript and test scores, we will be able to determine whether you qualify for financial assistance.

Save the file as DOC3.

After reviewing your application for financial assistance, we need additional information. Please call the financial aid office at 555-0120 regarding your application.

Save the file as DOC4.

Within one month after we receive your complete application, we will contact you regarding your qualifications for financial assistance.

Save the file as DOC5.

Your interest in attending East Central University is appreciated. We look forward to seeing you at the fall orientation that will be held August 19, 19--.

Save the file as DOC6.

FINISH

Slide 4 (slide with a table)
College Savings Plan

Future Value			
Amt. of Deposit	Interest Rate	No. of Deposits	Future Value
$3,000.00	6%	18	92,716.96

3. Use the ellipse tool to place an ellipse over the amount of deposit on each slide (1,000; 2,000; 3,000).

4. Bring the numbers forward.

5. Add a piece of clip art to the lower right-hand corner of the first slide. The clip art should represent banking, savings, etc.

6. Check your work using the Spell Check function.

7. Switch to the Slide Show View and review your work.

8. Save your presentation as COLLEGE.

9. Print all slides of your presentation.

JOB 77

Create Documents Using Document Assembly

1. Record a macro for the closing lines as shown below.

2. Set the page to center vertically, and set the left and right margins at 1.5 inches.

3. Create block style letters with the data shown below. Name the macro CLOSE.

   Sincerely yours,

   Merle Jackson
   Financial Aid Director

4. Save the first letter as ECU1 and the second letter as ECU2.

5. Print the documents.

(Current Date)   (Current Date)

Mr. John O'Dell   Ms. Debi Sehon
2233 Ridgecrest Drive   326 Hunter Drive
Buchanan, MI 45369-2233   Larsen, WI 54947-1326

Dear John: Dear Debi:

Retrieve DOC1   Retrieve DOC2

Retrieve DOC3   Retrieve DOC4

Retrieve DOC5   Retrieve DOC6

Retrieve DOC6   (Use the macro created for the closing)

(Use the macro created for the closing)

Create a Presentation with a Table

Mr. Furr will give a presentation about a college savings plan. He provided you with information to prepare the presentation.

1. Create a new presentation.

2. Create the following slides. Add tables and format the tables as shown by changing the point size, centering the titles, changing the line height, aligning the numbers, etc.

Slide 1 (title slide)
FIRST SECURITY BANK
Plan for College

Slide 2 (slide with a table)
College Savings Plan

Future Value			
Amt. of Deposit	Interest Rate	No. of Deposits	Future Value
$1,000.00	6%	18	30,905.65

Slide 3 (slide with a table)
College Savings Plan

Future Value			
Amt. of Deposit	Interest Rate	No. of Deposits	Future Value
$2,000.00	6%	18	61,811.31

Continued on Next Page

JOB 78

Use Line Sort

1. Key the list of names as shown below.

WORDPERFECT USER'S GROUP

March, 19--

Whitney Sanders
Kari Golightly
Mindy Boatwright
Joel Ward
MaeBeth Hodgkins
Kyle Tolin
Allison Stafford
Megan Miller
Katie Buxton
Rosa Medina
Matthew Joel Stafford
Joy Stafford
Rosa Martinez
Julie Norvill
Sky Nelson
Toni Pyrum
Drew Pyrum
Sunny Nelson
Summer Nelson
John Sanchez
Brent Boatwright
Kyle Sanders
Juan Alvarez
Shawn Stafford
Lindsey Golightly
Christy Tolin
Martin Polanski
Leon G. Martinez
John David Buxton

Continued on Next Page

JOB 29

Create a Presentation with a Table

The sales manager of AAA Manufacturing wants a slide presentation for the sales meeting. He provided you with the information below. Prepare a two-slide presentation.

1. Create a new presentation.

2. If available with your software, create a look for the presentation by selecting a predesigned presentation template.

3. Create the following slides:

   Slide 1 (title slide)
   AAA Manufacturing Co.
   First-Quarter Sales

   Slide 2 (slide with a table)
   First-Quarter, 19--

Month	January	February	March
Belts	15,629	18,141	19,022
Shoes	38,720	39,699	42,081
Purses	26,320	32,481	38,110

4. Check your work using the Spell Check function.

5. Add a transition to each slide.

6. Switch to the Slide Show View and review your work.

7. Save your presentation as AAA.

8. Print all slides of your presentation.

JOB 78

Continued

2. Sort the list in alphabetical ascending order by last name. If the last names are identical, use the first name as a secondary sort.

3. Center the list of names horizontally, and center the page vertically.

4. Save the document as GROUP.

5. Print the document.

7. Delete the third slide (Tee for Two).

8. Add the following slide as the last slide:

   <u>Slide 4 (bulleted list)</u>
   Pack Your Woods and Irons!
   - One low price
   - Only $99 per person (double occupancy)
   - Breakfast and dinner included
   - Available every weekend

9. Switch to the Slide Show View and review your work.

10. Resave your presentation.

11. Print all slides of your presentation.

JOB 79

Use Numeric Sort

1. Set the page to center vertically.

2. Clear all tabs. Set tabs at 1.75 inches, 3.5 inches, and 5 inches. Key the table as shown below.

3. Sort the list by population in numerical descending order.

4. Save the document as EUROPE.

5. Print the document.

POPULAR TOURIST SPOTS

European Countries

(population over 10,000,000)

Country	Population	Language	Capital
England	10,400,000	English	London
France	55,632,000	French	Paris
Germany	77,812,000	German	Bonn
Hungary	10,600,000	Hungarian	Budapest
Italy	57,355,000	Italian	Rome
Netherlands	14,660,000	Dutch	The Hague
Poland	37,664,000	Polish	Warsaw
Portugal	10,000,000	Portuguese	Lisbon
Spain	38,832,000	Spanish	Madrid
Turkey	51,350,000	Turkish	Ankara

JOB 28

Move and Delete Slides

The Oklahoma Tourism Director needs a presentation to promote Oklahoma Resorts.

1. Create a new presentation.

2. If available with your software, create a look for the presentation by selecting a predesigned presentation template.

3. Create the following slides. Add an appropriate piece of clip art to the title slide.

Slide 1 (title slide)
Get-a-Way for Two

Add appropriate clip art (move to balance the slide).

Slide 2 (bulleted list)
Tee for Two
- One low price
  - $99 per person (double occupancy)
  - breakfast and dinner
- Available year-round

Slide 3 (bulleted list)
Other Package Benefits
- Unlimited green fees and cart usage
  - from noon on day of arrival through noon on day of departure
- Sleeve of golf balls
- Pro shop for purchasing other needs
- Golf pro available for instructions

Slide 4 (slide with two columns)
Tee Off at an Oklahoma Resort!
- Arrowhead
- Beavers Bend
- Fountainhead
- Lake Murray
- Lake Texoma
- Quartz Mountain
- Roman Nose
- Sequoyah

4. Switch to the Slide Show View and review your work.

5. Save your presentation as GETAWAY.

6. Switch to Sorter View and move slide 4 to slide 2.

Continued on Next Page

JOB 80

Use Merge Sort

1. Open DATA1.

2. Sort the merge record in numerical ascending order according to the zip code.

3. Remove the page breaks and merge codes. Double space between the records.

4. Use Save As to save the document as ADDRESS.

5. Print the document.

JOB 27

Move and Delete Slides

Auto Security, Inc. needs to edit the May presentation to use for the June sale.

1. Open PROTECT.

2. Switch to the Sorter View.

3. Move slide 2 between slides 4 and 5.

4. Delete slide 5.

5. Add a new slide.

6. Change to Edit View and key the information as shown below. Add an appropriate piece of clip art on the right-hand side.

   Slide 5 (bulleted list)
   25% OFF DURING JUNE
   • All security features
   • All convenience features

7. Switch to the Slide Show View and review your work.

8. Use Save As to save your presentation as PROTECT2.

9. Print all slides of your presentation.

JOB 81

Use Sort and Select

1. Open EUROPE.

2. Sort the list by population in numerical ascending order.

3. If available with your software, extract all countries with populations greater than 50,000,000. Otherwise, delete all countries with populations less than 50,000,000.

4. Change the secondary title to (population over 50,000,000).

5. Use Save As to save the document as EUROPE2.

6. Print the document.

JOB 26

Add Clip Art to a Presentation

Enhance the presentation for Fisher Oil Company by adding another slide with clip art.

1. Open FISHER3.

2. Add a new slide with one title to the end of the presentation.

3. Add the title "Thanks for Attending!"

4. Add a piece of clip art to the center of the new slide. The clip art should be appropriate for the presentation.

5. Switch to the Slide Show View and review your work.

6. Use Save As to save your presentation as FISHER4.

7. Print all slides of your presentation.

JOB 82

Use Sort

1. Set the top margin at 1.5 inches. Clear all tabs, and set a decimal tab at 5 inches.

2. Key the memo as shown below.

3. Sort the salary column in numerical descending order. Move the currency ($) symbol to the first number in the column.

4. Save the document as SALARY.

5. Print the document.

TO: Accounting Department

FROM: Data Entry Department

DATE: Current Date

SUBJECT: Salaries, Art Department

Below is a list of the salaries of the people in the Art Department. Please check to be sure they are all correct before we enter them into the computer.

Karen Hector	$16,880.00 yearly
Phil Roberts	20,550.00 yearly
Lynn Gibson	8,125.00 yearly
Larry Roberts	22,000.00 yearly
Trent Dotson	31,850.00 yearly
Billy Dee Wade	14,880.00 yearly
V. L. Hall	12,000.00 yearly
Ginny Wilson	5.50 per hour
Suzy Finn	4.40 per hour

wa

JOB 25

Add Clip Art to a Presentation

Enhance the presentation for Western Technology's sales meeting by adding some clip art.

1. Open WESTERN2.

2. Add a piece of clip art to the lower right-hand corner of the fifth slide. The clip art should represent "tips" or "selling."

3. Add a piece of clip art to the middle of the sixth slide. The clip art should represent "questions and answers."

4. Switch to the Slide Show View and review your work.

5. Use Save As to save your presentation as WESTERN5.

6. Print all slides of your presentation.

JOB 83

Challenge Reinforcement

1. Create the Schedule of Accounts Receivable as shown below.

2. Save the table as CHOATE.

3. Create a merge document, and send a letter to all customers whose accounts are three months or more past due. Include in the letter that customers need to explain why the payment has not been made, or they need to settle the account. If customers are dissatisfied with the service they received, they need to notify the office. Otherwise, the payment should be received within 10 days from the date of the letter.

4. Create envelopes for the letters.

5. Use Save As to save the document as REPAIR.

6. Print the document.

Choate's Transmission
3323 Broadway
Allentown, WI 53002-1234

Schedule of Accounts Receivable

Customer Name	Customer Address	City, State, Zip	Amount Past Due	Months Past Due
Ms. Sally Wright	1234 West 59 Street	Allentown, WI 53002-1234	$278.50	5
Ms. Elizabeth Lowry	611 Sunset Road	Allentown, WI 53002-1234	$527.62	4
Mr. Yuan Sheng	4452 West Allison	Allentown, WI 53002-1234	$188.20	2
Mr. Darrell Jones	5502 McArthur	Allentown, WI 53002-1234	$640.02	4
Fred Bonar	326 Winged Foot	Allentown, WI 53002-1234	$525.30	2
Jamie Stephenson	1723 Augusta	Allentown, WI 53002-1234	$750.50	3
Lauren Moon	3326 Country Club	Allentown, WI 53002-1234	$666.75	2

FINISH

JOB 24

Add Clip Art to a Presentation

Edit the presentation you created for the local skill development center.

1. Open ADVANCE.

2. If you haven't already done so, select a very plain predesigned presentation template.

3. Add a piece of clip art to the lower right-hand corner of the last slide. The clip art should represent computers.

4. Check your work using the Spell Check function.

5. Switch to the Slide Show View and review your work.

6. Use Save As to save your presentation as ADVANCE2.

7. Print all slides of your presentation.

JOB 84

Challenge Reinforcement

1. Use the list created in Job 47 (TRAINING) to make name badges for the people attending the computer training class. Format the labels as desired.

2. Save the labels as BADGES.

3. Print the labels.

Create a Presentation with Two Columns of Text

Create a presentation for the Veasey Greenhouse to run at the county fair.

1. Create a new presentation.

2. If available with your software, create a look for the presentation by selecting a predesigned presentation template.

3. Create the following slides:

Slide 1 (title slide)
PLANT A BEAUTYBUSH
Be the Envy of Your Neighbors

Slide 2 (slide with two columns of text)
Beautybush at a Glance
- Size
  - 10 feet or more
- Light
  - full sun to
    partial shade
- Soil
  - well drained,
    acid to alkaline
- Pest
  - none serious
- Growth rate
  - rapid
- Pruning
  - immediately
    after
    flowering

Slide 3 (slide with two columns of text)
Beautybush . . .
- Range
  - Upper, Middle,
    and Lower South
- Expect to pay
  - $5 - $10 for a 1-gallon
    plant
  - $20 - $25 for a 5-gallon plant

4. Add a transition of your choice for each slide.

5. Switch to the Slide Show View and review your work.

6. Save your presentation with the name BUSH.

7. Print all slides of your presentation.

1. Merge the information as shown below with the file FORM4 created in Job 73.

2. Use Save As to save the document as MEETING.

3. Print the document.

Shawn Stafford

Britny Garrett

Current Date

at 6:30 p.m. on (Determine the date ten days from the current date)
in the Oklahoma State Bank Community Room.
(Determine the date five days from the current date)

cb

JOB 22

Create a Presentation with Two Columns of Text

Prepare a presentation for the area skill development center to advertise a new computer class.

1. Create a new presentation.

2. If available with your software, create a look for the presentation by selecting a predesigned presentation template.

3. Create the following slides:

<u>Slide 1 (title slide)</u>
YOUR PERSONAL COMPUTER
Learn to Use Advanced Features

<u>Slide 2 (slide with two columns of text)</u>
Advanced Word Processing Features
- Bookmarks
- Customized toolbars
- Footnotes
- Indexes and tables of contents
- Macros
- Mail merge
- Master documents
- Sort
- Tables
- Templates

<u>Slide 3 (slide with two columns of text)</u>
Advanced Spreadsheet Features
- Templates
  - create your own
  - buy ready-made templates
- Macros
- Spreadsheet charts
  - bar charts
  - line charts
  - pie charts
  - variations of the charts

<u>Slide 4 (slide with two columns of text)</u>
Advanced Database Management Features
- Query
- Create charts

4. Add a transition of your choice for each slide.

5. Switch to the Slide Show View and review your work.

6. Save your presentation as ADVANCE.

7. Print all slides of your presentation.

JOB 86

Challenge Reinforcement

1. Create the Division Order for Cantrell Oil as shown below. Use a macro to create the form.

2. Save the document as ORDER.

3. Print the document.

CANTRELL OIL
DIVISION ORDER

(Gas)

Owner _____ Address _____ Tax ID No. _____

Owner _____ Address _____ Tax ID No. _____

Owner _____ Address _____ Tax ID No. _____

Owner _____ Address _____ Tax ID No. _____

Owner _____ Address _____ Tax ID No. _____

Owner _____ Address _____ Tax ID No. _____

Owner _____ Address _____ Tax ID No. _____

Owner _____ Address _____ Tax ID No. _____

Owner _____ Address _____ Tax ID No. _____

Owner _____ Address _____ Tax ID No. _____

FINISH

CHAPTER 15

Jobs 22–42
Create Presentations Using
Automatic Slide Layouts

Time Estimate: 8 hrs.

OBJECTIVES

In this chapter, students will:

1.   Create a presentation with two columns of text
2.   Add clip art to a presentation
3.   Move and delete slides
4.   Create a presentation with a table
5.   Create a presentation with a bar chart
6.   Create a presentation with a line chart
7.   Create a presentation with a pie chart
8.   Create a presentation with text and a chart
9.   Create a presentation with an organization chart

Challenge Reinforcement

1. Create the memo as shown below. Use a memo template or wizard if your software has this feature.

2. Use the Table function to create and format the table as shown below.

To: Ron O'Neal
CC: Ralph Evans
From: Ken Turner
Date: Current Date
Subject: Office Buildings, Orchard Street

Below is a list of people who might be interested in the two office buildings we have listed on Orchard Street. Please contact each person. Send them the location, description, and price of each building.

FAX/PHONE LIST

Name	Company	Phone No.	Fax No.
Vandiver, Bill	Ames Services	555-0106	(918) 555-0110
Gurley, Treva	Evans Realty	555-0107	(918) 555-0111
Cummings, Mary	Martin, Wass & Co.	555-0108	(405) 555-0112
Hobbs, Jeff	Hobbs' Catering	555-0109	(918) 555-0113

Our contract on these buildings will expire in 60 days. It is urgent that we make every effort to sell.

le

Continued on Next Page

JOB 21

Use the Print Options

In this exercise, you will use some of the presentation print options. If your software does not accommodate a particular option, substitute an option of your choice.

1. Print slide 2 of NEWS.

2. Print slides 1 and 3 of WESTERN2.

3. Print slide 2 with builds of PROTECT.

4. Print handouts with slides 2, 4, and 7 of UNITED2. Print three to a page.

3. Record a macro that will remove all lines and borders from the table and will set the position of the table to center. Name the macro ERASE.

4. Sort the names in the table in ascending alphabetical order by the last name.

5. Use Save As to save the document as OFFICE.

6. Prepare a fax cover sheet for Ron O'Neal to accompany the memo on the previous page. The fax will consist of 2 pages. Save the fax cover sheet as FAX2.

7. Print the document and the fax cover sheet.

FINISH

JOB 20

Add Transitions, Build, and Sound Effects

Create a sales presentation for Computer Depot.

1. Create a new presentation.

2. If available with your software, create a look for the presentation by selecting a predesigned presentation template.

3. Create the following slides:

Slide 1 (title slide)
COMPUTER DEPOT
Sell, Upgrade, Install

Slide 2 (bulleted list)
All Major Brands Available
- No money down
- No payments
- No interest

Slide 3 (bulleted list)
Service Essentials
- 4-year warranty
- In-store setup
- Upgrades/installation
- In-home setup

Until August, 19-- (6 months)

4. Add a transition for each slide. If available with your software, use the uncover down transition. If not, use a transition of your choice.

5. If available with your software, use build slide text on slide 2. Have the text fly from the bottom.

6. Switch to the Slide Show View and review your work.

7. Save your presentation as DEPOT.

8. Print all slides of your presentation.

1. Set the page to center vertically, and use the Table function to create and format the table as shown below.

2. Play the macro ERASE to remove the lines from the table and to set the position of the table to center.

3. Sort the table in descending order according to square miles.

4. Save the document as PARKS.

5. Print the document.

NATIONAL PARKS OF THE UNITED STATES

Park	Location	Square Miles
Kings Canyon	Central California	708
Lassen Volcanic	Northern California	163
Mammoth Cave	Central Kentucky	79
Mesa Verde	Southwest Colorado	80
Mount Rainier	West-Central Washington	377
Mount McKinley	Central Alaska	3,030
Olympic	Northwest Washington	1,323
Petrified Forest	Northern Arizona	147
Rocky Mountain	Central Colorado	405
Sequoia	Central California	604
Shenandoah	Northern Virginia	301
Virgin Islands	Eastern Caribbean	148
Yellowstone	Northwest Wyoming	3,458
Yosemite	Central California	1,182
Zion	Southwest Utah	148

FINISH

JOB 19

Add Transitions, Build, and Sound Effects

Edit the presentation for the Western Technology sales meeting and add special effects.

1. Open WESTERN3.

2. Add the following bulleted items to the second slide:

   • Camcorder with color viewfinder
   • Color hand-held scanner

3. Add a transition for each slide. If available with your software, use the checkerboard or jigsaw transition. If not available, use a transition of your choice.

4. Add sound to each slide transition. If available with your software, use the laser or a similar .wav (sound) file.

5. If available with your software, use build slide text on slide 2. Have the text split vertical out.

6. Change the predesigned template. If available with your software, use the color boxes. If not, use a template of your choice.

7. Switch to the Slide Show View and review your work.

8. Use Save As to save your presentation as WESTERN4.

9. Print all slides of your presentation.

JOB 89

Challenge Reinforcement

1. Write to five universities, colleges, or vocational schools you are interested in attending. Request information on scholarships, grants, or financial aid. Use the Mail Merge function to create the documents.

2. Save the documents as HIGHER.

3. Print the letters.

JOB 18

Add Transitions, Build, and Sound Effects

Add some special effects to the presentation for United Tire Company.

1. Open UNITED.

2. Change the position of slides 5 and 6.

3. Add a transition for each slide. If available with your software, use the box transition. If not, use a transition of your choice.

4. Add sound to each slide transition. If available, use the whoosh or a similar .wav (sound) file.

5. If available with your software, use build slide text on slides 2, 3, 4, 5, 6 and 7. Have the text fly from the bottom.

6. Switch to the Slide Show View and review your work.

7. Use Save As to save your presentation as UNITED2.

8. Print all slides of your presentation.

CHAPTER 5

Jobs 90–102
Enhance a Document

Time Estimate: 4 hrs.

OBJECTIVES

In this chapter, students will:

1. Create a text box
2. Create border styles
3. Create a watermark
4. Create a paragraph border
5. Change the size of a graphic
6. Create a horizontal line
7. Create a vertical line
8. Use TextArt or WordArt
9. Create check boxes

JOB 17

Add Transitions and Build Effects

Edit and add special effects to the presentation concerning the production of a company newsletter.

1. Open NEWS2.

2. Edit slide 1 and change the title to "Producing a Newsletter" and the subtitle to "By Jack Reed Wilson."

3. Edit slide 2 and make the first bullet "To generate new business."

4. Edit slide 4 and make the first bullet "Add to the current list to compile a new mailing list."

5. Add a transition for each slide. If available with your software, use the wipe or close transition. If not, use a transition of your choice.

6. If available with your software, use build slide text on slides 2, 3, and 4. Have the text dissolve.

7. Switch to the Slide Show View and review your work.

8. Use Save As to save your presentation as NEWS3.

9. Print all slides of your presentation.

JOB 90

Create a Text Box

1. Set the left, right, and top margins at 1.5 inches. Center the title of the article and quadruple space below.

2. Key the article as shown below.

3. Create a text box for the quotation similar to the one shown below.

4. Save the document as PICNIC.

5. Print the document.

COMPANY PICNIC A HUGE SUCCESS

Several of the employees commented on the success of this year's company outing which was held at Marlee's Amusement Park on June 16.

> "Everyone had a wonderful time today. This was our best company picnic ever!"
>
> Jan Roberts

Bill Evers won the pie-eating contest by putting away three whole blackberry pies. The two-legged race trophy went to Kim and Jay Chin. The Strikers (marketing department) won the softball game by defeating the accounting department 7-3. Larry Pfister and Sandy Goins won the putt-putt golf tournament. Kim and Howell Hill won the egg-toss with a toss of 50 feet.

Special thanks go to the Social Committee for planning such a fun-filled day. Everyone had a wonderful time. If you did not get to attend, make plans to attend the Fall Follies to be held September 1.

JOB 16

Add Transitions and Build Effects

Auto Security, Inc. needs a presentation to promote its products.

1. Create a new presentation.

2. If available with your software, create a look for the presentation by selecting a predesigned presentation template.

3. Create the following slides:

<u>Slide 1 (title slide)</u>
AUTO SECURITY, INC.

Security and Convenience Systems

<u>Slide 2 (bulleted list)</u>
PERSONAL SAFETY WHEN YOU ARE ALONE OR IN THE DARK
- Illuminated entry
- Remote panic button
- Remote door lock/unlock

<u>Slide 3 (bulleted list)</u>
PROTECT YOUR VEHICLE AND DETER THEFT
- Shock sensors
- Intrusion sensors
- Starter kill

<u>Slide 4 (bulleted list)</u>
ADD CONVENIENCE FEATURES TO YOUR SYSTEM
- Keyless entry
- Remote car start
- Remote trunk pop
- Flashing parking lights

<u>Slide 5 (slide with one title)</u>
MAY IS SALE MONTH!
Add security or convenience features to your security system or purchase them separately.

4. Add a transition for each slide. If available with your software, use the horizontal blind transition. If not, use a transition of your choice.

5. If available with your software, use build slide text on slides 2, 3, and 4. Have the text fly from the left.

6. Switch to the Slide Show View and review your work.

7. Save your presentation as PROTECT.

8. Print all slides of your presentation.

JOB 91

Create Border Styles

1. Create an advertisement similar to the one shown below using a text box and borders.

2. Save the document as WASH.

3. Print the document.

Car Wash

Saturday, May 3

Roy's Service Station
5407 N. 81st Street

$3.00 per car

Fast Service!

Held by the
Mid-High Band Fundraisers

JOB 15

Use a Predesigned Presentation Template

Make additions to the sale presentation prepared for Field's Department Store.

1. Open FIELDS2.

2. Add "Dress shoes" and "Athletic shoes" under "<u>Women</u>" on the third slide.

3. Change the point size to 88 for the title of the fourth slide. Change the point size to 44 for the line of text under the title on the fourth slide. Center this line.

4. If available with your software, select a look for the presentation by selecting a predesigned presentation template. Select one that will be appropriate for the material.

5. Use Save As to save your presentation as FIELDS3.

6. Print all slides of your presentation.

1. Key the memo as shown below.

Date: October 21, 19--

From: Ted N. Chandler, Chairman

To: Corporate Management Members

Subject: Board of Directors Meeting, October 5, 19--

Marwick Medical completed the first decade of its history with another outstanding year. Sales increased 31%, net income 50%, and earnings per share 29%. This was done while we invested in global expansion, new ventures, and research.

Every member of our management team had a part in this success. Therefore, all members of the management team will receive a 14.5% salary increase.

The following salary increases have been approved for non-management associates. These increases were decided by each associate's contribution to our success. Please be sure they know they are vital to the success of our company.

Lee Chandler, 11%
Joseph Cotson, 12.2%
Richard Hutchinson, 14%
Brad O'Donnel, 10.5%
Leslie Petkat, 10%
Larry Rossi, 6.5%
Geoffrey D. Seen, 9.6%
Sandra Simpson, 8.8%
J. R. Tarbet, 8.9%
Susan Watkins, 8.4%

Other associates will receive a 6% increase in salary. Increases will be effective January 1, 19--.

ss

Continued on Next Page

JOB 14

Use a Predesigned Presentation Template

Add a design to the presentation for the accountant of Cunningham Family Furniture Store.

1. Open CUNNING2.

2. Change the layout of the third slide to a slide with only one title. Add the title "Cunningham Family Furniture."

3. If available with your software, select a look for the presentation by selecting a predesigned presentation template. Select one that will be appropriate for the material.

4. View your slides in the following ways:

   Outline View
   Slide Show View
   Sorter View

5. Use Save As to save your presentation as CUNNING3.

6. Print all slides of your presentation.

JOB 92

Continued

2. Create a confidential watermark for the memo.

3. Save the document as CHANDLER.

4. Print the document.

JOB 13

Use a Predesigned Presentation Template

Improve the appearance of the presentation for the sales meeting by adding a predesigned template.

1. Open WESTERN2.

2. Select Sorter View. Delete the second slide.

3. If available with your software, select a look for the presentation by selecting a predesigned presentation template. Select one that will be appropriate for the material.

4. View your slides in the following ways:

   Outline View
   Slide Show View
   Sorter View

5. Use Save As to save your presentation as WESTERN3.

6. Print all slides of your presentation.

JOB 93

Create a Paragraph Border

1. Set the page to center vertically. Set the left and right margins at 1.5 inches.

2. Change the font to Arrus BT or one of your choice. Key the travel advertisement as shown below with a bold 24-point font for the title and a 12-point font for the body.

3. Create a paragraph border around the last paragraph. Use a dotted border with a 20% shaded fill.

4. Save the document as TOUR.

5. Print the document.

COME ALONG WITH US!

With our tour, TASTE OF EUROPE, you'll visit the highlights of great cities like London, Paris, Amsterdam, Rome, Venice, Florence, and Vienna.

While traveling between cities, you will see England's thatched cottages, castles, and ancient universities. You'll get to look at the crooked castles along the Rhine River and view Italy's beautiful landscapes of Tuscany and Umbria. You will see the gorgeous Mediterranean seascapes and the most beautiful snow-capped mountains in the world.

Contact us today for dates and prices.

TRAVEL, INC.
14522 Montgomery Blvd. NE
Albuquerque, NM 87111
1-800-555-0114

We are planning a wonderful tour of "New Europe," whose members include Moscow, Berlin, Prague, and Budapest. Watch your mail for exciting information!

JOB 12

Use a Predesigned Presentation Template

Make additional changes to the presentation for Fisher Oil Company.

1. Open FISHER2.

2. To improve the appearance of the slides, move the last bulleted item on slide 2 to the first bulleted item on slide 3.

3. Add the following level-two bulleted items under this bullet:

   - Follow all federal and state regulations
   - Address each concern immediately

4. Change the point size of the bulleted items on slide 3 to 28.

5. If available with your software, select a look for the presentation by selecting a predesigned presentation template. Select one that will be appropriate for the material.

6. View your slides in the following ways:

   Outline View
   Slide Show View
   Sorter View

7. Use Save As to save your presentation as FISHER3.

8. Print all slides of your presentation.

JOB 94

Change the Size of a Graphic and Create a Horizontal Line

1. Set the top margin at .5 inch.

2. Create a user box with a graphic. Select an appropriate graphic or clip art of your choice.

3. Size the graphic to fit your document.

4. Change the font to Arial or one of your choice. Use a bold 24-point font for the company name, an 18-point font for the second line, and a 12-point font for the address. Center all lines. After the address is keyed, press Enter until the cursor is under the box at the left margin.

5. Create a horizontal line under the address.

6. Save the document as FLOWER.

7. Print the document.

| Insert Graphic or Clip Art Image | **Barringer's Flower Shop**
Full Service Florist
544 Westminster Circle
Buffalo, NY 14215-1592 |

4. View your slides in the following ways:

   Outline View
   Slide Show View
   Sorter View

5. Save your presentation as UNITED.

6. Print all slides of your presentation.

JOB 95

Create a Vertical Line

1. Open FLOWER.

2. Change the horizontal line to a vertical line. Select a line style of your choice.

3. Use Save As to save the document as FLOWER2.

4. Print the document.

JOB 11

Use a Predesigned Presentation Template

You have been asked to prepare a presentation for a workshop for the Public Relations Department of United Tire Company.

1. Create a new presentation.

2. If available with your software, select a look for the presentation by selecting a predesigned presentation template. Read through this exercise so you can select one that will be appropriate for the material.

3. Create the following slides:

Slide 1 (title slide)
United Tire Company
Secrets of Power Presentations

Slide 2 (bulleted list)
Know Your Audience
- Size of the group
- Makeup of the audience
- Expertise of the audience

Slide 3 (bulleted list)
Get Ready for the Presentation
- Clarify your topic
- Identify your theme
- Research your topic
- Locate appropriate visuals

Slide 4 (bulleted list)
Prepare the Presentation
- The opening
- Transitions
- The body
- Call to action

Slide 5 (bulleted list)
Rehearse Your Presentation
- Talk through your presentation
- Tape record your presentation
- Video tape your presentation
- Visualize yourself giving a successful presentation

Slide 6 (bulleted list)
Logistics and Visual Aids
- Schedule a convenient time and place
- If the presentation is long, arrange for refreshments
- Select a complementary seating arrangement

Slide 7 (bulleted list)
Deliver the Presentation
- Speak lower and slower than normal
- Watch your tone of voice
- Deliver your presentation with confidence

Continued on Next Page

1. Set the page to center vertically.

2. Create the sign as shown below using TextArt or WordArt for the title.

3. Place the title in the center of the page.

4. Key the remainder of the sign with each line centered using an 18-point font.

5. Save the document as HUNTER.

6. Print the document.

Gun Safety for Hunters

Instructors:

Jeff Anderson
&
Steve Henry

Date: September 2, 19--
Time: 6:00 to 8:30 p.m.
Place: County Extension Building
No charge

Open and Edit a Presentation

Add information to your presentation concerning the production of a company newsletter.

1. Open NEWS.

2. Add a new slide.

3. Use a bulleted list slide.

4. Key the following title:

   How to Produce a Newsletter

5. Key the following bulleted list:

   • Gather information
   • Write copy/design format
   • Work with the printer

6. Add a new slide.

7. Use a bulleted list slide.

8. Key the following title:

   Distributing Newsletters

9. Key the following bulleted list:

   • Compile mailing list
   • Check postal regulations
   • Work with a mail house

10. View your slides in the following ways:

    Outline View
    Slide Show View
    Sorter View

11. Use Save As to save your presentation as NEWS2.

12. Print all slides of your presentation.

1. Use TextArt or WordArt for the title as shown below.

2. Key the remainder of the document.

3. Save the document as NEW.

4. Print the document.

New Business?

Do you know where people get ideas for new businesses? Most of the time it is from prior jobs. Of course, sometimes it is just something they like to do.

```
Prior job .............................................. 45%
Personal interest/hobby .................................. 16%
Chance happening ........................................ 11%
Education course/family business ......................... 6%
Friends/relatives ........................................ 5%
Other ................................................... 17%
```

Source: NFIB Foundation.

JOB 9

Open and Edit a Presentation

The accountant for Cunningham Family Furniture Store decided to add information to his presentation.

1. Open CUNNING.

2. Add the date December 31, 19-- as the second line of the subtitle on the first slide.

3. On the second slide, add the following level-two bulleted items under the fourth level-one bullet:

   - Window treatments
   - Floor coverings
   - Accessories

4. Add a new slide.

5. Use a slide with no title.

6. Move the fifth and sixth level-one bulleted items to the new slide.

7. Add the following level-two bulleted items under the fifth level-one bullet:

   - Raising interest rates
   - Local competition

8. Add the following level-two bulleted items under the sixth level-one bullet:

   - Employment of a collection agency
   - Aggressive advertising campaign

9. View your slides in the following ways:

   Outline View
   Slide Show View
   Sorter View

10. Use Save As to save your presentation as CUNNING2.

11. Print all slides of your presentation.

JOB 98

Retrieve a Graphic Image

1. Set the top margin at 2 inches and the left and right margins at 1.5 inches.

2. Create a custom horizontal line.

3. Press Enter twice and create a user box. Use a clip art or graphic of your choice.

4. Make the user box 2 inches wide and 1.5 inches high. Position the graphic at the left margin.

5. Contour the text flow on the right side with the shape of the art.

6. Bold the first line, and key the text with the line spacing as shown below.

7. Create a second horizontal line.

8. Save the document as REMINDER.

9. Print the document.

REMINDER FOR: MARTIN PEREZ

| Use Clip Art or Graphic of your choice | It's time to visit Dr. Bell for your post-surgery checkup! |

Please call our office at 555-0115 to schedule an appointment.

JOB 8

Open and Edit a Presentation

Field's Department Store is having another sale. Update the presentation announcing a sale.

1. Open FIELDS.

2. Change the date of the first slide to August 22, 19--.

3. Change the rate on the second slide to 15%.

4. Add a new slide.

5. Use a slide with only one title.

6. Key the following title:

   Big Discounts On All Items

7. Key the following data (tab for the second column):

Women	Men
Career dresses and suits	Cotton sport shirts
Career-related separates	Casual pants
Cotton denim shorts	Shorts
	Athletic shoes

8. Add a title slide.

9. Key the following title and subtitle:

   Hurry!
   Just 13 Hours to Save!

10. Use Save As to save your presentation as FIELDS2.

11. Print all slides of your presentation.

1. Set the page to center vertically. Set the left and right margins at 1.5 inches.

2. Change the font to 12 point Courier New, or a comparable font.

3. Key the block style letter with the check boxes as shown below.

(Current Date)

Ms. Kari Garcia
339 West Highland Street
Tulsa, OK 73011-3391

Dear Ms. Garcia:

Thank you very much for applying for the data-entry position with our company.

The position has been filled, but we were very impressed with your application. If you desire, we will keep the application on file so that you can be called as soon as another opening occurs. Please check the appropriate box below and return this letter to us in the self-addressed envelope.

☐   Yes, please keep my application on file.

☐   No, I'm no longer interested in a position.

Sincerely,

Mr. Bill Nelson
Personnel Director

sg

Enclosure

Continued on Next Page

14. Add another slide.

15. Use a slide with only one title.

16. Key the following title:

    Questions and Answers

17. Use Save As to save your presentation as WESTERN2.

18. Print all slides of your presentation.

JOB 99

Continued

4. Create an envelope with the USPS Postnet Bar Code, and use your own address for the return address. Use the envelope size 9.5 inches wide x 4.13 inches deep, unless otherwise instructed by your teacher. Insert the envelope information in the current document.

5. Save the document as POSITION.

6. Print the letter and the envelope.

JOB 7

Open and Edit a Presentation

Add to the presentation for the Western Technology sales meeting.

1. Open WESTERN.

2. Add a new slide.

3. Use a bulleted list slide.

4. Key the following title:

   Introduction of New Products

5. Key the following bulleted list:

   - Wireless mice
   - PC blood pressure check and pulse meter
   - 6X CD-ROM drive
   - Mini-tower, no tools

6. Add another slide.

7. Use a slide with only one title.

8. Key the following title:

   Demonstration of New Products

9. Center the following line under the title:

   By William Brunk and Bill Skinner

10. Add another slide.

11. Use a slide with only one title.

12. Key the following title:

    Tips on Selling New Products

13. Center the following line under the title:

    By Sara K. Edison

Continued on Next Page

Challenge Reinforcement

1. Create an announcement using an appropriate graphic.

2. Use your own judgment to design the announcement. Include the following information:

   Name of the course: A Writing Adventure

   Dates: July 22-26

   Time: 1:30 p.m. to 3:30 p.m.

   Location: Arts and Heritage Center

   Activities: Keep a Journal, Write Poetry, Write a Short Story.

   When and where to enroll: July 19-21, Arts and Heritage Center, 1 p.m. to 4 p.m.

3. Save the document as WRITING.

4. Print the document.

JOB 6

Open and Edit a Presentation

The board meeting for Fisher Oil Company has been changed to May 18, 19--. Update your presentation for the meeting.

1. Open FISHER.

2. Change the date of the first slide to May 18, 19--.

3. On the second slide, change the point size of the bulleted items to 28.

4. Add the following level-two bulleted items under the first level-one bullet:

   - Insurance premiums
   - Public relations

5. Add the following level-two bulleted items under the third level-one bullet:

   - Safety training sessions
   - Close supervision by department heads

6. Delete the last level-one bullet.

7. Add a new slide.

8. Use a bulleted list slide.

9. Key the following title:

   Question and Answer Session

10. Key the following bulleted list:

    • Presentation by the department heads
      - John Wilson
      - Shawn Stafford
      - Allison Stafford
      - Montana Anderson
    • Questions directed to the department heads

11. Use Save As to save your presentation as FISHER2.

12. Unless otherwise instructed, print all slides of your presentation on one page with a frame around each slide. Submit the printout for your instructor's evaluation. Follow this plan throughout this section.

    NOTE: The object of a presentation program is to help you prepare slides for display on the computer screen, for projection directly from the computer, for the development of 35mm slides, or for use with overhead projectors. You may never need to print a presentation. However, you should be aware that most presentation programs will print outlines, speaker notes, and audience handouts.

Challenge Reinforcement

Create your own letterhead, including your name, address, phone number, and any other information that is appropriate. Change the fonts and attributes as desired. Consider using a graphic, clip art, or a graphic line to emphasize the letterhead. Save the document as LETHEAD. Print the document.

JOB 5

Create and Save a Presentation

Your department has been asked to produce a company newsletter. Prepare a presentation to inform other members of the department about the newsletter.

1. Create a new presentation.

2. Use a blank presentation or the default presentation.

3. Use a title slide.

4. Key the following title:

   Plan for Producing a Newsletter

5. Key the following subtitle:

   By Student's Name

6. Add a new slide.

7. Use a bulleted list slide.

8. Key the following title:

   Why Produce a Newsletter?

9. Key the following bulleted list:

   - To generate business
   - To keep clients informed
   - To advertise our products

10. Save your presentation as NEWS.

11. The presentation will be printed in a future job.

12. Close the presentation.

JOB 102

Challenge Reinforcement

The Board of Directors of the First National Bank is hosting a reception for William Parker, the retiring president. The reception is at seven o'clock on Friday evening, June 1, 19-- at the Oak Hills Golf and Country Club. Guests should RSVP. Create a formal invitation for this event. Consider using a graphic or clip art to accentuate the invitation. Change the font, font size, and attributes as desired. Save the document as RECAP. Print the document.

JOB 4

Create and Save a Presentation

You have been asked to prepare a presentation for the accountant of Cunningham Family Furniture Store. This presentation is about the financial status of the company.

1. Create a new presentation.

2. Use a blank presentation or the default presentation.

3. Use a title slide.

4. Key the following title:

   Cunningham Family Furniture

5. Key the following subtitle:

   Financial Status of the Company

6. Add a new slide.

7. Use a bulleted list slide.

8. Key the following title:

   Cunningham Family Furniture

9. Key the following bulleted list:

   - Current financial condition
   - Challenges to the industry
   - Strengths of company's financial position
   - Areas of growth
   - Issues of concern
   - Proposal to strengthen position during the next quarter

10. Save your presentation as CUNNING.

11. The presentation will be printed in a future job.

12. Close the presentation.

SPREADSHEET

JOB 3

Create and Save a Presentation

Prepare a presentation announcing a one-day sale for Field's Department Store.

1. Create a new presentation.

2. Use a blank presentation or the default presentation.

3. Use a title slide.

4. Key the following title:

   FIELD'S DEPARTMENT STORE

5. Key the following subtitle on two lines:

   One-Day Sale
   Thursday, May 15, 19--

6. Add a new slide.

7. Use a slide for text with a title. You will not need a subtitle.

8. Key the following title:

   Door Buster Bonus!

9. Key and center the following text:

   Early hours: 8:00 - 10:00 a.m.
   Late hours: 7:00 - 9:00 p.m.

   Take an extra 10% off everything in the store

10. Save your presentation as FIELDS.

11. The presentation will be printed in a future job.

12. Close the presentation.

CHAPTER 6

Jobs 1–22
Create, Format, Edit,
and Print a Spreadsheet

Time Estimate: 6 hrs.

OBJECTIVES

In this chapter, students will:

1. Create and format a spreadsheet
2. Adjust column widths
3. Create and copy a formula
4. Use the Autosum feature
5. Use Page Setup to print

JOB 2

Create and Save a Presentation

You have been asked to create a presentation for the Western Technology sales meeting.

1. Create a new presentation.

2. Use a blank presentation or the default presentation.

3. Use a title slide.

4. Key the following title:

   WESTERN TECHNOLOGY

5. Key the following subtitle on two lines:

   Sales Presentation
   Thursday, March 6, 19--

6. Add a new slide.

7. Use a bulleted list slide.

8. Key the following title:

   Agenda

9. Change the point size of the bulleted items to 24. Tab twice after the time. Key the following agenda:

   - 8:00 - 8:30 a.m.   Continental breakfast
   - 8:30 - 9:00 a.m.   Introduction of new products
   - 9:00 - 9:30 a.m.   Demonstration of new products
   - 9:30 - 10:15 a.m.   Tips on selling new products
   - 10:15 - 10:30 a.m.   Break
   - 10:30 - Noon   Questions and answers

10. Save your presentation as WESTERN.

11. The presentation will be printed in a future job.

12. Close the presentation.

JOB 1

Create and Format a Spreadsheet

Prepare an inventory of hi-tech equipment for Wilson Jones.

1. Create the spreadsheet as shown below.

2. Center the title (rows 1, 2, and 3) across columns A–G.

3. Right align the heading in column F.

4. Make the title and all column headings bold.

5. Format column F for commas with zero decimal places.

	A	B	C	D	E	F	G
1	WILSON JONES AND COMPANY						
2	HI-TECH EQUIPMENT INVENTORY LIST						
3	DECEMBER, 19--						
4							
5	ITEM			PURCHASE			SERVICE/
6	NAME		MANUF	DATE	DEPT	COST	REPAIRS
7							
8	Typewriter		US Bus.	90/11/12	Sales	680	EZ Repair
9	Typewriter		Echo	91/09/01	Sales	700	EZ Repair
10	Computer		Exec.	95/12/01	Sales	1,840	Options
11	Computer		Exec.	96/12/01	Sales	1,840	Options
12	Computer		Pack	96/07/12	Admin.	2,400	Options
13	Modem		Echo	95/10/01	Sales	640	Top Repair
14	Modem		Echo	96/10/01	Admin.	640	Top Repair
15	DM Printer		Express	95/12/01	Sales	410	Options
16	DM Printer		Express	96/12/01	Prod.	410	Options
17	L Printer		Express	96/01/11	Admin.	1,200	Options
18	Copier		Pro Copy	96/01/01	Admin.	1,100	Pro Copy
19	Calculator		OCC Cal	92/10/01	Sales	110	EZ Repair
20	Calculator		OCC Cal	92/10/01	Sales	110	EZ Repair
21	Check Protector		Protect	94/03/20	Admin.	140	Deltacorp
22	Dictating Machine		Ace Co.	88/04/26	Admin.	485	Teleco

Continued on Next Page

JOB 1

Create and Save a Presentation

As an employee of Fisher Oil Company, you have been asked to prepare a presentation about product liability for the upcoming board meeting.

1. Create a new presentation.

2. Use a blank presentation or the default presentation.

3. Use a title slide.

4. Key the following title:

   FISHER OIL COMPANY

5. Key the following subtitle on two lines:

   Allen Fisher
   May 15, 19--

6. Add a new slide.

7. Use a bulleted list slide.

8. Key the following title:

   Product Liability Report

9. Key the following bulleted list:

   - Why product liability is a concern for the company
   - Components of the threat
   - How it has been addressed in the past
   - How this relates to your department
   - Questions

10. Save your presentation as FISHER.

11. The presentation will be printed in a future job.

12. Close the presentation.

6. Use Print Preview to see how the printed page will look without actually printing it.

7. Save the spreadsheet as WILSON.

8. Print the spreadsheet.

CHAPTER 14

Jobs 1–21
Create, Edit, Format, and Print a Presentation

Time Estimate: 5 hrs.

OBJECTIVES

In this chapter, students will:

1. Create a presentation
2. Save a presentation
3. Open and edit a presentation
4. Use a predesigned presentation template
5. Print a presentation
6. Add transitions
7. Add build effects
8. Add sound effects
9. Use the print options

JOB 2

Create and Format a Spreadsheet

1. Key the information below in your spreadsheet to prepare a stock analysis.

2. Center the column headings.

3. Format columns B, C, and D for fixed format with three decimal places.

4. Save the spreadsheet as STOCK.

5. Print the spreadsheet.

	A	B	C	D
1		STOCK ANALYSIS		
2		PRICE PER SHARE		
3				
4	Date	OSA	MNR	TWA
5				
6	Jan 9	29.75	12.25	75.125
7	Jan 16	32.5	15.25	70.25
8	Jan 23	38.125	20.875	50.25
9	Jan 30	44.5	25.5	35.5

FINISH

PRESENTATION GRAPHICS

JOB 3

Adjust Column Widths

Prepare a list of accounts receivable for Sanders' Clothiers.

1. Key the information as shown below in your spreadsheet.

2. Center the title across columns A–C as shown.

3. Adjust column widths to fit content. Column widths can be changed individually or globally. If the width is adjusted individually, only the specified column will change. If the width is adjusted globally, all the columns will change.

4. Make the title bold, and change the font in row 1 to 18 point Times New Roman or a comparable font.

5. Center the headings in columns A and B, and right align the heading in column C.

6. Make all headings bold.

7. Save the spreadsheet as SANDERS.

8. Print the spreadsheet.

	A	B	C
1		SANDERS' CLOTHIERS	
2		ACCOUNTS RECEIVABLE	
3			
4			ACCOUNT
5	CUSTOMER	ADDRESS	BALANCE
6			
7	Black and Associates	1818 Lindsey Drive, Denton, TX	2999.88
8	Denim Specialties	1522 Whispering Hills, Dallas, TX	3000.25
9	Dick Cope Clothiers	1233 Lake Drive, San Francisco, CA	10003.25
10	Jean's Wear	1322 Darby Drive, Ardmore, OK	11500.89
11	Lake Wood, Inc.	1223 Harding Drive, Denver, CO	3777.91

JOB 64

Challenge Reinforcement

The Registry Office at East Central University is responsible for notifying students when they are on academic probation (students whose GPA is less than a 2.0). Prepare a query and calculate the students' GPA. Use the database STUDENT4. Include in the query the information needed to calculate each student's GPA and the mailing address information so you can prepare mailing labels. Sort the query by last name in ascending order. Save the query and database as ACDEMIC. Print the query.

Use the query to prepare mailing labels. Use Save As to save the labels as LABELS. Print the labels.

Compose a letter notifying the student that he or she is on academic probation for the next semester of attendance. If the student's average is above the minimum 2.0 GPA at the end of the probationary semester, he or she may continue course work with the university. Otherwise the student will be suspended from the university. Have the student contact the East Central University Registry Office if he or she has any questions. Sign the letter with your name. Save the letter as PROB. Print the letter.

JOB 4

Adjust Column Widths

Mr. Fischer needs a second quarter report on the sales of new and used cars.

1. Key the information as shown below in your spreadsheet.

2. Center each region heading as shown.

3. Adjust column widths as needed to fit content.

4. Make the titles (rows 1 and 2) bold and the regional titles (rows 4, 8, 12, and 16) bold and italic.

5. Format the spreadsheet for commas with two decimal places.

6. Save the spreadsheet as AUTO.

7. Print the spreadsheet.

	A	B	C	D
1	FISCHER AUTO ENTERPRISES			
2	CAR SALES, SECOND QUARTER			
3				
4	EASTERN REGION:			
5	New Cars			1777883.23
6	Used Cars			777322.22
7				
8	WESTERN REGION:			
9	New Cars			1654328.89
10	Used Cars			445768.99
11				
12	NORTHERN REGION:			
13	New Cars			2345342.88
14	Used Cars			755233.77
15				
16	SOUTHERN REGION:			
17	New Cars			1112334.88
18	Used Cars			655288.98

FINISH

Challenge Reinforcement

The people that work in sales at AAA Motors receive a base salary of $1,000 a month and a commission of 3% of their total sales. Use the database PAYROLL to prepare a query to determine each person's commission and total salary for the pay period. Add the following information to the database, and then use the database to prepare a query. List each person's last name, first name, department, salary, and sales. Add the fields "COMMISSION" and "TOTAL SALARY." Calculate each person's commission based on total sales. Determine total salary by adding the commission and salary. Use Save As to save the query and database as COMMISS. Print the query.

Last	**First**	**Sales**
Coleman	Jack	$66,500
Key	Kyle	$52,555
McCain	Vicki	$33,000
Hisle	Claudia	$99,336
Sali	Angela	$23,055
Miller	Susan	$15,500

Use the query to prepare a report. List each person's last name, first name, sales, commission, and total salary in the report. Sort the last names in alphabetical order. Select the layout and style of the report. The title of the report should be "Sales Commission Report." Use Save As to save the report and database as COMREP. Print the report. Close the report and the database.

JOB 5

Adjust Column Widths

Prepare an employee record for West Real Estate and Auction.

1. Key the information as shown below in your spreadsheet.

2. Adjust column widths as necessary to fit content.

3. Format cells C6..C15 for fixed format with two decimal places.

4. Center all column headings.

5. Save the spreadsheet as WEST.

6. Print the spreadsheet.

	A	B	C	D	E
1	WEST REAL ESTATE AND AUCTION				
2	REGIONAL EMPLOYEE RECORDS				
3					
4	LAST	FIRST	WAGE	DEPARTMENT	LOCATION
5					
6	McFarlane	Ben	10.2	Accounting	Amarillo
7	Melton	Amy	10.95	Accounting	Houston
8	Fischer	Barbara	9.05	Sales	Houston
9	Brown	John	12.2	Sales	Dallas
10	Rhoads	Kurt	11.55	Accounting	Dallas
11	Cassell	Ed	10.5	Advertising	Dallas
12	Farmer	John	10.25	Sales	Amarillo
13	Fleming	Kay	9.95	Accounting	Dallas
14	Albright	Kari	9.75	Advertising	Houston
15	Cannon	Lindsey	10.25	Advertising	Amarillo

JOB 62

Challenge Reinforcement

The Denver office of Star Manufacturing is having a meeting for all employees that have insurance with the company. Use the database EMPLOY5 to prepare a query of the people that are employed in the Denver office and have insurance. Include the following fields: last name, first name, location, department, and insurance. Sort the names by last name in alphabetical order. Save the query as REGIONAL.

Use the query to prepare name labels. Include on the label their name and the department in which they work. Change the font of the labels as desired. Use Save As to save the labels and database as LABREG. Print the labels. Close the report and the database.

JOB 6

Create and Copy a Formula

A local business needs an inventory price sheet.

1. Create the spreadsheet as shown below.

2. Center the title (row 1) across columns A–F.

3. Center the heading in column A. Right align the heading in column C. Also, right align the headings in columns D and F.

	A	B	C	D	E	F
1	COMPUTER SOFTWARE COST SHEET					
2						
3						Total
4	Program		Cost	Inventory		Cost
5						
6	Sports		14.95	11		*formula*
7	Religion		14.95	34		
8	Holidays		14.95	65		
9	Borders & Boxes		29.95	76		
10	Cartoons		29.95	36		
11	Cartoons II		39.95	49		
12	Business I		29.95	77		
13	Business II		39.95	104		
14	Business III		39.95	112		
15	Calendar Creator		49.95	34		
16	Organizer		19.95	98		
17	Label Creator		49.95	201		
18	Paint Power		99.95	22		
19	Time Management		14.95	48		
20	Schedule Creator		19.95	38		
21	Careers		49.95	14		
22	DOS Tutor		29.95	88		
23	Utilities		29.95	26		

Continued on Next Page

JOB 61

Challenge Reinforcement

The librarian at your school would like a report showing all books in the library. Use the database (BOOKS) created in Job 36 to create the report. Include the name of the book, the author, the copyright date, and the type of book. Group the list by the type of book. The title of the report should be the *"Name of Your School* Library Books" (for example, Jackson High School Library Books). Use Save As to save the report and database as LIBRARY. Print the report. Close the report and the database.

4. Create a formula that multiplies cost by inventory to calculate a total cost in cell F6.

5. Copy the formula in cell F6 and paste to cells F7..F23.

6. Format column F for commas with two decimal places.

7. Save the spreadsheet as SOFT.

8. Print the spreadsheet.

JOB 60

Challenge Reinforcement

The principal's office would like to prepare a report of all teachers in the building. Use the database (TEACHER) created in Job 20 to create the report. Group the report by the areas in which they teach. List their names, the areas in which they teach, and the number of years taught. Use Save As to save the report and database as FACULTY. Print the report. Close the report and the database.

JOB 7

Create and Copy a Formula

1. Create the spreadsheet as shown below.

2. Center the titles (the first three rows) across columns A–E.

3. Center all column headings.

	A	B	C	D	E
1	INVENTORY				
2	Western Heights High School				
3	Room 129				
4					
5	Quantity	Description		Cost	Extension
6					
7	5	Sonic Monitor		150	*formula*
8	5	Bell Monitor		195	
9	1	Gold Star Monitor		167	
10	1	Edison Monitor		200	
11	2	Sonic Monitor		235	
12	1	Okla Data Systems		1000	
13	10	Executive Computer		600	
14	12	Keyboard		99	
15	1	Podium		75	
16	10	Student desks		55	
17	12	Student chairs		24	
18	10	Typing stands		2	
19	1	Wastebasket		5	
20	1	Paper cutter		35	
21	1	Overhead projector		150	
22	1	Screen		75	
23	2	Locked disk file cabinets		40	
24	1	Small table		115	
25	1	Swell LCD Unit		1159	

Continued on Next Page

Star Manufacturing needs to mail some information to all who have applied for a position with the company. Create a mailing label for each person.

1. Open the database APPLI5.

2. Use the database APPLI5 to create a report to print labels. Use the Label Wizard if available with your software.

3. Select the desired label size. Change the font size to 10 points and sort the labels by the zip code. Include the following fields for the label:

   First and Last Name
   Address
   City, State Zip

4. Use Save As to save the label report as LABELS.

5. Print the labels.

6. Close the report and the database.

4. Create a formula that multiplies cost by quantity to calculate extension.

5. Format columns D and E for commas with two decimal places.

6. Save the spreadsheet as HEIGHTS.

7. Print the spreadsheet.

FINISH

JOB 58

Create a Report

The president's office would like a report showing the students who made the President's Honor Roll (students who have maintained a 3.5 or higher GPA).

1. Open the database HONOROLL.

2. Use the query HONOROLL to create the report. If available with your software, use a Report Wizard to create the report.

3. Use the following information to create the report:

   Use the following fields: "MAJOR" "LAST," "FIRST," and "CLASSIFICATION."
   Group the data by major.
   Sort the list according to the last name then first name, both in ascending order.
   Select a layout and style of your choice.
   Key the title "President's Honor Roll" in the title text box.

4. Preview the report, and make any necessary adjustments to the layout of the report.

5. Use Save As to save the report and database as HONOROL2.

6. Print the report.

7. Close the report and the database.

JOB 8

Create and Copy a Formula

1. Create the spreadsheet as shown below.

2. Center the title (rows 1 and 2) across columns A–G as shown below.

3. Right align all column headings.

4. Create a formula that multiplies the number of books sold by the average price to calculate total sales.

5. Create a formula that multiplies the number of movies rented by the average rental to calculate total rental.

6. Format columns C, D, F, and G for commas with two decimal places.

7. Save the spreadsheet as DANBURY.

8. Print the spreadsheet.

	A	B	C	D	E	F	G
1				Danbury's			
2				Book & Movie Count			
3							
4	Store	Books	Average	Total	Movies	Average	Total
5	Number	Sold	Price	Sales	Rented	Rental	Rental
6							
7	1023	1300	9	*formula*	600	1.5	*formula*
8	1047	1000	8.8		300	1.65	
9	2019	500	9.05		100	1.55	
10	3055	1800	8.65		750	1.7	

JOB 57

Create a Report

Star Manufacturing wants a report that shows how much money was spent on each expense.

1. Open the database EXPENSE.

2. Use the database EXPENSE to prepare the report. If available with your software, use a Report Wizard to create the report.

3. Use the following information to create the report:

   Use the following fields: "EXPENSE," "PAYEE," and "AMOUNT."
   Group the data by expense.
   Sort the list according to the payee in ascending order.
   Select a layout and style of your choice.
   Sum the amounts for each expense.
   Key the title "Expense Report" in the title text box.

4. Preview the report, and make any necessary adjustments to the layout of the report.

5. Use Save As to save the report and database as EXPENSE2.

6. Print the report.

7. Close the report and the database.

JOB 9

Create and Copy a Formula

Wintersmith Insurance needs a claims report for January.

1. Key the information as shown below in your spreadsheet.

2. Adjust column widths as needed.

3. Make the title in row 1 bold, and change the font to 18 point Times New Roman or a comparable font.

4. Add the label "Total" in cell F4 and "Cost" in cell F5.

5. Center the column headings.

6. Create a formula to multiply the number of claims filed by the average cost per claim to get the total cost in column F.

7. Format columns B and F for commas with zero decimal places.

8. Recenter the title across columns A–F.

9. Save the spreadsheet as CLAIM.

10. Print the spreadsheet.

	A	B	C	D
1	WINTERSMITH INSURANCE COMPANY			
2	CLAIMS FILED FOR JANUARY, 19--			
3				
4		No. of		Average
5	Location	Claims Filed		Cost/Claim
6				
7	Atlanta, GA	2400		550.87
8	Oklahoma City, OK	918		546.66
9	Tulsa, OK	821		668.93
10	Dallas, TX	3456		567.99
11	Austin, TX	998		439.99
12	Denver, CO	968		588.45
13	Kansas City, KS	3324		548.97

FINISH

JOB 56

Create a Report

The Oaks Real Estate Company needs a report listing the houses for sale according to the development in which the houses are located.

1. Open the database LISTING5.

2. Use the database LISTING5 to create the report. If available with your software, use a Report Wizard to create the report.

3. Use the following information to create the report:

   Use the following fields: "DEVELOPMENT," "COST," "ADDRESS," and "SQUARE FEET."
   Group the data by development.
   Sort the list according to the cost of the house in ascending order.
   Select a layout and style of your choice.
   Key the title "The Oaks" in the title text box.

4. Preview the report, and make any necessary adjustments to the layout of the report.

5. Use Save As to save the report and database as OAKS.

6. Print the report.

7. Close the report and the database.

JOB 10

Create and Copy a Formula

1. Change the width of column A to 20 spaces, and create the spreadsheet as shown below.

2. Center all column headings.

3. Create a formula that multiplies sales by the commission rate to calculate the commission earned.

4. Format columns B and D for commas with two decimal places.

5. Format column C for percent with zero decimal places.

6. Save the spreadsheet as FOOD.

7. Print the spreadsheet.

	A	B	C	D
1	WHOLESOME FOOD COMPANY			
2	COMMISSION SUMMARY			
3				
4			Comm.	Comm.
5	Name	Sales	Rate	Earned
6				
7	Axline, Lisa	3750	0.25	*formula*
8	Dingwall, Trudie	2700	0.21	
9	Dixon, Patricia	2600	0.21	
10	Hagen, Kristine	3200	0.25	
11	Hass, Carol	2850	0.21	
12	Hergman, William	1900	0.17	
13	Herning, Julie	2200	0.21	
14	Hyman, Leesa	2100	0.21	
15	Newbern, Linda	1600	0.17	
16	Schauss, Gordon	1800	0.17	
17	Whittaker, Chris	1800	0.17	

FINISH

JOB 55

Create a Report

The alumni office for East Central University needs a report showing the alumni who have graduated from East Central University according to their degrees.

1. Open the database ALUMNI2.

2. Use the database ALUMNI2 to create a report. If available with your software, use a Report Wizard to create the report.

3. Use the following information to create the report:

   Use the following fields in your report: "DEGREE," "YEAR," "LAST," "FIRST," "ADDRESS," "CITY," and "STATE."
   Group the data by degree.
   Sort the list according to the year graduated and then last name, both in ascending order.
   Select a layout and style of your choice.
   Key the title "ECU Alumni" in the title text box.

4. Preview the report, and make any necessary adjustments to the layout of the report.

5. Use Save As to save the report and database as ECUALUMN.

6. Print the report on one page.

7. Close the report and the database.

JOB 11

Create and Copy a Formula

Prepare an earnings record for Jerry Hammond.

1. Globally change the column widths to 12.

2. Key the information as shown below in your spreadsheet.

3. Center the heading and data in column A.

4. Right align the headings in columns B, C, and D.

5. Create a formula to add columns B and C to get the totals in column D.

6. Copy the formula in cell D7 and paste to cells D8..D14.

7. Save the spreadsheet as EARN.

8. Print the spreadsheet.

	A	B	C	D
1	JERRY HAMMOND'S EARNINGS			
2	PAY PERIOD FOR APRIL-JULY			
3				
4	Pay Period			
5	Ended	Bimonthly	Overtime	Total
6				
7	4/15	650	19.55	*formula*
8	4/30	650	9.75	
9	5/15	650	30.35	
10	5/31	650	19.55	
11	6/15	715	48.75	
12	6/30	715	9.75	
13	7/15	715	39.25	
14	7/31	715	30.75	

JOB 54

Create a Query with a Calculated Field

The president's office would like to prepare a list of the students who made the President's Honor Roll (students who have maintained a 3.5 or higher GPA).

1. Open the database STUDENT4.

2. Create a query using the database STUDENT4.

3. Include the following information in the query:

   Use the following fields: "LAST," "FIRST," "POINTS," "CREDITS," "MAJOR," and "CLASSIFICATION."
   Select the students who have maintained a 3.5 or higher GPA.
   Do not show the "POINTS" or "CREDITS" records.
   Sort the "LAST" and "FIRST" columns in ascending order.
   Insert a GPA column between "MAJOR" and "CLASSIFICATION." Determine the GPA (POINTS/CREDITS).
   Change the GPA field properties to fixed format (two decimal places).

4. Use Save As to save the query and database as HONOROLL.

5. Print the query or database in List View.

6. Close the query and the database.

FINISH

JOB 12

Create and Copy a Formula

Prepare an interest table for the First State Bank.

1. Key the information as shown below in your spreadsheet. It is not necessary to key the leading zeroes in column C.

2. Adjust column widths to fit content.

3. Center the column headings.

	A	B	C	D	E
1			FIRST STATE BANK		
2			INTEREST COMPUTATION TABLE		
3					
4	Loan		Interest	Time	Interest
5	No.	Principal	Rate	(Days)	Due
6					
7		1	10400	0.125	360	*formula*
8		2	5500	0.088	720	
9		3	11650	0.105	720	
10		4	3300	0.133	90	
11		5	2800	0.095	90	
12		6	19000	0.185	720	
13		7	23000	0.21	720	
14		8	6600	0.125	360	
15		9	8876	0.125	360	
16		10	500	0.085	30	
17		11	750	0.085	60	
18		12	3400	0.105	180	
19		13	3000	0.103	180	
20		14	7500	0.12	360	
21		15	15000	0.175	390	

Continued on Next Page

JOB 53

Create a Query with a Calculated Field

Based on the sales for the year, the employees who work in sales receive a bonus at the end of the year. This year Star Manufacturing is planning to give a 15% bonus. Determine the bonus and total salary for each employee.

1. Open the database EMPLOY5.

2. Create a query using the database EMPLOY5.

3. Include the following information in the query:

    Use the following fields: "LAST," "FIRST," "DEPARTMENT," and "SALARY."
    Select the employees who work in sales.
    Sort the "SALARY" column in descending order.
    Add a field for the "BONUS" that will calculate a 15% bonus.
    Add a field for "TOTAL SALARY" that will add the salary plus the bonus.
    Change the bonus and total salary field properties to currency with two decimal places.

4. Use Save As to save the query and database as BONUS.

5. Print the query or database in List View.

6. Close the query and the database.

4. Create a formula in cell E7 to calculate the interest due (B7*C7*D7/365). Copy and paste the formula to complete column E.

5. Format columns B and E for commas with two decimal places.

6. Format column C for percent with two decimal places.

7. Format cells B7 and E7 for currency with two decimal places.

8. Save the spreadsheet as FIRST.

9. Print the spreadsheet.

JOB 52

Create a Query with a Calculated Field

Star Manufacturing wants to give all employees with 15 or more years of employment a 6% salary increase. Determine the salary increase for each employee.

1. Open the database EMPLOY5.

2. Create a query using the database EMPLOY5.

3. Include the following information in the query:

   Use the following fields: "LAST," "FIRST," "SALARY," and "YEARS EMPLOYED."
   Select the employees with 15 or more years of employment with the company.
   Sort the "YEARS EMPLOYED" column in descending order.
   Add a field for SALARY INCREASE that will compute a 6% increase.
   Change the salary and salary increase field properties to currency with two decimal places.

4. Use Save As to save the query and database as INCREASE.

5. Print the query and database in List View.

6. Close the query and the database.

JOB 13

Create and Copy a Formula

American Securities, Inc. needs a list of commissions earned by each broker.

1. Key the information as shown below in your spreadsheet.

2. Adjust column widths to fit content.

3. Center the column headings.

4. Make the title and all column headings bold and italic.

5. Format column B for commas with zero decimal places.

6. Format column C for percent with zero decimal places.

7. Create a formula to multiply sales times the rate of commission to determine the commission amount for column D.

8. Format column D for currency with two decimal places.

9. Save the spreadsheet as COMM.

10. Print the spreadsheet.

	A	B	C	D
1		AMERICAN SECURITIES, INC.		
2		COMMISSION REPORT		
3				
4			RATE OF	COMMISSION
5	BROKER	SALES	COMMISSION	AMOUNT
6				
7	Woods, P.	12344	0.03	*formula*
8	Youngs, B.	18344	0.03	
9	Moss, K.	44233	0.03	
10	Nicols, R.	21343	0.03	
11	Cowan, M.	22444	0.03	
12	Myers, K.	29960	0.03	
13	Jacobs, L.	8321	0.03	

FINISH

JOB 51

Create a Query with a Calculated Field

The Oaks Real Estate Company needs to know the price per square foot on the houses listed.

1. Open the database LISTING5.

2. Create a query using the database LISTING5.

3. Include the following information in the query:

   Use the following fields: "ADDRESS," "DEVELOPMENT," "COST," and "SQUARE FEET."
   Add a field "PRICE PER SQ FT," and enter a formula to calculate the price per square foot.
   Sort the "PRICE PER SQ FT" column in descending order.
   Change the price and cost field properties to currency with two decimal places.

4. Use Save As to save the query or database as PRICE.

5. Print the query and database in List View.

6. Close the query and the database.

JOB 14

Create and Copy a Formula

Prepare a price list for Fun Track Company.

1. Key the information as shown below in your spreadsheet.

2. Center the column headings and all item numbers.

3. Adjust the width of column B to fit the content.

4. Create a formula to multiply the price by 10% to complete column D.

5. Create a formula to subtract a 10% cash discount from price to complete column E.

6. Format columns C, D, E, and F for commas with two decimal places.

7. Save the spreadsheet as FUN.

8. Print the spreadsheet.

	A	B	C	D	E	F
1			FUN TRACK			
2			PRICE LIST, 19--			
3						
4				10% Cash	Cash	Shipping
5	Item No.	Name	Price	Discount	Price	Charge
6						
7	1300F	Fun Track Elite	1099	*formula*	*formula*	33
8	344F	Fun Track 600 Achiever	699			33
9	1001F	Fun Track 530 Pro	599			33
10	1002F	Fun Track 505	499			33
11	1600F	Fun Track 303	399			33
12	328G	Ski Pole Grips and Straps	12			2
13	384M	XR210 Pulse Meter	99			3
14	395M	Sport PE-300 Pulse Meter	199			3
15	1187V	Video-Getting Started on	695			2
16		Your Fun Track				
17	875B	Storage Bag	149			5

JOB 50

Create a Query

The Oaks Real Estate Company would like a separate listing of the houses that are in the Meadowood and Silver Leaf developments. The listing should include the date the house was listed, the address of the house, the development, and the cost.

1. Open the database LISTING5.

2. Create a new query using the database LISTING5.

3. Create a query that shows the houses in the Meadowood and Silver Leaf developments. List the date, the address, the development, and the cost. Sort the query in descending order according to cost.

4. Use Save As to save each query or database separately with the name of the development (MEADOWOD and SLVRLEAF).

5. Print the query or database in List View.

6. Close the query and the database.

JOB 15

Use the Autosum Feature

1. Create the spreadsheet as shown below.

2. Adjust the column widths as needed.

3. Center the column headings.

4. Make the title, headings, and the data in cell A9 bold.

5. Create a formula or use the Autosum feature to calculate the totals for North, South, East, and West in column E. The Autosum feature will add all numbers directly above the cell or directly to the left of the cell.

6. Create a formula or use the Autosum feature to calculate the totals for January, February, and March in cells B9, C9, D9, and E9.

7. Format the spreadsheet for commas with zero decimals.

8. Save the spreadsheet as TRI.

9. Print the spreadsheet.

	A	B	C	D	E
1	Tri-Tech Incorporated				
2	1st Quarter Sales				
3					
4	Sales Region	January	February	March	Total
5	North	155325	153666	156333	*formula*
6	South	175808	178987	177545	
7	East	177225	179445	178383	
8	West	188325	189450	190323	
9	TOTAL	*formula*			

JOB 49

Create a Query

East Central University needs a list of each student's personal information.

1. Open the database STUDENT4.

2. Create a new query using the database STUDENT4.

3. Create a query that shows the student's personal information. List the student's last name, first name, major, telephone number, address, city, state, and zip. Sort the list in ascending order by the last name and then by first name.

4. Use Save As to save the query or database as STUDENT5 depending upon the software you are using.

5. Print the query or database in List View.

6. Close the query and the database.

JOB 16

Use the Autosum Feature

Prepare a payroll register for Floyd's Department Store for the month of March.

1. Globally change the column widths to 10 spaces.

2. Key the information as shown below in your spreadsheet. Use bold and italic print as shown.

3. Add the label "Total" in cell E5.

4. Create a formula or use autosum in column E to add the regular and overtime pay.

5. Format columns C, D, and E for fixed format with two decimal places.

6. Center the heading for column A. Right align the headings for columns C, D, and E.

7. Center the title across columns A–E.

8. Save the spreadsheet as FLOYD.

9. Print the spreadsheet.

	A	B	C	D
1	*FLOYD'S DEPARTMENT STORE*			
2	*PAYROLL REGISTER FOR MARCH*			
3				
4	Employee			
5	Name		Regular	Overtime
6				
7	Allen, S.		484	10.55
8	Weeks, M.		374	12.75
9	Andrew, T.		506	15.55
10	Floyd, K.		850	20.25
11	Jones, G.		462	8.85
12	Cobb, E.		466	12.25

JOB 48

Create a Query

The scout for the Jackson Kangaroos would like a list of the recruits showing who has averaged at least 15 points per game (PPG) and has had 5 or more rebounds per game (RPG).

1. Open the database DRAFT4.

2. Create a new query using the database DRAFT4.

3. Create a query of the players that averaged at least 15 points per game and had 5 or more rebounds per game. List each player's last and first name, the university, points per game, and rebounds per game. Sort the query in descending order according to the points per game. Do a secondary sort in descending order by RPG.

4. Use Save As to save the query or database in List View as PPG.

5. Print the query or database in List View.

6. Close the query and the database.

JOB 17

Use Page Setup to Print on One Page

1. Globally change the column widths to 11 spaces, and create the spreadsheet as shown below.

2. Use underline and italic print as shown.

3. Center all column headings.

4. Create a formula or use the Autosum feature to calculate the weekly sales.

5. Globally format the spreadsheet for commas with two decimal places.

6. Use Page Setup so that the spreadsheet prints on one page.

7. Save the spreadsheet as YARDLEY.

8. Print the spreadsheet.

	A	B	C	D	E	F	G
1			*YARDLEY COLLECTIONS*				
2			*Weekly Sales Summary*				
3			*September 5, 19--*				
4							*Weekly*
5	*Employee*	*Monday*	*Tuesday*	*Wednesday*	*Thursday*	*Friday*	*Sales*
6							
7	Pickford, L.	582.5	426.3	128.33	460.75	446.86	*formula*
8	Truman, P.	426.3	128.33	460.75	380.2	426.3	
9	Tyson, G.	128.33	460.75	380.2	426.3	128.33	
10	Taylor, S.	460.75	380.2	446.86	128.33	460.75	
11	Ellis, C.	380.2	426.3	505.72	460.75	380.2	
12	Foley, J.	446.86	128.33	586.35	380.2	426.3	
13	Rivera, C.	505.72	460.75	430.3	446.86	427.82	
14	Blue, B.	586.35	380.2	582.5	426.3	128.33	
15	Berryman, M.	430.3	446.86	426.3	128.33	460.75	

JOB 47

Use Advanced Filter

Star Manufacturing needs an alphabetical list of all employees who work in the accounting department or administration department, earn at least $30,000, and have been employed for five or more years.

1. Open the database EMPLOY5.

2. Use the Filter (Find) function to determine which employees work in the accounting department or administration department, earn at least $30,000, and have been employed for five or more years.

3. Print the database.

4. Close the database.

JOB 18

Use Page Setup to Print

1. Adjust the column widths as necessary, and create the spreadsheet as shown below.

2. Use bold print as shown.

3. Center the titles and column headings.

4. Create a formula that adds June charges to the past due balance to calculate the account balance.

5. Format columns C, D, and E for fixed format with two decimal places.

6. Use Print Preview. If necessary, use Page Setup so that the spreadsheet prints on one page.

7. Save the spreadsheet as SHIPE.

8. Print the spreadsheet.

	A	B	C	D	E
1		SHIPE'S SHOE STORE			
2		ACCOUNTS RECEIVABLE			
3					
4			JUNE	PAST DUE	ACCOUNT
5	CUSTOMER	ADDRESS	CHARGES	BALANCE	BALANCE
6					
7	Bourland, Gary	1818 Lindsey Dr., Boulder, CO 80321-2136	29.99	80.95	*formula*
8	Caldwell, Glenda	1522 Whispering, Boulder, CO 80322-1522	30.25	9.82	
9	Baulch, Donna	1233 Lake Dr., Boulder, CO 80321-2208	100.32	110.44	
10	Witkin, Gordon	1322 Darby Dr., Denver, CO 84331-1306	115	29.18	
11	Blevins, Randall	1223 Harding Dr., Denver, CO 84336-1223	377.79	106.62	

JOB 46

Use Advanced Filter (Find)

The Office Place has notified Star Manufacturing that payment of $325.00 for some equipment that Star Manufacturing had purchased has not been received. Determine if a check for $325.00 to The Office Place has been written.

1. Open the database EXPENSE.

2. Use the Filter (Find) function to see if Star Manufacturing has written a check to The Office Place for $325.00. If they did, what was the date and the check number? Type or write your answer on a separate sheet of paper.

3. Do not save changes to the database.

4. Close the database.

Create a report for the board of directors of a hospital.

1. Key the information as shown below in your spreadsheet.

2. Center column A.

3. Right align the headings in columns C, D, and E.

4. Format column C for commas with zero decimal places and column D for percent with zero decimal places.

5. Adjust the column widths to make the table more attractive.

6. Adjust Page Setup so that the spreadsheet is centered both vertically and horizontally.

7. Save the spreadsheet as HOSP.

8. Print the spreadsheet.

	A	B	C	D	E
1	ADMISSIONS, OCCUPANCY, AND LENGTH OF STAY				
2	STATISTICS FOR HOSPITALS				
3					
4	Type		Patient	Average	Average
5	of		Admissions	Percent of	Length of
6	Hospital		Number	Occupancy	Stay (Days)
7					
8	A-1		2682	0.72	6.2
9	A-2		1824	0.81	6.9
10	A-3		1498	0.88	5.9
11	A-4		986	0.79	4.7
12	A-5		494	0.62	6.1
13	A-6		201	0.91	6.2

FINISH

JOB 45

One of AAA Motors' customers is looking for an Accord or Prelude. The color does not matter, but it needs to be in excellent condition, must have fewer than 50,000 miles, and must cost $15,000 or less. Determine if AAA Motors has a car that meets this criteria.

1. Open the database USED4.

2. Use the Filter (Find) function to determine if there is an Accord or Prelude in excellent condition, that costs $15,000 or less, and has fewer than 50,000 miles. List any cars that meet this criteria. Type or write your answers on a separate sheet of paper.

3. Do not save the changes to the database.

4. Close the database.

JOB 20

Challenge Reinforcement

Entertainment Today, Inc. would like a list of video rentals for June, July, and August. Below is a list of the kind and number rented for each of the three months. Use this information to create a spreadsheet. A row labeled "Total" will also be needed. Enter a formula or use the Autosum feature to get a total for each month. If your program has an Autoformat or Format Gallery, choose an appropriate format.

	Jun	Jul	Aug
New Releases	1208	1291	1233
Western	188	150	191
Comedy	186	189	176
Exercise	128	119	131
Sports	133	119	126
Disney	1307	1422	1509
Science Fiction	119	131	126
49-Cent Special	1306	1324	1402

Save and print the spreadsheet. Name the file RENTALS.

Use Advanced Filter (Find)

There are some customers looking at property listed with the Oaks Real Estate Company.

1. Open the database LISTING5.

2. Use the Filter (Find) function to find the houses that meet the following criteria. Remove the filter (show all records) after each selection to answer the next question. Type or write your answers on a separate sheet of paper.

   One customer needs a house that is at least 1,500 square feet and costs less than $90,000. Which houses meet this criteria?

   A customer wants a house in the Oak Tree Development. The square footage needs to be at least 1,000 square feet, and it must cost less than $88,000. Which houses meet this criteria?

   Another customer wants a house in the Meadowood Division. It must have at least 1,500 square feet, be less than 5 years old, and cost less than $110,000. Which houses meet this criteria?

3. Do not save the changes to the database.

4. Close the database.

Challenge Reinforcement

Wiley Standfield would like a spreadsheet with payroll information about his student workers. He needs the names in column A, the high school they attend in column B, the rate of pay ($5.00 per hour) in column C, the number of hours worked for week 1 in column D, the number of hours worked for week 2 in column E, the number of hours worked for week 3 in column F, and the number of hours worked for week 4 in column G. He also needs the total hours worked for each student in column H. Multiply the total hours in column H by the rate in column C to get the salary for each student in column I.

Name	High School	Week 1	Week 2	Week 3	Week 4
Logan, D.	Bixby	20	15	18	20
Bare, K.	Midwest	21	10	10	10
Kemp, J.	Douglas	8	10	15	10
Roark, B.	Norman	15	12	12	12
Bingham, K.	Shawnee	10	8	10	15

If desired, change the font and type size and use bold print.

Save and print the spreadsheet. Name the file WILEY.

East Central University needs to obtain some information on the alumni from the university.

1. Open the database ALUMNI2.

2. Use the Filter (Find) function to determine the answers to the following questions. Remove the filter (show all records) after each selection to answer the next question. Type or write your answers on a separate sheet of paper.

   How many students have graduated with an Associate degree since 1993?

   How many female students have graduated from the state of Texas with a Bachelor of Science degree since 1991?

   How many students graduated from the state of Oklahoma with a Master of Science degree in the year 1995?

   How many male students have graduated with a Master of Science or a Master of Art degree after 1993?

3. Do not save the changes to the database.

4. Close the database.

Entertainment Today, Inc. needs its spreadsheet updated.

Open RENTALS and add the information for September, October, and November to the spreadsheet. Create a formula to show the total number of rentals for each category and the total for the period of June through November.

	Sep	Oct	Nov
New Releases	2288	2321	2313
Western	97	159	81
Comedy	196	76	284
Exercise	29	24	54
Sports	186	87	176
Disney	2490	1654	2609
Science Fiction	21	32	43
49-Cent Special	1891	1623	1599

Use Save As to save the spreadsheet as RENTALS2. Print the spreadsheet using Page Setup to print in landscape orientation.

JOB 42

Filter (Find) Records

Star Manufacturing has some job openings in different cities. Identify the people who have applied for positions in these areas.

1. Open the database APPLI5.

2. Use the Filter (Find) function to determine the answers to the following questions. Remove the filter (show all records) after each selection to answer the next question. Type or write your answers on a separate sheet of paper.

   List the people who have applied for an accountant position in Chicago.

   List the people who have applied for a graphic artist position in Chicago.

   List the people who have applied for a sales representative position in Texas.

3. Do not save the changes to the database.

4. Close the database.

CHAPTER 7

Jobs 23–41
Delete Columns and
Rows and Use Formulas

Time Estimate: 6 hrs.

OBJECTIVES

In this chapter, students will:

1. Insert a row and delete a column
2. Delete and insert multiple rows
3. Insert a column
4. Insert multiple columns
5. Insert rows and a column
6. Use the Sum function
7. Use the Average function
8. Use the Maximum and Minimum functions
9. Use the Payment function
10. Use an absolute reference in a formula
11. Use the Count function

JOB 41

Filter (Find) Records

East Central University needs to obtain some information about its alumni.

1. Open the database ALUMNI.

2. Use the Filter (Find) function to determine the answers to the following questions. Remove the filter (show all records) after each selection to answer the next question. Type or write your answers on a separate sheet of paper.

   How many students graduated with a Bachelor of Art degree?

   How many students graduated with a Bachelor of Science degree?

   How many students who graduated were from the state of Texas?

   How many students were female?

   How many students graduated in the year 1995?

3. Do not save the changes to the database.

4. Close the database.

JOB 23

Delete a Single Row or Multiple Rows

The computer software list needs to be updated.

1. Open SOFT.

2. Center columns C and D.

3. Make the main heading, column headings, and the data in column A italic.

4. The company has eliminated Business I, Business II, and Business III from its software line. Delete rows 12, 13, and 14 from your spreadsheet.

5. Use Page Setup to center the page horizontally and vertically and to create a centered header using the text "Cost Sheet Report."

6. Create a footer with the current date on the left and the page number on the right.

7. Use Save As to save the spreadsheet as SOFT2.

8. Print the spreadsheet.

JOB 40

Filter (Find) Records

AAA motors needs to obtain some information from the used car database.

1. Open the database USED4.

2. Use the Filter (Find) function to determine the answers to the following questions. Remove the Filter (show all records) after each selection to answer the next question. Type or write your answers on a separate sheet of paper.

   How many Berettas are there for sale?

   How many Camaros are there for sale?

   How many Accords are there for sale?

   How many Chevrolets are there for sale?

   How many Hondas are there for sale?

3. Do not save the changes to the database.

4. Close the database.

JOB 24

Insert a Row and Delete a Column

The manager of Fischer Auto Enterprises would like to have a total for each region.

1. Open AUTO.

2. Center the word "TOTAL" in cells A7, A11, A15, and A19.

3. Use Autosum or key a formula in cells D7, D11, D15, and D19 to calculate the total for each region.

4. The spreadsheet would be more attractive if there were a blank row following the total for each region. Insert a blank row after these totals.

5. To decrease the width of the spreadsheet, delete column B from your spreadsheet.

6. Use Page Setup to center the spreadsheet horizontally and to create a header with the current date aligned at the right.

7. Use Save As to save the spreadsheet as AUTO2.

8. Print the spreadsheet.

JOB 39

Sort Multiple Records

Star Manufacturing would like an alphabetical list of all employees.

1. Open the database EMPLOY4.

2. Sort the names in ascending order by the last name and then ascending order by the first name.

3. Print the database in List View.

4. Use Save As to save the database as EMPLOY5.

5. Close the database.

JOB 25

Delete and Insert Multiple Rows

Jerry Hammond would like a report to reflect his earnings for the pay period of February through June.

1. Open EARN.

2. Delete the pay period information for 7/15 and 7/31.

3. Insert four rows above row 7.

4. Key the additional data shown below in rows 7, 8, 9, and 10.

5. Copy and paste the formula from D11 to complete column D for the additional data.

6. Change the heading to "PAY PERIOD FOR FEBRUARY - JUNE."

7. Format columns B, C, and D for fixed format with two decimal places.

8. Use Save As to save the spreadsheet as EARN2.

9. Print the spreadsheet.

	A	B	C
7	2/15	650	10.5
8	2/28	650	48.5
9	3/15	650	20.25
10	3/31	650	30.3

FINISH

JOB 38

Sort Records in Descending Order

The Jackson Kangaroos would like a list to show which recruits have scored the most points per game.

1. Open the database DRAFT3.

2. Sort the column "PPG" in descending order. Use a secondary sort by RPG in descending order.

3. Print the database in List View.

4. Use Save As to save the database as DRAFT4.

5. Close the database.

JOB 26

Insert a Column

The manager of Floyd's Department Store would like additional information on the payroll register.

1. Open FLOYD.

2. The manager would like to include columns for marital status and number of allowances. Center the headings "Marital" in cell B4 and "Status" in cell B5.

3. Insert a column between columns B and C.

4. Center the headings "No. of" in cell C4 and "Allowances" in cell C5.

5. Key the additional data as shown below in columns B and C.

6. Center the headings and the data in columns B and C.

7. Use Page Setup to center the page horizontally and to create a centered header using the text "March Register."

8. Use Save As to save the spreadsheet as FLOYD2.

9. Print the spreadsheet.

	B	C
7	M	2
8	M	2
9	S	1
10	M	3
11	S	1
12	S	1

Sort Records in Alphabetical Order

East Central University would like an alphabetical list of its alumni.

1. Open the database ALUMNI.

2. Sort the names in alphabetical order according to the last name.

3. Print the database in landscape orientation in List View.

4. Use Save As to save the database as ALUMNI2.

5. Close the database.

JOB 27

Insert Multiple Columns

West Real Estate and Auction needs additional data for the regional employee records.

1. Open WEST.

2. The manager needs to include columns for the employee ID number and sex of the employee. Insert two columns between columns B and C.

3. Insert a blank row above row 3. Center the column headings "EMPLOYEE" in cell C4 and "ID NUMBER" in cell C5. Center the heading "SEX" in cell D5.

4. Key the additional data as shown below.

5. Adjust the widths of columns C and D to fit the content. Right align column D.

6. Recenter the headings in rows 1 and 2 across the columns.

7. Create a footer with the current date at the bottom center.

8. Use Save As to save the spreadsheet as WEST2.

9. Print the spreadsheet.

	C	D
7	443-78-9876	M
8	442-78-7888	F
9	980-54-7895	F
10	300-78-7892	M
11	456-89-7888	M
12	676-88-8999	M
13	555-90-8976	M
14	215-98-8976	F
15	233-67-7654	F
16	556-23-5678	F

CHAPTER 13

Jobs 37–64
Extract and Report Databases

Time Estimate: 7 hrs.

OBJECTIVES

In this chapter, students will:

1. Sort records in alphabetical order
2. Sort records in descending order
3. Sort multiple records
4. Filter records
5. Use advanced filtering
6. Create a query
7. Create a query with a calculated field
8. Create a report
9. Create a label

Insert Rows and a Column

1. Open SANDERS.

2. Insert rows as necessary to add the data as shown below so that the customer names will be in alphabetical order.

Casey's Fashions	1545 E. 1st Street, Ponca City, OK	2432.35
Cowboy Cuts	1124 Stadium Dr., Miami, FL	3824.56
Dillon's	803 Mockingbird Lane, Atlanta, GA	5543.27
K & L Clothing	903 West Main Street, Oakland, CA	3245.77
Marny's Accessories	808 Cherry Blvd., Reno, NV	892.56

3. The manager would like to include a column for the customer's account number. Insert a column between columns A and B.

4. Add the headings "ACCOUNT" in cell B4 and "NUMBER" in cell B5.

5. Add the data as shown below in column B.

	B
7	1144
8	1123
9	1238
10	803
11	1001
12	1154
13	565
14	2001
15	1233
16	235

Continued on Next Page

JOB 36

Challenge Reinforcement

You are the school librarian, and you would like to set up a database for the books in the library. Include the name of the book, the author, the type of book (fiction, nonfiction, science fiction, biography, etc.), and the copyright date. Include at least 20 books in the database. Save the database as BOOKS. Print the database on one page in List View.

6. Change the column width of column B to 9 spaces, and center the data in the column.

7. Reformat column D for commas with two decimal places to include the data added.

8. Use Save As to save the spreadsheet as SANDERS2.

9. Print the spreadsheet.

JOB 35

Challenge Reinforcement

AAA motors would like to put all of the company's payroll data into a database. Create a database from the information below that shows the employee first name, last name, social security number, department, salary, and whether he or she has insurance through the company. If available with your software, use the Lookup Value when possible. Save the database as PAYROLL. Print the database on one page in List View.

Jeff Kopczynski
443-56-8055
Accounting
$1,562
Insurance

Jack Coleman
445-82-1257
Sales
$1,000

Larry McBroom
449-23-8611
Service
$1,250
Insurance

Anthony Pyrum
773-58-8908
Marketing
$1,700
Insurance

Kyle Key
445-62-1238
Sales
$1,000
Insurance

Chuck Roberts
446-62-8011
Service
$1,200
Insurance

Vicki McCain
443-89-6789
Sales
$1,000
Insurance

Kylie Byrd
443-99-7890
Accounting
$1,900
Insurance

Claudia Hisle
446-42-8033
Sales
$1,000

Felix Perez
665-93-2133
Service
$1,300
Insurance

Angela Sali
662-38-1231
Sales
$1,000

Susan Miller
446-92-8011
Sales
$1,000

FINISH

JOB 29

Use the Sum Function

The owner of the Sports Stuff store needs a post-closing trial balance.

1. Key the information as shown below in your spreadsheet.

2. Change the width of column A to 30 spaces and columns B and C to 14 spaces.

3. Center the column headings.

	A	B	C
1	SPORTS STUFF		
2	POST-CLOSING TRIAL BALANCE		
3	NOVEMBER 30, 19--		
4			
5	Account Title	Debit	Credit
6			
7	Cash	21554.2	
8	Accounts Receivable	25572	
9	Merchandise Inventory	75400	
10	Supplies	541	
11	Office Equipment	5400	
12	Prepaid Insurance	805	
13	Accounts Payable		7576.2
14	Sales Tax Payable		2889
15	Kari Hennigan, Capital		52242.9
16	Lindsey Hennigan, Capital		66564.1
17			
18	TOTALS	*formula*	*formula*

Continued on Next Page

JOB 34

Challenge Reinforcement

Star Manufacturing is growing rapidly and would like to monitor expenses to see where money is being spent. Below is its checkbook register. Using this register, create a database to set up this information. Save the database as EXPENSE. Print the database in List View.

Check Number	Date	Payee	Amount	Expense
501	1/01/--	City Utilities	$99.21	Utilities
502	1/02/--	Thompson's	$25.25	Supplies
503	1/04/--	PEC Electric	$156.55	Utilities
504	1/05/--	The Office Place	$1,326.55	Equipment
505	1/06/--	The Copy Doctor	$128.55	Repair
506	1/07/--	Paper Supply	$55.25	Supplies
507	1/08/--	KTLS Radio	$127.00	Advertising
508	1/10/--	PC Computer	$1,525.25	Equipment
509	1/10/--	B & B Telephone	$229.33	Utilities
510	1/11/--	Thompson's	$157.00	Supplies
511	1/11/--	City Utilities	$46.46	Utilities
512	1/12/--	Daily Tribune	$125.66	Advertising
513	1/12/--	The Office Place	$325.00	Equipment
514	1/15/--	Helping Hands	$150.00	Contribution
515	1/16/--	Daily News	$175.00	Advertising
516	1/18/--	Paper Supply	$52.23	Supplies
517	1/22/--	Postal Plus	$26.26	Supplies
518	1/25/--	Salvation House	$150.00	Contribution
519	1/28/--	PC Computer	$1,575.75	Equipment
520	1/30/--	The Office Place	$750.00	Equipment

FINISH

4. Create a formula in cell B18 or use the Autosum feature to total the "Debit" column (B7..B12).

5. Create a formula in cell C18 or use the Autosum feature to total the "Credit" column (C13..C16).

6. Format columns B and C for commas with two decimal places.

7. Save the spreadsheet as SPORTS.

8. Print the spreadsheet.

East Central University would like to add the student's major, points, credits, and classification to the student list. Add these fields to the right of the zip code. If available with your software, use a Lookup Value to enter the major and classification. Use the database STUDENT3. Add the information shown below to the database. Use Save As to save the database as STUDENT4, and print the database on one page in landscape orientation in List View.

ZIP	MAJOR	POINTS	CREDITS	CLASSIFICATION
94131	Accounting	352	95	Senior
73116	Engineering	80	66	Junior
77062	Education	343	98	Senior
77062	Education	158	45	Sophomore
77062	Engineering	247	130	Senior
80303	Computer Science	320	120	Senior
40513	Chemistry	112	62	Sophomore
74011	Engineering	55	29	Freshman
92801	Education	360	100	Senior
73034	Chemistry	216	60	Sophomore
22305	Chemistry	108	30	Freshman
76133	Accounting	192	64	Junior
65089	Accounting	112	32	Sophomore
74074	Engineering	367	102	Senior
74105	Computer Science	250	66	Junior
74037	Chemistry	114	30	Freshman
77062	Engineering	329	94	Senior
75231	Chemistry	186	62	Sophomore
75061	Chemistry	224	64	Junior
77062	Engineering	42	32	Sophomore
85948	Education	56	16	Freshman
94131	Accounting	150	100	Sophomore
82601	Chemistry	155	62	Sophomore
71115	Education	270	90	Junior
75231	Education	512	128	Senior
76133	Accounting	289	76	Junior
60620	Accounting	128	64	Junior
33176	Computer Science	240	96	Senior
94114	Engineering	350	100	Senior
73069	Chemistry	210	60	Sophomore

Use the Sum Function

Watkins Supply needs a six-month budget.

1. Globally change the column widths to 7 spaces. Change the width of column A to 18 spaces.

2. Right align the column headings, and key the data as shown below. Center the title across all columns. Copy and paste duplicate amounts such as the amounts for auto expense and miscellaneous expense.

3. Use the Autosum feature or create a formula in cell B9 to determine the total income. Copy and paste the formula to complete row 9.

	A	B	C	D	E	F	G
1		WATKINS SUPPLY					
2		SIX-MONTH BUDGET					
3							
4		JAN	FEB	MAR	APR	MAY	JUN
5							
6	INCOME:						
7	Sales	21800	20000	21800	21800	21800	20000
8	Services	1000	800	1000	1000	1000	800
9	TOTAL INCOME	formula					
10							
11	EXPENSES:						
12	Advertisement	150	150	140	130	130	130
13	Auto Expense	125	125	125	125	125	125
14	Insurance Expense	425			425		
15	Miscellaneous Expense	150	150	150	150	150	150
16	Office Expense	200	200	200	200	200	200
17	Purchases	10900	10000	10900	10900	10900	10000
18	Rent	550	550	550	550	550	550
19	Utilities	220	220	220	220	220	220
20	TOTAL EXPENSES	formula					
21							
22	BALANCE	formula					

Continued on Next Page

JOB 32

Hide and Unhide a Column

Star Manufacturing's insurance company needs a list of its employees, their office locations, departments, and number of years employed. Since salary is confidential, this column must be hidden.

1. Open the database EMPLOY4.

2. Hide the column for salary.

3. Print the database in List View.

4. Unhide the column for salary.

5. Close the database.

4. Use the Autosum feature or create a formula in cell B20 to determine the total expenses. Autosum should not be used if it includes the amounts under "INCOME." Copy and paste the formula to complete row 20.

5. Subtract total expenses from total income for the balance in row 22. Copy and paste the formula to complete row 22.

6. Globally format the spreadsheet for commas with two decimal places.

7. Create a double horizontal line above and below row 4 as shown.

8. Use Page Setup to center the page vertically and horizontally and to create a footer with the date at the bottom right.

9. Save the spreadsheet as WATKINS.

10. Print the spreadsheet.

4. Adjust the column widths as necessary.

5. Print the document in portrait style on one page in List View.

6. Use Save As to save the table as USED4.

7. Close the database.

JOB 31

Use the Sum Function

The manager of Cathy's Card Shop needs an order summary.

1. Key the information as shown below in your spreadsheet.

2. Center the title, column headings, and the data in columns A and D.

3. Create a formula to multiply price times quantity to obtain the total amounts in column E.

	A	B	C	D	E
1	CATHY'S CARD SHOP				
2	Order Summary				
3					
4	Item	Description	Price	Quantity	Total
5					
6	123	Select-A-Card	1.95	20	*formula*
7	190	Craft	5.95	10	
8	203	Poster	5.4	15	
9	210	Rubber Stamp	4.8	5	
10	232	Birthday Card	1.5	25	
11	332	Postcard	1.95	25	
12	322	Organizer	10.95	5	
13					
14	Merchandise Total				*formula*
15	Handling Fee				3
16					
17	Subtotal				*formula*
18	Sales Tax (6.75%)				*formula*
19					
20	TOTAL AMOUNT DUE				*formula*

Continued on Next Page

JOB 31

Use the Lookup Value

AAA motors would like to include a category in its list of used cars for the condition of the car.

1. Open the database USED3.

2. Insert a field between "MILEAGE" and "PRICE" to include "CONDITION." If available with your software, use a Lookup Value for the data type for the condition field. Type in the values from which you want to select, and use the default (one) for the number of columns.

   Type the following values for the condition:
   Fair
   Good
   Excellent

3. Enter the data as shown below. If you created a Lookup Value, use it to fill in the condition of the car.

MILEAGE	CONDITION
12,000	Fair
18,000	Fair
25,000	Excellent
67,000	Fair
71,000	Excellent
52,000	Good
69,000	Excellent
47,000	Excellent
63,000	Good
59,000	Excellent
34,000	Fair
81,000	Good
75,000	Fair
65,000	Fair
79,000	Good
76,000	Good
88,000	Excellent

Continued on Next Page

4. Create a formula or use the Autosum feature to obtain the merchandise total in cell E14.

5. Add the merchandise total and the handling fee to obtain the subtotal in cell E17.

6. Determine the sales tax in cell E18 by multiplying the subtotal by 6.75%.

7. Determine the total amount due in cell E20.

8. Adjust the column widths as needed to fit content.

9. Format columns C and E for fixed format with two decimal places.

10. Create a single-line border at the bottom of cells E12, E15, and E18.

11. Save the spreadsheet as CARD.

12. Print the spreadsheet.

JOB 30

Continued

4. Preview the document. Adjust column widths as necessary. Print the document in portrait style on one page.

5. Use Save As to save the database as ALUMNI.

6. Close the database.

Use the Average Function

B & D Enterprises would like a weekly sales summary for the activities of its employees.

1. Globally change the width to 12 spaces. Change the width of column A to 14 spaces.

2. Key the information as shown below in your spreadsheet.

3. Right align the column headings for columns B–G.

4. Create an average formula to determine the weekly averages in column G.

5. Use average formulas to determine the daily averages for columns B–F in row 16.

6. Globally format the spreadsheet for commas with two decimal places.

7. Save the spreadsheet as WEEKLY.

8. Use Page Setup so that the spreadsheet prints on one page.

9. Print the spreadsheet.

	A	B	C	D	E	F	G
1			B & D ENTERPRISES				
2			WEEKLY SALES SUMMARY				
3			March 4, 19--				
4							Weekly
5	Salesperson	Monday	Tuesday	Wednesday	Thursday	Friday	Average
6							
7	Atkinson, K.	555.6	750.36	950.52	1001.25	887.75	*formula*
8	Asbury, L.	1234.6	1299.88	1005.82	1556.89	998.45	
9	Asklund, R.	335.78	450.52	1003.85	950.45	750.63	
10	Babb, V.	567.8	1234.88	1005.99	1226.89	999.25	
11	Baldwin, J.	460.75	1459.88	1567.77	1345.25	1002.69	
12	Lossan, A.	1225.55	1288.63	1432.88	1433.45	1088.99	
13	Meharg, J.	1235.67	1889.82	2001.89	2005.63	1006.33	
14	Snow, L.	1263.12	1558.25	988.25	1023.89	888.88	
15							
16	DAILY AVERAGE	*formula*					

JOB 30

Create a Database with a Lookup Value

East Central University would like to create a list of its alumni.

1. Create a new database.

2. If available with your software, use the Lookup Value for the data type for sex and degree. Type in the values from which you want to select. Use the default (one) for the number of columns.

Type the following values for sex:
F
M

Type the following values for degree:
Associate Degree
Bachelor of Art
Bachelor of Science
Master of Art
Master of Science

3. Enter the records as shown below. If you created a Lookup Value, use it to fill in the data in the appropriate columns. Otherwise, key the information as shown.

LAST	FIRST	SEX	ADDRESS	CITY	STATE	DEGREE	YEAR
Short	Kari	F	105 W. Cottage	Albuquerque	NM	Bachelor of Science	1995
Vasquez	Shawn	M	232 Belmont	Abilene	TX	Bachelor of Art	1993
Buxton	Katie	F	467 Stadium Drive	Dallas	TX	Bachelor of Science	1996
Miller	Meagan	F	1433 Gardina Drive	Tulsa	OK	Master of Art	1994
Boatwright	Dale	M	1233 Willowbrook	Little Rock	AR	Associate Degree	1992
Cowart	Andrew	M	1544 Fairview	Jenks	OK	Master of Science	1993
Smith	Reagan	F	1325 Stockton	Bartlesville	OK	Associate Degree	1995
Larsh	Mary	F	456 Townsend	Arlington	TX	Master of Science	1992
Anderson	Nick	M	236 Valley View	Ft. Worth	TX	Associate Degree	1991
Fischer	Matt	M	1325 Broadway	Denton	TX	Bachelor of Science	1994
Muncrief	Kevin	M	807 Laurel Drive	Springfield	MO	Master of Art	1996
Bowers	Loyd	M	789 Duke Street	Ardmore	OK	Bachelor of Science	1993
Housel	Hilary	F	1635 Dogwood	Shreveport	LA	Bachelor of Art	1995
Hodgkins	Mae	F	333 Sandy Creek	Bartlesville	OK	Bachelor of Art	1994
Smith	Leann	F	256 Highland	Houston	TX	Master of Science	1996
Hoover	Stephanie	F	300 Ridgecrest	Atlanta	GA	Bachelor of Art	1995
Tracy	Chae	M	333 Wintersmith	Topeka	KS	Bachelor of Art	1994
Meharg	Jason	M	333 Kickapoo	Norman	OK	Bachelor of Art	1994
Cox	Darryl	M	326 Raintree	St. Louis	MO	Associate Degree	1995

Continued on Next Page

JOB 33

Use the Maximum and Minimum Functions

Mr. Smith would like a weekly stock analysis of the stock he owns to determine the average, low, and high stock prices.

1. Key the information as shown below in your spreadsheet.

2. Right align the column headings. Adjust column widths as necessary to fit content.

3. Create a formula in cell F7 to determine the average of cells B7..E7. Copy and paste the formula to cells F8..F16.

	A	B	C	D	E	F
1	STOCK ANALYSIS					
2	WEEKLY PRICE COMPARISON					
3						
4						Weekly
5		Week 1	Week 2	Week 3	Week 4	Average
6						
7	Ardy's	8.25	8	8.75	9.25	*formula*
8	Haliburten	29.5	30.5	30.25	33.75	
9	Holman	3.25	4.25	5.75	5.25	
10	Kerr Pumps	45.2	47.25	54.25	54	
11	Maxell	62.75	61.2	62.5	60.5	
12	Penney	17.25	17	16.75	15.75	
13	Legal Press	34.5	35.5	35.75	34.25	
14	ABC Oil	78.25	78.125	79.5	77.75	
15	J & F Corp.	25.2	25.125	30.25	29.625	
16	Jones Petroleum	17.25	16.25	16	15.5	
17						
18	Weekly High	*formula*				
19	Weekly Low	*formula*				
20	Weekly Average	*formula*				

Continued on Next Page

4. Change the font size to 8 points, center Yes/No, and adjust the column widths to fit the table on one page in portrait style.

5. Print the database in List View.

6. Use Save As to save the database as EMPLOY4.

7. Close the database.

4. Create a formula in cell B18 to determine the weekly high price (maximum formula). Copy and paste the formula to cells C18, D18, and E18.

5. Create a formula in cell B19 to determine the weekly low price (minimum formula). Copy and paste the formula to cells C19, D19, and E19.

6. Create a formula in cell B20 to determine the weekly average price. Copy and paste the formula to cells C20, D20, and E20.

7. Globally format the spreadsheet for fixed format with three decimal places.

8. Save the spreadsheet as PRICE.

9. Print the spreadsheet.

FINISH

Change the Data Type and Font Size

The payroll department would like a list of employees who have insurance with the company.

1. Open the database EMPLOY3.

2. Insert a field between "SALARY" and "YEARS EMPLOYED." Name the field "INSURANCE." If available with your software, select the Yes/No option for the data type.

3. Enter the information as shown below.

SALARY	INSURANCE	YEARS EMPLOYED
$15,500.00	Yes	1
$17,000.00	No	6
$16,500.00	Yes	4
$22,500.00	No	8
$17,000.00	No	2
$34,000.00	Yes	10
$25,000.00	No	20
$29,000.00	Yes	5
$24,500.00	Yes	19
$65,000.00	No	3
$20,500.00	Yes	12
$22,000.00	Yes	15
$32,000.00	No	10
$29,000.00	Yes	5
$17,500.00	No	6
$45,000.00	No	25
$21,500.00	No	13
$19,500.00	No	10
$20,500.00	Yes	12
$19,000.00	Yes	9
$22,000.00	No	15
$24,500.00	Yes	10
$26,000.00	No	22
$21,500.00	No	14
$39,000.00	No	15
$18,000.00	Yes	7
$23,000.00	No	2
$15,000.00	Yes	1

JOB 34

Use the Maximum and Minimum Functions

BG's Sports Grill would like a summary of its weekly payroll expenses.

1. Key the information as shown below in your spreadsheet.

2. Right align the headings in columns B–H. Adjust column widths as necessary to fit content.

3. Create a heavy line across the table under the column headings (columns A–H).

	A	B	C	D	E	F	G	H
1				BG'S SPORTS GRILL				
2				WEEKLY PAYROLL				
3								
4		Hourly	Hours			Federal	State	Net
5	Employee	Rate	Worked	Salary	SS Tax	Tax	Tax	Pay
6								
7	Bender, Jessica	6.5	20	*formula*	*formula*	*formula*	*formula*	*formula*
8	Claxton, Lindsay	5.25	25					
9	Doepke, Kellye	6.5	30					
10	Gray, Sari	5.75	40					
11	Jones, Julie	6.5	25					
12	Kruger, Denise	6.5	20					
13	Penwright, Michelle	6.5	25					
14	Puls, Erin	5.25	33					
15	Rich, Jaime	5.75	40					
16	Stephenson, Ashley	5.75	20					
17	Traugutt, Amy	5.25	25					
18	Weeks, Krista	5.25	20					
19								
20	TOTAL			*formula*				
21	HIGHEST SALARY			*formula*				
22	LOWEST SALARY			*formula*				
23	AVERAGE SALARY			*formula*				

Continued on Next Page

JOB 28

Move a Field

Star Manufacturing would like the list of job applicants displayed in a different format.

1. Open the database APPLI4.

2. Move the field "POSITION" to follow the field "FIRST" (the third field).

3. Print the database on one page in landscape orientation in List View.

4. Use Save As to save the database as APPLI5.

5. Close the database.

4. Determine the salary in column D by multiplying the hourly rate by hours worked.

5. Determine the social security tax in column E. The social security tax is 7.65% of the salary.

6. Determine the federal tax in column F. The federal tax is 15% of the salary.

7. Determine the state tax in column G. The state tax is 6% of the salary.

8. Determine the net pay in column H (salary less all taxes).

9. Determine the totals for columns D, E, F, G, and H in row 20.

10. Use the maximum formula to determine the highest salary in cell D21.

11. Use the minimum formula to determine the lowest salary in cell D22.

12. Use the average formula to determine the average salary in cell D23.

13. Format columns B, D, E, F, G, and H for commas with two decimal places.

14. Save the spreadsheet as GRILL.

15. Print your spreadsheet.

4. Preview the database. Adjust column widths as necessary to print the database in portrait style on one page in List View.

5. Use Save As to save the database as STUDENT3.

6. Close the database.

Use the Maximum and Minimum Functions

Update your stock list.

1. Open STOCK.

2. Insert a row above row 4. Center the heading "Market" in cell E4 and "Average" in cell E5.

3. Use the average formula to determine the market average in column E.

4. Key the label "Average" in cell A12. Use the average formula to determine the average for columns B, C, D, and E.

5. Key the label "High" in cell A13. Use the maximum formula to determine the high price in columns B, C, D, and E.

6. Key the label "Low" in cell A14. Use the minimum formula to determine the low price in columns B, C, D, and E.

7. Recenter the heading over the columns.

8. Use Save As to save the spreadsheet as STOCK2.

9. Print the spreadsheet.

JOB 27

Add a Field

East Central University would like the student list to include the student's address, city, state, and zip.

1. Open the database STUDENT2.

2. Add the fields "ADDRESS," "CITY," "STATE," and "ZIP."

3. Add the data as shown below.

LAST	FIRST	PHONE NO	ADDRESS	CITY	STATE	ZIP
Meharg	John	415-555-3692	1778 Noe Street	San Francisco	CA	94131
Sutton	Pat	405-555-3689	4101 Santa Fe	Oklahoma City	OK	73116
Key	Mary Jane	713-555-3876	6620 Apalachee	Houston	TX	77062
Walbrick	Lafton	713-555-5609	2840 Oak Harbor	Houston	TX	77062
Bodine	Larry	713-555-3289	2967 Southridge	Houston	TX	77062
Clark	Charles	303-555-3678	4855 Broken Fence	Boulder	CO	80303
Brendle	Ronnie	606-555-6678	2215 Woodland	Lexington	KY	40513
Kedy	Paula	918-555-6654	3117 Cornelia	Broken Arrow	OK	74011
Boatwright	Marcia	714-555-6656	4550 Mill Run	Anaheim	CA	92801
Anderson	Devon	405-555-9089	6404 Circle Hill Rd.	Edmond	OK	73034
Stafford	Allison	703-555-3245	6404 Blackberry Rd.	Alexandria	VA	22305
Sanders	Whitney	817-555-9876	6356 Wales Ct.	Ft. Worth	TX	76133
Stafford	Shawn	314-555-6765	3089 Manor Mall	Springfield	MO	65089
Stafford	Matt	405-555-7897	2533 Woodlake	Stillwater	OK	74074
Hoover	Angie	918-555-3691	300 Cherokee Dr.	Tulsa	OK	74105
Choate	Lauren	918-555-6621	2355 Fox Run Circle	Jenks	OK	74037
Leddy	Toby	713-555-9987	34 Raintree	Houston	TX	77062
Davis	Nick	214-555-2212	642 Golf Lake Trails	Dallas	TX	75231
Anderson	Tanner	214-555-8362	833 Foster	Denton	TX	75061
Vasquez	Roy	713-555-9826	1833 Faith Blvd.	Houston	TX	77062
Cranford	Taylor	602-555-9818	72 Stone Street	Tucson	AZ	85948
Lough	Debbie	415-555-6323	2410 Fletcher	San Francisco	CA	94131
Landrum	Tanner	307-555-6260	4566 N. Lake Dr.	Casper	WY	82601
Gomez	Robert	318-555-6260	1412 Lakehurst	Shreveport	LA	71115
Sehon	Debi	214-555-6854	1910 Camelot	Dallas	TX	75231
Hill	Carly	817-555-6854	3020 Broadway	Ft. Worth	TX	76133
Webb	Jessica	312-555-3688	3365 Augusta	Chicago	IL	60620
Akita	Yuki	305-555-9254	962 Stockton	Miami	FL	33176
Mariano	Marcus	415-555-6663	332 Peach Street	San Francisco	CA	94114
Cranford	Lauren	405-555-8908	1325 Kickapoo	Norman	OK	73069

Continued on Next Page

JOB 36

Use the Payment Function

Jake Tracy would like to purchase a new car. He needs a loan comparison table to determine the interest paid for the various rates and times.

1. Key the information below in your spreadsheet.

2. Globally change the column widths to 8 spaces.

3. Center the column headings.

	A	B	C	D	E	F	G	H
1			LOAN COMPARISON ANALYSIS					
2			BASED ON NUMBER OF MONTHS AND INTEREST RATE					
3								
4		Down	Amount	Interest	No. of		Amount	Interest
5	Price	Payment	Financed	Rate	Months	Payment	Paid	Paid
6								
7	15000	1500	*formula*	0.08	36	*formula*	*formula*	*formula*
8	15000	1500		0.085	36			
9	15000	1500		0.09	36			
10	15000	1500		0.095	36			
11	15000	1500		0.1	36			
12								
13	15000	1500		0.08	48			
14	15000	1500		0.085	48			
15	15000	1500		0.09	48			
16	15000	1500		0.095	48			
17	15000	1500		0.1	48			
18								
19	15000	1500		0.08	60			
20	15000	1500		0.085	60			
21	15000	1500		0.09	60			
22	15000	1500		0.095	60			
23	15000	1500		0.1	60			

Continued on Next Page

4. Add the data as shown below.

5. Use Save As to save the database as EMPLOY3.

6. Print the database on one page in List View.

7. Close the database.

DEPARTMENT	SALARY	YEARS EMPLOYED
Advertising	$15,500.00	1
Sales	$17,000.00	6
Art	$16,500.00	4
Accounting	$22,500.00	8
Advertising	$17,000.00	2
Accounting	$34,000.00	10
Sales	$25,000.00	20
Accounting	$29,000.00	5
Sales	$24,500.00	19
Administration	$65,000.00	3
Sales	$20,500.00	12
Sales	$22,000.00	15
Advertising	$32,000.00	10
Accounting	$29,000.00	5
Sales	$17,500.00	6
Accounting	$45,000.00	25
Art	$21,500.00	13
Advertising	$19,500.00	10
Sales	$20,500.00	12
Sales	$19,000.00	9
Sales	$22,000.00	15
Advertising	$24,500.00	10
Art	$26,000.00	22
Sales	$21,500.00	14
Accounting	$39,000.00	15
Sales	$18,000.00	7
Accounting	$23,000.00	2
Art	$15,000.00	1

4. Determine the amount financed in column C by subtracting the down payment from the price.

5. Use the Payment function to determine the payment in column F. (**Note:** The Payment function calls for three variables: principal, interest rate, and number of months.)

6. Determine the amount paid in column G by multiplying the payment by the number of months.

7. Determine the interest paid by subtracting the amount financed from the amount paid.

8 Format columns A, B, C, F, G, and H for commas with two decimal places.

9. Format column D for percent with two decimal places.

10. Save the spreadsheet as COMP.

11. Print the spreadsheet.

FINISH

JOB 26

Add a Field

Star Manufacturing wants to include salary and years of experience in its list of employees.

1. Open the database EMPLOY2.

2. Add the fields "SALARY" and "YEARS EMPLOYED" to the right of "DEPARTMENT."

3. Make the following changes to the database's format:

Field Name	Data Type	Format	Decimal Places
SALARY	Number (with comma)	Currency	Auto (2)
YEARS EMPLOYED	Number		

Continued on Next Page

JOB 37

Use an Absolute Reference in a Formula

Add additional information to the spreadsheet for American Securities, Inc.

1. Open COMM.

2. Using bold and italic print, key the heading "PERCENT OF" in cell E4 and "TOTAL SALES" in cell E5.

3. Key the label "TOTAL SALES" in cell A15.

4. Create a formula in cell B15 to total the sales.

5. Format cells B7 and B15 for currency with zero decimal places.

6. Adjust the column widths as necessary to fit content.

7. To determine each broker's percent of the total sales, divide the broker's sales (column B) by the total sales (B15). Key a formula in E7 using mixed references (relative for the broker's sales and absolute for the total sale) so that the formula can be copied (B7/B15).

8. Copy and paste the formula to the remaining cells in column E.

9. Format column E for percent with zero decimal places.

10. Recenter the title across the columns.

11. Use Save As to save the spreadsheet as COMM2.

12. Print the spreadsheet.

JOB 25

Add a Field

AAA motors would like to add a field (column) to its database to include the car color.

1. Open the database USED2.

2. Insert the car color between the model and mileage fields. Name the field "COLOR." Add the colors for the cars listed below.

3. Use Save As to save the database as USED3.

4. Print the database in List View.

5. Close the database.

MODEL	COLOR
Camaro	Red
Silverado	Maroon
Beretta	White
Beretta	White
Blazer	Red
Beretta	Silver
Accord	Maroon
Accord	Black
Accord	Black
Prelude	White
Camaro	Red
Camaro	Maroon
Mustang	Black
Probe	Black
Mustang	White
Accord	Blue
Accord	Red

JOB 38

Use the Count Function

Wilson Jones and Company needs a count of inventory items.

1. Open WILSON.

2. Key the label "Total Inventory Cost" in cell A24. Create a formula in cell F24 to determine the total inventory cost.

3. Format cell F24 for currency with zero decimal places. Adjust the column width as necessary to fit content.

4. Key the label "Total Inventory Items" in cell A25.

5. Create a count formula in cell F25 to count the number of items in the inventory.

6. To improve the appearance of the spreadsheet, center the column headings and add double horizontal lines above row 5 and below rows 6 and 22.

7. Use Save As to save the spreadsheet as WILSON2.

8. Use Page Setup so that the spreadsheet prints on one page.

9. Print the spreadsheet.

Delete a Field

The Jackson Kangaroos basketball team wants to eliminate the weight column for its listing of potential draft picks.

1. Open the database DRAFT2.

2. Delete the field for weight.

3. Use Save As to save the database as DRAFT3.

4. Print the database on one page in List View.

5. Close the database.

JOB 39

Challenge Reinforcement

The manager at Quality Used Cars wants a spreadsheet with payment options for the following automobiles. The buyer can pay $500 for a down payment and can pay $250 per month on a car. Quality Used Cars' credit policy is 24 months at 8% interest or 30 months at 7.5% interest.

Automobile	Cost
1990 Jeep	$6,000.00
1991 Pickup	$7,000.00
1992 Sports Car	$8,000.00

Create a spreadsheet to determine the payments on each automobile for both credit plans. The title should have "Quality Used Cars" on the first line and "Payment Plan" on the second line.

Save and print the spreadsheet. Name the file CAR.

JOB 23

Find and Replace Data

Star Manufacturing has discovered that some zip codes in its list of applications have been listed incorrectly. Update their records to fix the errors.

1. Open the database APPLI3.

2. Use the Find and Replace function to make the following changes:

   Find the zip code "65089" and replace with "66101."
   Find the zip code "80302" and replace with "80202."

3. Use Save As to save the database as APPLI4.

4. Print the database on one page in landscape orientation in List View.

5. Close the database.

JOB 40

Challenge Reinforcement

Ace Skating Rink needs a pay report prepared for its five assistants for the week of February 15–19 (Monday–Friday). Each assistant gets paid $6 per hour. Determine the total hours and the total salary for each assistant.

Feb.	Mon.	Tue.	Wed.	Thur.	Fri.
Devon Anderson		8	9	8	11
Kari Fowler	8	8	8	9	9
Jill Santo	8	8			
Maria Valdez	8	8	9		8
Frank Tomosh	8		8		11

Save and print the spreadsheet. Name the file ACE.

JOB 22

Find and Replace Data

The Oaks Real Estate Company needs to make some changes to its listings.

1. Open the database LISTING4.

2. Use the Find and Replace function to make the following changes:

   Find "Dr." and replace with "Drive."
   Find "St." and replace with "Street."
   Find "Oaktree" and replace with "Oak Tree."

3. Adjust the column widths as necessary.

4. Use Save As to save the database as LISTING5.

5. Print the database in List View.

6. Close the database.

JOB 41

Challenge Reinforcement

First State Bank needs additional information on its outstanding loans.

Open FIRST. Center the label "Total Due" in column F. Create a formula in column F to add the principal and interest due to get the total due for each loan. Format the column to match the spreadsheet.

Add the label "Total" in cell A23. Create formulas to show the total principal, total interest due, and total due.

Format row 23 for currency with two decimal places.

Save and print the spreadsheet. Use Save As to save the file as FIRST2.

FINISH

JOB 21

Copy and Paste Data

Star Manufacturing is opening a new branch office in Chicago, Illinois, and several people have applied for positions in that area. Update the company's list of applicants.

1. Open the database APPLI2.

2. Add the information as shown below. Copy and paste the city, state, and zip code (Chicago, IL 60616).

3. Use Save As to save the database as APPLI3.

4. Print the database on one page in landscape orientation and in List View.

5. Close the database.

LAST	FIRST	ADDRESS	PHONE	POSITION
Meharg	Jason	1212 Arlington	312-555-9889	Sales Rep
Bowers	Don	223 Pine	312-555-9090	Advertising Manager
Cranford	Kathryn	1213 Emerson Way	312-555-6767	Sales Rep
Wilfong	Larry	1420 Ivy	312-555-0912	Accountant
Stewart	Neva	1325 Charles Circle	312-555-2367	Graphic Artist
Floyd	Ruth	1415 Blake Way	312-555-1826	Accountant
Procter	Billie	434 Country Place	312-555-2954	Sales Rep
Werner	Marie	236 Mockingbird Lane	312-555-6935	Advertising Manager
Ray	Steve	289 Wintersmith	312-555-2948	Accountant
Kedy	Scott	1326 Spruce	312-555-8082	Graphic Artist
Moon	Jon	1456 Hemingway	312-555-3786	Accountant

FINISH

CHAPTER 8

Jobs 42–57
Use Windows and Macros

Time Estimate: 8 hrs.

OBJECTIVES

In this chapter, students will:

1. Freeze panes
2. Use windows
3. Use windows with unsynchronized (split) scroll
4. Use the Fill feature
5. Use windows to input data
6. Create command macros
7. Use command macros
8. Create label macros
9. Create a formula macro
10. Use label and formula macros

CHAPTER 12

Jobs 21–36
Edit and Manipulate a Database

Time Estimate: 5 hrs.

OBJECTIVES

In this chapter students will:
1. Copy and paste data
2. Find and replace data
3. Delete a field
4. Add a field
5. Move a field
6. Change the data type
7. Change the font size
8. Create a database with a Lookup Value
9. Use the Lookup Value
10. Hide and unhide a column

JOB 42

Freeze Panes

Create a video price list for Outstanding Video Network.

1. Center all column headings, and key Table A as shown below. Adjust column widths as necessary to fit content.

2. Move the cell pointer to row 8 and freeze the horizontal titles.

	A	B	C	D	E	F
1		OUTSTANDING VIDEO NETWORK				
2		5868 19TH STREET				
3		HUNTSVILLE, TX 77340				
4						
5			Tapes		Price	Cost
6	Cat		per	Developed	per	per
7	No	Title	Pkg	By	Tape	Pkg
8						
9	001V	Your Self Esteem	2	Columbia	39.95	*formula*
10	002V	Parliamentary Procedures	1	Lou & Lou Co.	39.95	
11	003V	Cleaning Your VCR	2	Hi Tec Co.	49.95	
12	007V	Conduct the Meeting	1	Lou & Lou Co.	29.95	
13	015V	Understanding Inflation	3	Fitz Co.	29.95	
14	109V	Tool Loader Plus	1	Hi Tec Co.	59.95	
15	110V	Magic Wand Today	1	Hi Tec Co.	29.95	
16	111V	Your Rubber Stamp	1	King Fortner Co.	39.95	
17	113V	Your Name Stamp	1	King Fortner Co.	39.95	
18	118V	Your Time Stamp	1	King Fortner Co.	39.95	
19	145V	Two-Color Airbrush	1	King Fortner Co.	69.95	
20	211V	SAT Prep for Math	1	Columbia	39.95	

Table A

Continued on Next Page

JOB 20

Challenge Reinforcement

You are the secretary for the principal at your school. The principal needs a list of the teachers in your building, the areas in which they teach, and the number of years they have taught. Obtain this information from your teachers, and compile a database. Save the database as TEACHER. Print the database in List View. Close the database.

3. Add the information from Table B as shown below to the spreadsheet.

	A	B	C	D	E	F
21	213V	SAT Prep for English	1	Columbia	39.95	
22	256V	Big Thesaurus	1	King Fortner Co.	49.95	
23	259V	Know Your Computer	4	Hi Tec Co.	29.95	
24	266V	Utility Tool Package	1	Hi Tec Co.	39.95	
25	288V	Capitalism	5	Fritz Co.	19.95	
26	300V	Facts about Drugs	1	Sullivan Video	29.95	
27	531V	Spelling Coach	1	King Fortner Co.	39.95	
28	589V	Design Tool Package	1	Hi Tec Co.	39.95	
29	595V	High on Life	1	Columbia	39.95	
30	596V	Make Good Grades	1	Columbia	49.95	
31	599V	Imaging Tool Package	1	Hi Tec Co.	39.95	
32	604V	Power Back	1	King Fortner Co.	69.95	
33	605V	Wall Street Today	2	Fritz Co.	29.95	
34	606V	Peer Pressure	1	Columbia	39.95	
35	607V	Personal Success	1	Columbia	49.95	
36	671V	How to Study	3	Columbia	29.95	
37	682V	Introduction to the PC	2	Hi Tec Co.	29.95	
38	683V	Introduction to MS-DOS	2	Hi Tec Co.	29.95	
39	684V	The Club Officers	1	Lou & Lou Co.	49.95	
40	780V	The Entrepreneurs	3	Videos for Now	19.95	
41	804V	Know Wall Street	2	RT Development	29.95	
42	805V	Decision Making	1	Columbia	49.95	
43	806V	Guide--Job Hunters	1	Videos for Now	39.95	
44	807V	Build Self Esteem	1	Columbia	69.95	
45	946V	Test Taking Without Fear	1	Columbia	39.95	
46	947V	Persuasive Speaking	1	Videos for Now	39.95	
47	993V	High Tech/High Touch	1	Hi Tec Co.	39.95	

Table B

Continued on Next Page

You have a problem with forgetting your friends' and family members' birthdays. Compile a list of at least 15 of your friends and family members. Include each person's first name, last name, address, and date of birth. Save the database as BIRTH. Print the database in List View. Close the database.

4. Create a formula in column F to multiply the number of tapes per package by the price per tape to get the cost per package. Copy and paste the formula to complete column F.

5. Format columns E and F for fixed format with two decimal places.

6. Clear the titles.

7. Save the spreadsheet as TAPES.

8. Use Page Setup so that the spreadsheet prints on one page.

9. Print the spreadsheet.

JOB 18

Challenge Reinforcement

Create a database of the students in your classroom. Enter each student's last name, first name, grade, sex, and classification. Save the database as CLASS. Print the database in List View. Close the database.

Create a checkbook analysis for John Meharg. Some of the entries from his checkbook will then be used to calculate tax-deductible expenditures.

1. Globally format the column widths for 9 spaces, and then change the width of column C for 18 spaces.

2. Key the spreadsheet in Table A as shown on the next page. Use the Fill feature for the check numbers. However, this must be done twice since cell A28 is empty. (Key "101" in cell A11, and use the Fill feature. Next, key "118" in cell A29, and use the Fill feature.)

3. All column headings should be right aligned except column C. This column heading should be centered.

4. Move the cell pointer to cell F10 and create a formula to determine the balance after each check or deposit. Copy and paste the formula to complete column F.

5. Key the spreadsheet in Table B as shown on p. 199 in the columns adjacent to the checkbook analysis. At this time, key *only* the data in rows 1–8. "TAX-DEDUCTIBLE EXPENDITURES" should be in cell I4.

6. Right align the headings for columns G–L.

7. Move to cell E8, and freeze both horizontal and vertical panes.

8. Key the remaining data for the tax-deductible expenditures.

9. Clear the panes and format columns D–L for commas with two decimal places.

10. Add double underlines above row 6 and below row 7.

11. Use Page Setup so that the spreadsheet fits on one page in landscape orientation.

12. Save the spreadsheet as CHECK.

13. Print the spreadsheet in landscape orientation.

Continued on Next Page

JOB 17

Edit a Record

The Oaks Real Estate Company needs to make some changes to the listing of houses currently on the market.

1. Open the database LISTING3.

2. Make the changes indicated to the following records:

   Find the property located at 1223 Augusta Dr. Change the square footage to 2,300.
   Find the property located at 213 Sycamore St. Change the price to $160,000.
   Find the property located at 110 Willowbrook St. Change the price to $88,500.

3. Use Save As to save the database as LISTING4.

4. Print the database in List View.

5. Close the database.

	A	B	C	D	E	F
1			JOHN MEHARG			
2			CHECKBOOK ANALYSIS			
3						
4						
5						
6	Ck.					
7	No.	Date	Payee	Amount	Deposit	Balance
8						
9						237.25
10		01/01/97	Deposit		3200	
11	101	01/01/97	Home Savings and Loan	1100		
12	102	01/01/97	County Treasurer's Office	330		
13	103	01/01/97	City Utilities	75		
14	104	01/01/97	Food World	75.25		
15	105	01/08/97	Dr. Charles Stafford	30		
16	106	01/08/97	Floyd's Pharmacy	15		
17	107	01/15/97	O G & G Electric Co.	125.25		
18	108	01/16/97	Comet Cleaners	15		
19	109	01/20/97	Dr. Gary Bates	90		
20	110	01/25/97	Food World	125.25		
21	111	01/25/97	Tax Commission	65		
22	112	01/25/97	B & B Telephone	75.25		
23	113	01/25/97	Daily Tribune	7.5		
24	114	01/31/97	Playskool for Kids	200		
25	115	01/31/97	Card Services	155		
26	116	01/31/97	PC Computers	150		
27	117	01/31/97	South Community College	225		
28		02/01/97	Deposit		3200	
29	118	02/02/97	Home Savings and Loan	1100		
30	119	02/04/97	Salvation Army	125		
31	120	02/05/97	City Utilities	125		
32	121	02/08/97	Food World	125.85		
33	122	02/10/97	O G & G Electric Co.	175		
34	123	02/15/97	B & B Telephone	85.99		
35	124	02/20/97	Dr. Gary Bates	90		
36	125	02/25/97	Daily Tribune	7.5		
37	126	02/28/97	Playskool for Kids	200		
38	127	02/28/97	Food World	155.75		
39	128	02/28/97	Boy Scouts	75		

Table A

Continued on Next Page

JOB 16

Edit a Record

Some of the information was entered incorrectly for the people who applied for jobs with Star Manufacturing. Update the company's records to correct the mistakes.

1. Open the database APPLI.

2. Make the changes indicated to the following records:

   Terri Hoffman's address is 3436 Melody Lane.
   Sari Gray's telephone number is 405-555-6788.
   Jeff Johnson's address is 1812 Scenic Drive.
   David Smith's address is 333 Country Road.

3. Use Save As to save the database as APPLI2.

4. Print the database on one page in landscape orientation in List View.

5. Close the database.

		TAX-DEDUCTIBLE EXPENDITURES			
Mortgage Interest	Taxes	Child Care	Medical	Contributions	Other
550					
	330				
			30		
					15
			90		
	65				
		200			
					150
					225
548					
				125	
			90		
		200			
				75	

Table B

JOB 15

Delete a Record

Some of the players have withdrawn their names from the NBA draft. Update the Jackson Kangaroos' list of prospective players.

1. Open the database DRAFT.

2. Delete the following records:

   Derick Dampler
   Trent Knight
   Randy Rogers

3. Use Save As to save the database as DRAFT2.

4. Print the database on one page in List View.

5. Close the database.

JOB 44

Use Windows

Outstanding Video Network needs a sales invoice prepared.

1. Open TAPES.

2. To create a sales invoice at the end of the spreadsheet, key the following additional information below starting in cell A51.

3. Split the spreadsheet into horizontal windows between rows 50 and 51.

4. The window with the cell pointer is the active window. The cell pointer should be in the top window.

	A	B	C	D	E
51	FROM:	Outstanding Video Network			
52		5868 19th Street			
53		Huntsville, TX 77340			
54					
55	TO:	Lois Risner	Date:	December 8, 19--	
56		4421 Road 84			
57		Huntsville, TX 77342			
58					
59	Cat.		Tapes per		Pkg.
60	No.	Title	Pkg.		Price
61					
62	604V				
63	607V				
64	671V				
65					
66				Selling Price	*formula*
67				8% Sales Tax	*formula*
68				Amount Due	*formula*

Continued on Next Page

JOB 14

Delete a Record

Some of the houses with the Oaks Real Estate Company have been sold or taken off of the market. Update the company's list of houses on the market.

1. Open the database LISTING2.

2. Delete the following records:

   300 S. Hayden
   1522 Augusta Dr.
   500 N. Sycamore Dr.

3. Use Save As to save the database as LISTING3.

4. Print the database in List View.

5. Close the database.

5. In the top window, move the cell pointer to the row with the information about "Cat. No. 604V" (row 32).

6. Switch windows and move the cell pointer to row 62. Looking at the top window, key the information needed to complete the sales invoice for "Cat. No. 604V" (columns B, C, and E below).

7. Use the same method to locate the information to complete the sales invoice for the two additional items.

8. Create a formula in cell E66 to total the three amounts above the cell pointer to determine the selling price.

9. Create a formula in cell E67 to multiply the selling price by 8%.

10. Create a formula in cell E68 to add the selling price and the sales tax.

11. Right align the column headings on the sales invoice in columns C and E, and format column E for fixed format with two decimal places. Adjust column widths as necessary to fit content.

12. Clear the windows.

13. Use Save As to save the spreadsheet as TAPES2.

14. Print the sales invoice only (A51..E68).

JOB 13

Delete a Record

Several of the used cars at AAA Motors have been sold. Update AAA Motors' records to reflect these sales.

1. Open the database USED.

2. Delete the following records:

   1995 Chevrolet Beretta
   1992 Ford Explorer
   1991 GMC Jimmy

3. Use Save As to save the database as USED2.

4. Print the database in List View.

5. Close the database.

JOB 45

Use Windows

Create two additional sales invoices for Outstanding Video Network.

1. Open TAPES2.

2. To create additional sales invoices at the end of the spreadsheet, you will use the sales invoice you created in job 44.

3. Split the spreadsheet into horizontal windows between rows 50 and 51.

4. To edit the previous invoice, insert the information in Table A by typing over the existing data. You will need to fill in the missing information in columns B, C, and E.

5. Create a second invoice by copying the invoice (A51..E68) to cell A75.

	A	B	C	D	E
55	TO:	Phillip Stephens	Date:	December 12, 19--	
56		925 Kings Road			
57		Medford, CA 95780			
58					
59	Cat.		Tapes per		Pkg.
60	No.	Title	Pkg.		Price
61					
62	111V				
63	113V				
64	118V				

Table A

Continued on Next Page

JOB 12

Add Records in Form View

The Oaks Real Estate Company has obtained some new listings. These listings need to be added to the company's list of houses on the market.

1. Open the database LISTING.

2. If your software did not automatically create a form for this database create one now.

3. Starting with record 16, add the information shown below in Form View.

233 Augusta Dr.	1500	4	115,000	Meadowood	10/20/97
319 Timber Terrace	2500	1	251,000	Oak Hills	10/25/97
822 Mockingbird Lane	1300	10	84,000	Oaktree	10/31/97
210 Maple St.	1100	15	62,000	Silver Leaf	11/1/97

4. Change to List View.

5. Use Save As to save the database as LISTING2.

6. Print the database in List View.

7. Close the database.

FINISH

6. Move the cell pointer to cell B79, and insert the information in Table B by typing over the existing data. You will need to fill in the missing information in columns B, C, and E. Delete any unnecessary information.

7. Clear the windows.

8. Use Save As to save the spreadsheet as TAPES3.

9. Print the sales invoices only (A51..E92).

	A	B	C	D	E
79	TO:	Oashi Okita	Date:	December 13, 19--	
80		8400 Tenth Street			
81		Berkeley, CA 94710			
82					
83	Cat.		Tapes per		Pkg.
84	No.	Title	Pkg.		Price
85					
86	211V				
87	213V				

Table B

JOB 11

Add Records

Star Manufacturing has added some new personnel who need to be added to the list of employees.

1. Open the database EMPLOY.

2. Add the data shown below.

3. Use Save As to save the database as EMPLOY2.

4. Print the database in List View.

5. Close the database.

LAST	FIRST	LOCATION	DEPARTMENT
Cristelli	Jamie	Dallas	Sales
Mayes	Mikella	Denver	Advertising
Mitchell	Kristen	Dallas	Art
Mayhue	Megan	Tulsa	Sales
Gifford	Brittany	Oklahoma City	Accounting
Patrizi	Meghan	Kansas City	Sales
Ross	Channing	Dallas	Accounting
Kedy	Mark	Tulsa	Art

FINISH

Use Windows with Unsynchronized (Split) Scroll

John Meharg wants a list of all tax-deductible expenditures.

1. Open CHECK.

2. Insert a column between columns F and G. Key "TOTALS" in cell G41.

3. Move the cell pointer to cell H41, and use the Sum function to determine the total for mortgage interest (cells H9..H39).

4. Copy and paste the formula to columns I–M.

5. Format the totals for commas with two decimal places.

6. Create a vertical *unsynchronized* (split) window.

7. In the (upper) right window, key the additional data as shown below in the spreadsheet starting in cell O1.

8. Move the cell pointer to cell H41 in the (lower) left window to display data needed to complete the report.

	O	P	Q	R
1	JOHN MEHARG			
2	TAX-DEDUCTIBLE EXPENDITURES			
3				
4	Mortgage Interest			
5	Taxes			
6	Child Care			
7	Medical			
8	Contributions			
9	Other			

Continued on Next Page

JOB 10

Add Records

Several students' names were left off of the list of students attending East Central University and need to be added.

1. Open the database STUDENT.

2. Add the data shown below.

3. Use Save As to save the database as STUDENT2.

4. Print the database in List View.

5. Close the database.

LAST	FIRST	PHONE NO
Hoover	Angie	918-555-3691
Choate	Lauren	918-555-6621
Leddy	Toby	713-555-9987
Davis	Nick	214-555-2212
Anderson	Tanner	214-555-8362
Vasquez	Roy	713-555-9826
Cranford	Taylor	602-555-9818
Lough	Debbie	415-555-6323
Landrum	Tanner	307-555-6260
Gomez	Robert	318-555-6260
Sehon	Debi	214-555-6854
Hill	Carly	817-555-6854
Webb	Jessica	312-555-3688
Akita	Yuki	305-555-9254
Mariano	Marcus	415-555-6663
Cranford	Lauren	405-555-8908

9. Switch back to the right window to key the needed data starting in cell Q4. Continue this process until all of the totals are determined.

10. When all totals are keyed, clear the window.

11. Use Save As to save the spreadsheet as CHECK2.

12. Print the range O1..R9.

JOB 9

Use Print Setup to Print in Landscape Orientation

Star Manufacturing would like a printed list of the people who have applied for jobs there.

1. Open the database APPLI.

2. Use Page Setup to change orientation to landscape. Print the database on one page in List View.

3. Close the database.

Create a sales report for ABC Department Store for the current year.

1. Change the width of column A to 20 spaces.

2. Key the titles below in cells A1 and A2. Center these titles across columns A–M.

ABC DEPARTMENT STORE
SALES FOR THE YEAR 19--

---

3. The information for the sales report appears on the following pages in Tables A and B. At this time, key *only* the data for column A. Center the data in cells A6, A11, A17, A23, and A28.

4. Key "JAN" in cell B4, and use the Fill feature for the column headings in columns B–M.

5. Position the cursor in cell B5 (one column to the right of the row headings and one row under the column headings), and freeze both horizontal and vertical panes.

6. Key the number columns of the spreadsheet, and key formulas where necessary to complete the department totals and monthly totals.

7. Clear the panes.

8. Format the entire spreadsheet for commas with zero decimal places.

9. Use Page Setup so that the spreadsheet prints on one page in landscape orientation.

10. Save the spreadsheet as STORE.

11. Print the spreadsheet in landscape orientation.

Continued on Next Page

JOB 8

Move to a Specific Record

You are employed by AAA Motors, and a prospective buyer needs information on some of the used cars.

1. Open the database USED.

2. Place the database in Form View.

3. Move from record to record to answer the following questions. Either write or type your answers on a separate sheet of paper.

   How many miles does the 1995 Chevrolet Camaro have, and how much does it cost?

   How many miles does the 1994 Chevrolet Beretta have, and how much does it cost?

   How many miles do the 1993 Chevrolet Berettas have, and how much do they cost?

   How many miles does the 1992 Honda Prelude have, and how much does it cost?

4. Close the database.

Continued

	A	B	C	D	E	F
4	DEPARTMENT	JAN				
5						
6	ACCESSORIES					
7	Men	2810	1925	2064	2295	3100
8	Women	3211	1482	1529	1783	2083
9	Total					
10						
11	CLOTHING					
12	Men	10254	11529	11783	12083	12216
13	Women	17264	18536	18788	17093	17228
14	Children	8255	9554	9792	10091	10293
15	Total					
16						
17	SHOES					
18	Men	5452	5925	5387	6380	6612
19	Women	8462	9635	9887	8390	8822
20	Children	4552	4455	4297	5190	5392
21	Total					
22						
23	PURSES					
24	Women	4264	4536	4788	4093	4228
25	Children	2255	2554	2972	2093	2972
26	Total					
27						
28	FRAGRANCES					
29	Men	4556	4455	4277	5190	5398
30	Women	8462	9698	9887	8930	8332
31	Total					
32						
33	MONTHLY TOTALS					

Table A

Continued on Next Page

JOB 7

Move to a Specific Record

You are employed by the Oaks Real Estate Company, and a prospective buyer needs information on some of the property listed.

1. Open the database LISTING.

2. Place the database in Form View.

3. Move from record to record to answer the following questions. Either write or type your answers on a separate sheet of paper.

   How many square feet does the house located at 410 E. Smith have?

   How long has the house located at 1223 Augusta Dr. been on the market?

   How much does the house located at 522 N. Magnolia cost?

   How old is the house located at 113 Sherry?

4. Close the database.

Continued

	G	H	I	J	K	L	M
4	JUN	JUL	AUG	SEP	OCT	NOV	DEC
5							
6							
7	1964	1995	2031	1931	3195	2031	4064
8	2164	900	984	1031	935	2195	3031
9							
10							
11							
12	11902	11984	11031	11935	12195	23031	28064
13	18922	18999	18036	18988	18197	28341	32096
14	9972	8948	8013	8953	9159	20013	25046
15							
16							
17							
18	5209	5489	5130	5539	6591	11130	14460
19	9229	9999	9630	9889	9791	14143	16698
20	4279	4643	4310	4359	4951	10310	12640
21							
22							
23							
24	4922	4999	4036	4988	4197	7341	8896
25	2972	2849	2013	2953	2159	5301	6046
26							
27							
28							
29	4279	4998	4310	4359	4961	10311	12650
30	9269	9989	9630	9869	9791	14144	16658

Table B

JOB 6

Print a Database

You are a scout for the Jackson Kangaroos, a professional basketball team. Compile a list of prospective players for the upcoming draft. Include their names, the universities they attend, height, weight, points per game, and rebounds per game.

1. Create a new database.

2. Enter the information shown below. Change the format of the database as needed.

3. Save the database as DRAFT.

4. Print the database on one page in List View.

5. Close the database.

LAST	FIRST	UNIVERSITY	HEIGHT	WEIGHT	PPG	RPG
Allen	Rusty	Connecticut	6-5	205	23	6
Barry	John	Georgia Tech	6-5	191	13	7
Camby	Marion	Massachusetts	6-11	220	20	8
Dampler	Derick	Mississippi State	6-11	200	14	9
Delk	Tom	Kentucky	6-1	193	18	4
Evans	Brent	Indiana	6-8	220	21	7
Fuller	Thomas	North Carolina State	6-11	255	21	10
Harrington	Luther	Georgetown	6-9	235	12	7
Henderson	Charles	LSU	6-4	206	22	5
Hendrickson	Howell	Washington State	6-9	220	16	10
Iverson	Mark	Georgetown	6-0	165	25	5
Kittles	Terry	Villanova	6-5	179	20	7
Knight	Trent	Connecticut	7-0	235	9	9
Marbury	Steven	Georgia Tech	6-2	180	19	4
McCarty	Kevin	Kentucky	6-10	230	11	6
Norris	Russell	West Florida	6-1	175	24	9
Riley	Michael	Arizona State	6-5	205	20	6
Rogers	Randy	Alabama	6-10	238	14	9
Sheffer	Devin	Connecticut	6-5	197	16	6
Walker	Anthony	Kentucky	6-8	224	15	8
Wallace	John	Syracuse	6-8	225	22	9

FINISH

ABC Department Store needs a sales report for the year. Include only the total sales for each month.

1. Open STORE.

2. Key the additional data as shown below in column A. Key January in cell A37, and use the Fill feature for the months (A37..A48).

3. Split the screen so you will have an *unsynchronized* (split) window at the bottom. Key the total sales for each month in column B. Use the top window to locate these amounts.

	A
35	Sales for the Year 19--
36	
37	January
38	
39	
40	
41	
42	
43	
44	
45	
46	
47	
48	
49	
50	Total

Continued on Next Page

JOB 5

Change a Database's Format

Create a list of the houses currently on the market for the Oaks Real Estate Company.

1. Create a new database.

2. Make the following changes to the database's format:

Field Name	Data Type	Format	Decimal Places
Address	Text		
Square Feet	Number	Standard (with commas)	0
Age	Number	Standard (with commas)	0
Cost	Currency	Currency (with comma)	Auto (2)
Development	Text		
Date on Market	Date/Time	Short Date (e.g., 10/1/96)	

3. Enter the records as shown below. Adjust the column widths as necessary.

4. Save the database as LISTING.

5. Close the database.

ADDRESS	SQUARE FEET	AGE	COST	DEVELOPMENT	DATE ON MARKET
204 N. Willow	1,200	5	$112,000.00	Meadowood	6/15/97
410 E. Smith	1,500	7	$89,000.00	Oaktree	6/20/97
300 S. Hayden	2,000	3	$96,000.00	Meadowood	6/21/97
1223 Augusta Dr.	2,200	1	$220,000.00	Oak Hills	7/13/97
100 E. Murray	2,400	2	$240,000.00	Oak Hills	7/15/97
522 N. Magnolia	2,500	1	$255,000.00	Oak Hills	7/22/97
331 S. Cottonwood	1,400	10	$85,000.00	Oaktree	8/15/97
100 Thompson Dr.	1,100	15	$66,000.00	Silver Leaf	8/22/97
110 Willowbrook St.	1,700	2	$89,000.00	Meadowood	8/31/97
1522 Augusta Dr.	2,600	1	$265,000.00	Oak Hills	9/1/97
200 Thompson Dr.	1,000	13	$59,000.00	Silver Leaf	9/3/97
213 Sycamore St.	1,700	3	$165,000.00	Oak Hills	9/15/97
113 Sherry	1,500	16	$62,000.00	Silver Leaf	10/2/97
220 S. Cottonwood	1,500	5	$85,000.00	Oaktree	10/5/97
500 N. Sycamore Dr.	2,000	2	$195,000.00	Oak Hills	10/15/97

FINISH

4. Clear the window.

5. Create a formula in cell B50 to total the sales for the year.

6. Use Save As to save the spreadsheet as STORE2.

7. Print the range A35..B50.

3. Enter the records as shown below.

4. Save the database as USED.

5. Close the database.

YEAR	MAKE	MODEL	MILEAGE	PRICE
1995	Chevrolet	Camaro	12,000	$14,988.00
1995	Chevrolet	Beretta	11,000	$12,995.00
1995	Chevrolet	Silverado	18,000	$14,000.00
1994	Chevrolet	Beretta	25,000	$10,995.00
1993	Chevrolet	Beretta	67,000	$7,000.00
1993	Chevrolet	Blazer	71,000	$14,000.00
1993	Chevrolet	Beretta	52,000	$7,892.00
1992	Honda	Accord	69,000	$10,588.00
1992	Honda	Accord	47,000	$12,500.00
1992	Honda	Accord	63,000	$11,988.00
1992	Honda	Prelude	59,000	$13,995.00
1992	Ford	Explorer	90,000	$13,000.00
1992	Chevrolet	Camaro	34,000	$8,980.00
1991	GMC	Jimmy	88,000	$9,600.00
1991	Chevrolet	Camaro	81,000	$8,150.00
1990	Ford	Mustang	75,000	$7,900.00
1990	Ford	Probe	65,000	$4,990.00
1989	Ford	Mustang	79,000	$4,295.00
1988	Honda	Accord	76,000	$4,250.00
1987	Honda	Accord	88,000	$4,650.00

FINISH

JOB 49

Use the Fill Feature

Create an earnings record for Arthur Anderson for April 1 through September 23 of the current year.

1. Adjust the column widths as needed, and key the information as shown below. Right align the column headings.

2. Key the date in cell A8 (04/01/96) and then use the Fill feature to enter the dates in cells A8..A33.

	A	B	C	D	E	F	G	H	I
1					ARTHUR ANDERSON				
2				EARNINGS RECORD FOR APRIL THROUGH SEPTEMBER, 1996					
3									
4	Wk	Total	Soc	Fed	St	Hosp	Total	Net	Accumulated
5	End	Earnings	Sec	Tax	Tax	Ins	Ded	Pay	Earnings
6									
7	03/31/96								
8	04/01/96	160	formula	formula	formula	55	formula	formula	formula
9		160							
10		168							
11		162							
12		170							
13		166				55			
14		160							
15		160							
16		162							
17		168				55			
18		160							
19		164							
20		180							
21		160				55			
22		160							
23		160							
24		168							
25		162							
26		170				55			
27		166							
28		160							
29		160							
30		162				55			
31		168							
32		160							
33		164							

Continued on Next Page

JOB 4

Change a Database's Format

Create a list of the used cars that AAA Motors currently has in stock. Include the year, make, model, mileage, and price.

1. Create a new database.

2. Enter the information shown below. Make the following changes to the database's format:

Field Name	Data Type	Format	Decimal Places
YEAR	Text		
MAKE	Text		
MODEL	Text		
MILEAGE	Number (with comma)	Standard (general)	0
PRICE	Currency		Auto (2)

Continued on Next Page

3. Use the Go To feature to move the cell pointer to cell B6, and freeze both horizontal and vertical panes.

4. Move the cell pointer to cell C8, and create a formula to multiply total earnings by 7.65% to determine the social security tax in column C. Copy and paste the formula to complete the column.

5. Move the cell pointer to cell D8 and create a formula to multiply total earnings by 15% to determine the federal income tax in column D. Copy and paste the formula to complete the column.

6. Move the cell pointer to cell E8 and create a formula to multiply total earnings by 6% to determine the state income tax in column E. Copy and paste the formula to complete the column.

7. Move the cell pointer to cell G8 and use the Sum function to add cells C8–F8 to determine the total deductions in column G. Copy and paste the formula to complete the column.

8. Move the cell pointer to cell H8 and create a formula to subtract total deductions from total earnings to determine the net pay in column H. Copy and paste the formula to complete the column.

9. Move the cell pointer to cell I8 and create a formula to add cells I7 and B8 to determine the accumulated earnings. Copy and paste the formula to complete the column.

10. Format columns B–I for commas with two decimal places.

11. Clear the panes.

12. Use Page Setup so that the spreadsheet prints on one page.

13. Save the spreadsheet as ARTHUR.

14. Print the spreadsheet.

JOB 3

Create and Save a Database

Star Manufacturing keeps a list in the main office of the people who have applied for jobs with its company. Create a list of these applicants. Include their names, addresses, phone numbers, and the positions for which they applied.

1. Create a new database.

2. Enter the information shown below. Adjust the column widths as necessary.

3. Save the database as APPLI.

4. Close the database.

LAST	FIRST	ADDRESS	CITY	STATE	ZIP	PHONE	POSITION
Young	Leonard	1105 N. Francis	Oklahoma City	OK	73127	405-555-3676	Advertising Manager
Wyche	Jenna	809 Gardenia	Tulsa	OK	73127	918-555-3678	Sales Rep
Hoffman	Terri	3336 Melody Lane	Kansas City	KS	65089	816-555-3987	Accountant
Williamson	Jason	6678 Cherry Street	Kansas City	KS	65089	816-555-3678	Advertising Manager
Parsons	Penny	806 S. Railway	Dallas	TX	75231	214-555-3789	Sales Rep
Jennings	Richard	333 S. Monta Vista	Denver	CO	80302	303-555-6666	Accountant
Floyd	Meredith	456 Sunny Lane Drive	Dallas	TX	75231	214-555-6543	Graphic Artist
Stephenson	Ashley	333 N. Country Club	Tulsa	OK	73127	918-555-3678	Graphic Artist
Gray	Sari	8678 Daniels Drive	Oklahoma City	OK	73127	405-555-6789	Accountant
Nimmo	Michael	3678 Wintersmith Drive	Dallas	TX	75231	214-555-9998	Accountant
Thompson	Jay	3378 Chestnut Street	Denver	CO	80302	303-555-6789	Sales Rep
Sanders	Kyle	656 Stadium Drive	Denver	CO	80302	303-555-6676	Accountant
Puls	Erin	6636 Kerr Lab Drive	Dallas	TX	75231	214-555-5489	Sales Rep
Weeks	Krista	3356 Arlington	Kansas City	KS	65089	816-555-4454	Graphic Artist
Johnson	Jeff	812 Scenic Drive	Denver	CO	80302	303-555-7787	Advertising Manager
Jones	Julie	8898 Jackson Drive	Kansas City	KS	65089	816-555-4432	Sales Rep
Jefferson	Reggie	1003 S. Stockton	Tulsa	OK	73127	918-555-7876	Sales Rep
Smith	David	333 County Road	Dallas	TX	75231	214-555-7090	Accountant
Woodward	Brent	690 Mongomery	Oklahoma City	OK	73127	405-555-8876	Accountant
Jackson	Jenny	888 Kings Road	Dallas	TX	75231	214-555-6777	Sales Rep

JOB 50

Use Windows to Input Data

Arthur Anderson needs a list of his accumulated earnings at the end of each month.

1. Open ARTHUR.

2. Delete columns C–H.

3. Key the additional data in cells A35–D43 as shown below.

4. Split the screen for horizontal windows.

5. Locate the accumulated earnings in the top window for March 31 (cell C7) and April 29 (cell C12). Key the information in column C in the bottom window.

6. Switch to the top window to display the needed data to complete the report.

7. Switch back to the bottom window to key the accumulated earnings through September.

8. When all totals are keyed, clear the windows. Format the totals for commas with two decimal places.

9. Use Save As to save the spreadsheet as ARTHUR2.

10. Print the range A35..D43.

	A	B	C	D
35	Accumulated Earnings for Arthur Anderson			
36				
37	March 31			
38	April 29			
39	May 27			
40	June 24			
41	July 29			
42	August 26			
43	September 23			

JOB 2

Create and Save a Database

Create a list of the employees of Star Manufacturing. Also include the office locations and departments in which they work.

1. Create a new database.

2. Enter the information shown below. Use text as the type of data to be entered. Use the default settings for the field size.

3. Save the database as EMPLOY.

4. Close the database.

LAST	FIRST	LOCATION	DEPARTMENT
Babb	Brandon	Oklahoma City	Advertising
Daniels	Brandon	Dallas	Sales
Tracy	Breca	Denver	Art
Eaves	Bridgette	Dallas	Accounting
O'Neal	Josh	Kansas City	Advertising
Quinlan	Julie	Denver	Accounting
Weems	Julie	Denver	Sales
Andrews	Kevin	Dallas	Accounting
Sanders	Kyle	Oklahoma City	Sales
Harper	Leslie	Tulsa	Administration
Pierce	Lindsey	Dallas	Sales
Hoover	Mandy	Kansas City	Sales
Taylor	Niki	Tulsa	Advertising
Page	Ryan	Tulsa	Accounting
Cristelli	Ryan	Dallas	Sales
Mettry	Shelley	Oklahoma City	Accounting
Compton	Susannah	Denver	Art
Moon	Todd	Denver	Advertising
Cristelli	Tony	Tulsa	Sales
Sanders	Whitney	Dallas	Sales

Macros can be created for commands that are used often. In the remaining jobs in this chapter, you will create macros by keying the macros first, then you will create the spreadsheets to use them.

1. Create a macro to change the width of column A to 10 spaces and column B to 35 spaces.

2. Save the macro as MACRO.

JOB 1

Create and Save a Database

Create a telephone list for the students enrolled at East Central University.

1. Create a new database.

2. Enter the information shown below. Use text as the type of data to be entered. Use the default settings.

3. Save the database as STUDENT.

4. Close the database.

LAST	FIRST	PHONE NO
Meharg	John	415-555-3692
Sutton	Pat	405-555-3689
Key	Mary Jane	713-555-3876
Walbrick	Lafton	713-555-5609
Bodine	Larry	713-555-3289
Clark	Charles	303-555-3678
Brendle	Ronnie	606-555-6678
Kedy	Paula	918-555-6654
Boatwright	Marcia	714-555-6656
Anderson	Devon	405-555-9089
Stafford	Allison	703-555-3245
Sanders	Whitney	817-555-9876
Stafford	Shawn	314-555-6765
Stafford	Matt	405-555-7897

JOB 52

Use Command Macros

1. With the cell pointer in cell A1 of a new spreadsheet, use the macro created in Job 51 (MACRO) to change the width of column A to 10 spaces and column B to 35 spaces.

2. Enter the information in your spreadsheet as shown below.

3. Format column C for fixed format with two decimal places.

4. Save the spreadsheet as LIST.

5. Print the spreadsheet.

	A	B	C
1		OFFICE SUPPLIES, INC.	
2		P.O. BOX 56905	
3		MIAMI, FL 33256-6905	
4			
5		Price List	
6			
7	Item #	Description	Price Each
8			
9	C45-1000	White Address 700 labels	17.9
10	C45-1012	Clear Address 130 labels	9.9
11	C45-1026	White 3.5" Disk 200 labels	9.9
12	C45-1024	White File Folder 260 labels	9.9
13	C45-1016	Shipping, 300 labels	17.9

FINISH

CHAPTER 11

Jobs 1–20
Create, Save, and
Print a Database

Time Estimate: 5 hrs.

OBJECTIVES

In this chapter, students will:

1. Create and save a database
2. Change a database's format
3. Print a database
4. Open an existing database and create a table
5. Move to a specific record
6. Use Print Setup to print in landscape orientation
7. Add records
8. Delete a record
9. Edit a record

(**Note to Microsoft Office Access users:** throughout this section, please ignore the "Save As" commands as this option is not available to you. In addition, Access requires that you create two files for each database. Use the same file name listed in the job for both files.)

JOB 53

Use Command Macros

1. With the cell pointer in cell A1 of a new spreadsheet, use the macro created in Job 51 (MACRO) to change the width of column A to 10 spaces and column B to 35 spaces.

2. Enter the information in your spreadsheet as shown below.

3. Right align the column headings in columns C, D, and E in row 7, and center the data in cells A7..A13.

4. Create a formula to multiply columns C and D to get the totals in column E.

	A	B	C	D	E
1					
2	Sold to:	Chiang Office System	Date:	June 19, 19--	
3		2556 Towne Road	Customer		
4		Hamden, CT 06514-4421	Order:	56 CC 8222	
5					
6					
7	Stock No.	Description/Stock No.	No.	Cost	Total
8					
9	82Z45	Desktop Calculator	4	77	*formula*
10	62Y35	Desktop Calculator	4	52	
11	66X45	Electronic Typewriter	2	365	
12	71W15	4-Drawer Desk	1	325	
13	78R85	Swivel Desk Chair	1	199	
14					
15					
16					
17		Subtotal			*formula*
18		Tax			*formula*
19		Total			*formula*
20					

Continued on Next Page

DATABASE

5. Create a formula to add the total for all five items to determine the subtotal in cell E17.

6. Create a formula to multiply cell E17 by 8.25% to get the tax for cell E18.

7. To determine the total for cell E19, create a formula to add the subtotal and the tax.

8. Format columns D and E for commas with two decimal places.

9. Add double underlines above rows 2 and 17 and below rows 4 and 19.

10. Use Page Setup so that the spreadsheet prints on one page.

11. Save the spreadsheet as OFFICE.

12. Print the spreadsheet.

Assume that you are the loan officer at Superior National Bank. Send a letter to the customers listed below. Congratulate them on the birth of their new sons, and tell them about a college savings plan. Insert the spreadsheet RICHIE illustrating the future value of $1,000, $2,000, and $3,000 annual deposits. Be sure to change the title on line one for the Kirkpatricks. Save as RICHIE2 and KIRKPATR.

Erin and Phil Richie
500 Arlington Center Blvd.
Columbus, OH 43220
Son: John David Richie

Kelly and David Kirkpatrick
102 Greenwood Ave.
Columbus, OH 43220
Son: Tanner Gale Kirkpatrick

JOB 54

Create Label Macros

The macro you created in Job 51 is used to execute commands. You can also create macros to enter labels. These macros are useful when you need to create a number of spreadsheets of a particular type or for a particular company. In this job, you will create label macros to be used in the following jobs.

1. Create a label macro that will enter the following company name and address.

Western Woods, Molding, and Millwork
Highway 44, East
San Francisco, CA 94109-4201

2. Save your macro as MACRO2.

   NOTE: Some programs require that you create all macros on one spreadsheet. If your program works this way, save all macros on the same page with the name MACRO. The solution manual shows an example of macros on the same page.

3. Create a label macro to enter the months of the year as shown below.

January
February
March
April
May
June
July
August
September
October
November
December

4. Save your macro as MACRO3

   NOTE: You will use the label macros above when you key the following spreadsheets.

FINISH

JOB 99

Integrate Spreadsheet, Word Processing, and Graphics

Create a sign for a real estate company advertising an open house.

1. Create a landscape-style sign with the information as shown below. If available, use a sign template in landscape style.

2. Use a graphic of your choice.

3. Insert the spreadsheet file WALKER2 as indicated.

4. The cells in rows 1 and 2 should be joined.

5. Center the column headings.

6. Save the sign as WALKER4.

7. Print the sign in landscape orientation.

Sunday, September 19, 19--

Insert spreadsheet file WALKER2.

JOB 55

Create a Formula Macro

Macros can also be used to execute formulas. In this job, you will create a formula macro to add 13 cells above the cell pointer and to format the total for commas with zero decimal places.

1. Move the cell pointer to a cell with at least 13 blank cells above the location.

2. Create a macro that will sum the amounts in the 13 cells above the location.

3. Save the macro as MACRO4.

   NOTE: You will use the label macros and the formula macro when you key the following spreadsheets.

JOB 98

Integrate Spreadsheet, Word Processing, and Graphics

Send a note and invoice for Arbuckle Sports Association.

1. Create the word processing document as shown below.

2. Insert a graphic of your choice in the heading.

3. Insert the spreadsheet file ARBUCK.

4. Adjust the width of column A.

5. The cells on the row with "Arbuckle Sports Association" should be joined.

6. All cells on the last row should be joined.

7. A single border should be around the invoice (and no internal gridlines).

8. Save the document as ARBUCK3.

9. Print the document.

Arbuckle Sports

Your invoice is below. We certainly appreciate doing business with you. We are enclosing a brochure listing our sale items for October and November. Let us know if we can be of service to you now or any time in the future. We look forward to serving you again.

Insert the spreadsheet file ARBUCK.

JOB 56

Use Label and Formula Macros

1. Key the spreadsheet as shown below.

2. Use a macro to enter the company name in cells A1..A3.

3. Use a macro to enter the months in cells A7..A18.

4. Use a macro for the totals in cells B20 and D20.

	A	B	C	D	E
1	*use macro*				
2					
3					
4					
5	Sales estimate, 1996			Actual sales, 1996	
6					
7	*use macro*	95000		96240	
8		96000		97380	
9		105000		99500	
10		110000		102380	
11		110000		106970	
12		120000		105990	
13		120000		137580	
14		130000		138850	
15		130000		137970	
16		110000		125690	
17		105000		110380	
18		95000		100450	
19					
20	Totals	*use macro*		*use macro*	

Continued on Next Page

May 9, 1996

Mr. Larry Kaebnick
4421 W. Harvest Dr.
Lincoln, NE 68521

Dear Mr. Kaebnick:

Welcome to our organization. As you know, the company makes an annual deposit into a retirement fund for each employee. The table below gives you an estimate of the growth of this fund. Of course, the interest rate may change, but we expect it to average 6%. You will receive an annual statement so you can keep up with the growth of your fund. Anytime you want to make additional deposits into this account, please let me know.

Insert spreadsheet file RETIRE.

If you have any questions, give me a call or stop by my office. I am on the sixth floor, office 622.

Sincerely,

Robert T. Huber

5. Center the title across the columns, and key the remainder of the spreadsheet as shown below.

6. The cash sales estimate, 1997 will be 40% of the actual sales, 1996. Enter a formula in cell B24 for this amount. Copy and paste the formula to complete the column.

7. Use a macro to enter the months in cells A24..A35

8. Use a macro to determine the total in cell B37.

9. Format the entire spreadsheet for commas with zero decimals.

10. Save the spreadsheet as WESTERN.

11. Print the spreadsheet.

	A	B
22	Cash sales estimate, 1997	
23		
24	*use macro*	*formula*
25		
26		
27		
28		
29		
30		
31		
32		
33		
34		
35		
36		
37	Total	*use macro*

Integrate a Spreadsheet and a Word Processing Document

Send a letter to a new employee concerning the retirement plan.

1. Create the word processing document on the next page. If available with your program, use a letter template. If needed, use the information below on a template.

Pipeline USA
400 East Woodward
Lincoln, NE 68501
Tele: (555) 500-5802
Fax: (555) 500-5900

---

2. Insert the spreadsheet file RETIRE as indicated. Center the spreadsheet horizontally.

3. Center the column headings of the spreadsheet.

4. The cells in rows 1 and 2 should be joined.

5. Center the letter vertically on the page.

6. Save the letter as RETIRE2.

7. Print the letter.

Continued on Next Page

JOB 57

Use Label and Formula Macros

1. Key the spreadsheet as shown below. Use the macros when needed to fill in the company name, month, and totals.

2. Center the title across the columns and center the column headings.

	A	B	C	D	E
1	*use macro*				
2					
3					
4					
5	SELLING EXPENSES				
6					
7		Adv.	Del.	Salary	Supplies
8		Expense	Expense	Expense	Expense
9					
10	*use macro*	800	990	8910	1200
11		610	1220	10980	915
12		790	810	7290	1185
13		520	710	6390	780
14		1050	1050	9450	1575
15		540	1540	13860	810
16		430	1380	12420	645
17		250	1250	11250	375
18		750	1090	9810	1125
19		810	810	7290	1215
20		720	790	7110	1080
21		530	660	5940	795
22					
23	Totals	*use macro*	*use macro*	*use macro*	*use macro*

Continued on Next Page

JOB 96

Integrate a Spreadsheet and a Word Processing Document

The accountant for BG's Sports Grill needs a list of employees and their hourly rates.

1. In a new word processing document, key the memo as shown below.

2. Insert the spreadsheet file GRILL as indicated.

3. Delete columns C, D, E, F, G, and H.

4. Delete rows 19, 20, 21, 22, and 23.

5. The cells in rows 1 and 2 should be joined.

6. Increase the width of column A so each employee name is on one line.

7. Turn cell gridlines off in the spreadsheet.

8. Save the memo as MARINO.

9. Print the memo.

DATE: August 20, 19--

TO: Bill Marino

FROM: Wendy Kelly

SUBJECT: Employee List

Below is the list of all employees and their hourly rates. Please keep this information confidential. If you need further information, please let me know.

Insert spreadsheet file GRILL.

3. Key the remainder of the spreadsheet using the data as shown below. Center the column headings. Use the macros when needed to fill in the months and the totals.

4. Format the entire spreadsheet for commas with zero decimals.

5. Save the spreadsheet as WESTERN2.

6. Print the spreadsheet.

	A	B	C	D	E	F
25	ADMINISTRATIVE EXPENSES					
26						
27		Ins.	Payroll	Rent	Salary	Utilities
28		Expense	Taxes	Expense	Expense	Expense
29						
30	use macro	110	9540	1500	7000	465
31		110	11610	1500	7000	495
32		110	7920	1500	7000	555
33		110	7065	1500	7500	585
34		110	10125	1500	7500	795
35		110	14535	1500	7500	720
36		110	13113	1500	7700	570
37		110	11943	1500	7700	870
38		110	10503	1500	7700	570
39		120	7983	1500	7700	435
40		120	7812	1500	7800	585
41		120	6642	1500	7800	615
42						
43	Totals	use macro	use macro	use macro	use macro	use macro

JOB 95

Integrate a Spreadsheet and a Word Processing Document

Send a letter to a potential customer giving payment options on an automobile.

1. Open a new word processing document.

2. Center the page vertically, and key the letter as shown below.

3. Insert the spreadsheet file CAR where indicated.

4. The cells in rows 1 and 2 should be joined.

5. Save the letter as CAR2.

6. Print the letter.

June 21, 19--

Mr. Jason Furr
4423 Carter Drive
Trumbull, CT 06611

Dear Mr. Furr:

The payment options for each of the automobiles we discussed yesterday are below.

Insert spreadsheet file CAR.

Please let me know if you are interested in any of these plans. If not, we have others available. Also, we received another Jeep, a 1992 model, that may interest you. Give me a call at 555-5000 or come by our office.

Sincerely,

QUALITY USED CARS

Bill K. McLean

CHAPTER 9

Jobs 58–68
Create Charts

Time Estimate: 6 hrs.

OBJECTIVES

In this chapter, students will:

1. Create and print a multiple-range column (bar) chart
2. Create a 3-D chart with gridlines
3. Create and modify a pie chart
4. Create a line chart and resize and move the chart
5. Create a chart and add attributes
6. Create an HLCO chart
7. Create an HLCO chart and add attributes
8. Create an XY (scatter) chart
9. Create a map

JOB 94

Integrate a Spreadsheet and a Word Processing Document

Fischer Auto Enterprises needs to send a quarterly report along with a memorandum to all regional managers.

1. In a new word processing document, key the memo as shown below.

2. Insert the spreadsheet AUTO2 at the bottom of the memo.

3. Format the spreadsheet. Center the title across the spreadsheet, and center the memo horizontally on the page.

4. Save the spreadsheet as AUTO3.

5. Print the memo.

MEMORANDUM

DATE: July 9, 19--

TO: All Regional Managers

FROM: Angela Logue
Sales Manager

SUBJECT: Car Sales, Second Quarter

Enclosed is our second quarter sales report. Congratulations to our sales representatives. We should all be proud of our success. Once again, the Northern Region is top in sales. However, all others have done an outstanding job. Because of this outstanding report, we are going forward with the expansion project that was outlined in the report of May 6, 19--. You will receive additional information on this project in the August report.

Insert spreadsheet file AUTO2.

JOB 58

Create and Print a Multiple-Range Column (Bar) Chart

Henson Company wants a chart to compare sales for each department during the months of January, February, and March.

1. Create the spreadsheet as shown below with right aligned headings. Format the values for commas with zero decimal places.

2. Create a vertical column chart with horizontal grid lines for the first quarter sales of 19-- in the range F6..K20. Make the title of the chart "HENSON COMPANY."

3. Save the document as HENSON.

4. Select and print the chart.

5. Add the title "Sales" in the y-axis.

6. Format the vertical axis (0; 5,000; 10,000; 15,000; etc.) for currency with zero decimal places.

7. Place the legend below the chart. If you are not satisfied with this final change, use the Undo feature. The legend will move back to its original position.

8. Change the title size to 16 points.

9. Use Save As to save the document as HENSON2.

10. Select and print the chart.

	A	B	C	D
1	HENSON COMPANY			
2	4489 West Rockport, Cambridge, MA 02142			
3				
4	Sales--First Quarter, 19--			
5				
6		Dept. 1	Dept. 2	Dept. 3
7				
8	January	22940	23987	23756
9	February	12987	20518	17596
10	March	11066	17322	16574

FINISH

JOB 93

Continued

4. Use Horizontal Lookup to enter the commission rates in column C. The amount of the sales is in cell B7, the range to look through is B24..H26 (absolute), and the rate is two rows under the "At least" row (row 24).

5. Multiply sales by commission rate to determine commission earned.

6. Format all commission rates for percent with zero decimal places, and format all other values for commas with two decimal places.

7. Save the spreadsheet as PIER.

8. Sort the broker names in alphabetical order by the last name.

9. Save and print the spreadsheet.

JOB 59

Create a 3-D Chart with Gridlines

1. Open HENSON2.

2. Change the chart type to a 3-D chart.

3. Add gridlines if the chart does not have them.

4. Use Save As to save the document as HENSON3.

5. Select and print the chart.

6. Change the Column (bar) chart to a line chart.

7. Use Save As to save the document as HENSON4.

8. Select and print the chart.

JOB 93

Use Horizontal Lookup

In order to determine the weekly commission for each broker, Pier Importing needs a spreadsheet that will give each broker's sales, the commission rate, and the commission earned.

1. Create the spreadsheet as shown below, and adjust the column widths as necessary.

2. Center the headings in columns B, C, and D.

3. Shade the commission rate table.

	A	B	C	D	E	F	G	H
1			PIER IMPORTING					
2			MONTHLY COMMISSION REPORT					
3								
4			Commission	Commission				
5	Broker	Sales	Rate	Earned				
6								
7	Andrews, Kevin	61208	*formula*	*formula*				
8	Bowers, Charlene	38261						
9	Carson, Stacy	8432						
10	Farris, Nicole	786						
11	Godwin, Tracey	10911						
12	Gunter, Jason	4401						
13	Haines, Kim	76001						
14	Holt, Erin	44380						
15	Isaacs, Danny	92421						
16	Lillard, Jefferson	39902						
17	Logan, Jim	106821						
18	Mason, David	3021						
19	Reese, Bob	40842						
20	Walters, Billy	31021						
21	Zachary, Mike	59921						
22								
23	COMMISSION RATE TABLE							
24	At least--	0	10000	20000	30000	40000	50000	75000
25	Not over--	9,999.99	19,999.99	29,999.99	39,999.99	49,999.99	74,999.99	
26	Rate	0.01	0.02	0.03	0.04	0.05	0.07	0.10

Continued on Next Page

JOB 60

Create and Modify a Pie Chart

A pie chart is made up of separate slices that fit together to make a circle. Different hatch patterns or colors for the pie slices can be specified, and individual slices can be exploded or separated from the rest of the pie for emphasis. Mr. Sanders wants a chart to compare each customer's account balance with the total amount due.

1. Open COMM.

2. A pie chart uses only two ranges of data—a range for labels for the legend and another containing numeric data for the chart. Create a pie chart with labels and percentages in the range E6..K22. Use the names in column A (A7..A13) for the labels and the sales in column B (B7..B13) for the numeric data.

3. Changes the title to "Sales—American Securities, Inc."

4. Use Save As to save the document as COMM3.

5. Select and print the chart.

6. Change the colors and/or patterns of the wedges in your chart.

7. Explode the largest slice.

8. Resize your chart as desired.

9. Use Save As to save the spreadsheet as COMM4.

10. Select and print the chart.

3. Use Horizontal Lookup to enter shipping and handling charges in cells C7..C19. Create a formula in cell C7 to use Horizontal Lookup to search through the range B23..I25 (absolute value in order to be copied) to find the data in cell B7 (12.95), and enter the amount located two rows under row 23. The search ends when the first value greater than the value in cell B7 is found. The program then returns to the next lower value in the column and enters the number two rows under the first row of the search.

4. Copy and paste the formula to complete column C.

5. To determine the total charges in column D, add shipping and handling to cost.

6. Shade the shipping and handling table with a shade of your choice.

7. Format the entire spreadsheet for fixed with two decimal places.

8. Save the spreadsheet as GIFT.

9. Print the spreadsheet.

JOB 61

Create a Line Chart and Resize and Move the Chart

Oklahoma Brokerage Company wants a line chart to show each broker's commission for the first and second quarters.

1. Create the spreadsheet as shown below.

2. Change the width of columns B and C to 12 spaces, and center the column headings.

3. Use the range A4..C9 to create a line chart with horizontal gridlines in the range A12..E28.

4. Add the title "OKLAHOMA BROKERAGE COMPANY." The title for the x-axis is "Employee Name," and the title for the y-axis is "Commission."

5. Format the vertical axis for currency with zero decimal places.

6. Resize or move the chart as desired.

7. Save the spreadsheet as BROKER.

8. Select and print the chart.

	A	B	C
1	OKLAHOMA BROKERAGE COMPANY		
2	Commission Report		
3			
4	Broker	1st Quarter	2nd Quarter
5	Poe	1209	908
6	Smith	1719	1353
7	Pyrum	690	726
8	Powell	1628	1750
9	Babb	559	732

FINISH

JOB 92

Use Horizontal Lookup

Create a spreadsheet with a shipping and handling charges table for The Gift Store.

1. Create the spreadsheet as shown below, and adjust the column widths as necessary.

2. Right align the column headings in columns B, C, and D.

	A	B	C	D	E	F	G	H	I
1			THE GIFT STORE						
2			Lebanon, New Hampshire						
3									
4			Shipping &	Total					
5	Item(s)	Cost	Handling	Charges					
6									
7	Set of 4 Magnets	12.95	*formula*	*formula*					
8	Set of 8 Magnets	24.95							
9	Set of 12 Magnets	34.95							
10	Set of 24 Magnets	69.95							
11	Microwave Rice Cooker	11.98							
12	Decorative Tablecloth	29.95							
13	Video Cassette Rewinder	15.85							
14	Flag Display Case	49.98							
15	Cast Iron Sundial	39.98							
16	Personalized Clock	22.98							
17	Indoor-Outdoor Rug	12.98							
18	Food Dehydrator	59.95							
19	Cast Iron Bird Bath	25.98							
20									
21	SHIPPING AND HANDLING CHARGES								
22									
23	At least--	10	20	30	40	50	60	75	100
24	Not over--	19.99	29.99	39.99	49.99	59.99	69.99	99.99	200
25	Rate	3.45	4.45	5.45	6.45	7.45	8.45	8.45	9.95

Continued on Next Page

JOB 62

Create a Chart and Add Attributes

Tom Logue, owner of Tom's Lunch Counter, wants a bar chart to compare his sales for April, May, and June.

1. Create the spreadsheet as shown below. Right align all column headings, and adjust column widths as necessary.

2. Use the spreadsheet to create a 3-D horizontal bar chart with vertical grid lines in a range of your choice.

3. Add the title "TOM'S LUNCH COUNTER" in a 14-point type.

4. Format the horizontal axis for currency.

5. Change the colors and patterns on the bars.

6. Save the document as TOM.

7. Select and print the chart.

	A	B	C	D
1	TOM'S LUNCH COUNTER			
2	SALES REPORT-SECOND QUARTER			
3				
4		April	May	June
5	Hamburger	1025	1163	986
6	Ham Sandwich	965	972	765
7	Chicken Sandwich	1076	1154	893

2. Create a formula in cell C9 to use Vertical Lookup to search through the range B27..E30 to find the data in cell B9 (Clerk). Enter the amount located one column to the immediate right of Clerk (the hourly rate).

3. Key a formula in cell D9 to use Vertical Lookup to search through the range B27..E30 to find the data in cell B9 (Clerk). Enter the amount located two columns to the immediate right of Clerk (the daily rate).

4. Key a formula in cell E9 to use Vertical Lookup to search through the range B27..E30 to find the data in cell B9 (Clerk). Enter the amount located three columns to the immediate right of Clerk (the weekly rate).

5. Copy and paste C9..E9 to cells C10..E19 to complete the billing rates.

6. Right align the column headings in columns C, D, and E on rows 6, 7, 24, and 25.

7. Save the spreadsheet as MCPHEE.

8. Format the spreadsheet for fixed format with zero decimal places.

9. Print the range A1..E19.

The employee charge schedule for McPhee Accounting Firm has been revised.

10. Change the rates in the Employee Charge Schedule as follows.

Clerk	9	72	325
CPA	65	520	
Secretary	11	88	425

11. Sort the spreadsheet so the positions (column B) are in ascending order.

12. Use Save As to save the spreadsheet as MCPHEE2.

13 Print the range A1..E19.

JOB 63

Create a Chart and Add Attributes

Hightime Department Store would like a chart to compare each department's sales to the total sales. Create a pie chart to show this information.

1. Create the spreadsheet as shown below. Right align the column headings.

2. Determine the totals in cells B9, C9, and D9.

3. Format all the numbers for commas with zero decimal places.

4. Select cells B4..D4 for the labels and cells B9..D9 for the numeric amounts, and create a pie chart with labels and percentages in a range of your choice.

5. Use the data in rows 1 and 2 of the spreadsheet for the main title.

6. Explode the wedge with the highest sales.

7. Save the document as HIGHTIME.

8. Select and print the chart.

	A	B	C	D
1	HIGHTIME DEPARTMENT STORE			
2	SALES REPORT - FIRST QUARTER			
3				
4		Men	Women	Children
5	January	10250	11630	9860
6	February	9650	9720	7650
7	March	10005	11540	8930
8				
9	Total			

FINISH

Use Vertical Lookup

Prepare a billing rate schedule for staff members at McPhee Accounting Firm.

1. Create the spreadsheet below, and adjust the column widths as necessary.

	A	B	C	D	E
1	MCPHEE ACCOUNTING FIRM				
2	SAN FRANCISCO, CALIFORNIA				
3					
4	BILLING RATES PER STAFF MEMBER				
5					
6			Hourly	Daily	Weekly
7	Staff	Position	Rate	Rate	Rate
8					
9	Kedy, Scott	Clerk	*formula*	*formula*	*formula*
10	Key, Chad	Accountant			
11	Meharg, Jonathan	CPA			
12	Mettry, Shelley	CPA			
13	Pyrum, Drew	Accountant			
14	Quinlan, Julie	Accountant			
15	Sanders, Chase	Accountant			
16	Sanders, Whitney	Accountant			
17	Taylor, Niki	Clerk			
18	Walbrick, Bo	Clerk			
19	Weems, Julie	Secretary			
20					
21					
22	EMPLOYEE CHARGE SCHEDULE				
23					
24			Hourly	Daily	Weekly
25		Position	Rate	Rate	Rate
26					
27		Accountant	40	320	1500
28		Clerk	8	64	300
29		CPA	60	480	2000
30		Secretary	10	80	400

Continued on Next Page

Create an HLCO Chart

The most common use of the HLCO (High-Low-Close-Open) chart is to show stock prices. Walt Azinger would like to evaluate his stock with Pacific Medical (PcMed). Prepare a five-day report for the week of February 7.

1. Create the spreadsheet as shown below. Right align the column headings, and format the values in the spreadsheet for fixed with three decimal places.

2. Create an HLCO chart. If the HLCO chart is not available, use a bar chart.

3. Use the data in rows 1 and 2 of the spreadsheet for the chart title.

4. The y-axis title is "Price" and the x-axis title is "Date."

5. To make the chart more readable, change the intervals on the y-axis (72.000, 74.000, etc.). Change the major interval to 2.

6. Add grids at the major intervals of the y-axis.

7. Save the document as PCMED.

8. Select and print the chart.

	A	B	C	D	E
1		PACIFIC MEDICAL			
2		Week of February 7 - February 11, 19--			
3					
4		High	Low	Close	Open
5					
6	2/7	75.125	72.5	74.5	74.375
7	2/8	76.625	74.5	76	74.5
8	2/9	79.875	76	77.5	76
9	2/10	80.125	77	79	77.5
10	2/11	82	79	80.75	79

FINISH

Erin and Phil Richie have decided to start a college savings plan for their new baby. Create a spreadsheet so they can determine how much money they will have if they deposit $1,000, $2,000, or $3,000 at the end of each year. They expect the money to earn an average interest of 6% and plan to make 18 payments.

Save the spreadsheet as RICHIE. Print the spreadsheet.

JOB 65

Create an HLCO Chart and Add Attributes

Walt Azinger wants to evaluate his stock with Safe Card (SafeCd). He will need another chart.

1. Create the spreadsheet as shown below. Right align the column headings, and format the values in the spreadsheet for fixed with three decimal places.

2. Create an HLCO chart for the week of February 7 through February 11 in the range All..F26. If the HLCO chart is not available, use a bar chart.

3. Use the data from rows 1 and 2 of the spreadsheet for the chart title.

4. The y-axis title is "Price," and the x-axis title is "Date."

5. Save the file with the name SAFECD.

6. Print the full document (spreadsheet and chart).

	A	B	C	D	E
1			SAFE CARD		
2		Week of February 7 - February 11, 19--			
3					
4		High	Low	Close	Open
5					
6	2/7	20.125	19	19.875	19
7	2/8	22.125	19.875	20.125	19.875
8	2/9	22	19.75	21.125	20.125
9	2/10	22.25	21.125	22	21.125
10	2/11	22.125	19.875	22.125	22

JOB 89

Use the Future Value Function

Larry Kaebnick is 25 years old, and he plans to retire at age 65. Create a spreadsheet for Larry Kaebnick to show how much money he will have for his retirement fund when he retires.

1. Create the spreadsheet as shown below.

2. Use the Future Value function to show how much money he would have at age 65 if he invested $1,000 per year in a retirement fund. Assume the interest rate is 6%.

3. Right align the column headings. Format column A for currency with zero decimal places, column B for percent with zero decimal places, and column D for currency with two decimal places. Adjust the column widths as necessary.

4. Save the spreadsheet as RETIRE.

5. Print the spreadsheet.

	A	B	C	D
1		LARRY KAEBNICK		
2		RETIREMENT FUND		
3				
4	Annual	Interest	No. of	Retirement
5	Deposit	Rate	Payments	Value
6				
7	1000			*formula*

JOB 66

Create an XY (Scatter) Chart

Computer Disk Outlet sells disks in bulk—the more disks purchased, the lower the unit price. Prepare a chart to show this relationship.

1. Create the spreadsheet as shown below. Right align the column headings, and format the values in column B for currency with two decimal places.

2. Select the range A10..B16, and create an XY (Scatter) chart with vertical and horizontal grid lines for the purchase price of a disk.

3. Add the title "COMPUTER DISK OUTLET." The title for the x-axis is "Number Purchased," and the title for the y-axis is "Price per Disk."

	A	B	C
1	COMPUTER DISK OUTLET		
2	Buy Bulk		
3			
4	Price Sheet for March, 19--		
5			
6		Price	
7	Number	per	
8	Purchased	Disk	
9			
10	1	0.98	
11	25	0.8	
12	50	0.7	
13	75	0.65	
14	100	0.6	
15	150	0.55	
16	200	0.5	

Continued on Next Page

2. In cell D7, key a Future Value formula to show the future value of an account when you save a regular amount at rates of 5 and 6 percent for periods of 5 and 10 years.

3. Copy and paste the formula to complete column D.

4. Right align the column headings. Format column A for commas with zero decimal places, column B for percent with zero decimal places, and column D for commas with two decimal places.

5. Save the spreadsheet as FUTURE.

6. Print the spreadsheet.

4. Change the major unit of the x-axis to 25.

5. Format the y-axis for currency with two decimal places.

6. Delete or hide the legend.

7. Increase the size of the chart.

8. Save the document as OUTLET.

9. Select and print the chart.

Use the Future Value Function

Create a spreadsheet for First State Bank to show the future value of a periodic savings plan.

1. Create the spreadsheet as shown below.

	A	B	C	D	E
1			FIRST STATE BANK		
2			FUTURE VALUE OF A PLANNED SAVINGS ACCOUNT		
3					
4		INTEREST	NUMBER OF		
5	AMOUNT	RATE	PAYMENTS	VALUE	
6					
7	100	0.05	5	*formula*	
8	500	0.05	5		
9	1000	0.05	5		
10	2000	0.05	5		
11					
12	100	0.05	10		
13	500	0.05	10		
14	1000	0.05	10		
15	2000	0.05	10		
16					
17	100	0.06	5		
18	500	0.06	5		
19	1000	0.06	5		
20	2000	0.06	5		
21					
22	100	0.06	10		
23	500	0.06	10		
24	1000	0.06	10		
25	2000	0.06	10		

Continued on Next Page

Create a Map

Instead of a standard chart, the management of Sunset Medical wants the sales information illustrated with a map.

1. Create the spreadsheet as shown below. Format the values in column C for commas with zero decimal places.

2. If available with your software, create a map in the range E1..L25 for Sales of the Southwestern Region.

	A	B	C
1	SUNSET MEDICAL SUPPLIES		
2	Sales Report, 19--		
3			
4	Southwestern Region		
5			
6	Arizona		23562000
7	New Mexico		26948000
8	Oklahoma		18220000
9	Texas		98849000
10			
11	Rocky Mountain Region		
12			
13	Montana		6589000
14	Idaho		3958000
15	Wyoming		13928000
16	Nevada		952000
17	Utah		1831000
18	Colorado		44000000

Continued on Next Page

JOB 87

Modify and Sort a Database

Westcox, Inc. wants you to add employee numbers to its spreadsheet.

1. Open WESTCOX.

2. Increase the salary of all employees in the sales department by 10%.

3. Increase the salary of all employees in the art department by 6%.

4. Bill F. Claxton in the Dallas office has been replaced with John L. Herndon. His salary is $80,000.

5. Sort the employee names in ascending order.

6. Insert one column to the left of what is now column A.

7. Use bold print and center the headings "Employee" in cell A5 and "Number" in cell A6. Adjust the column width as necessary.

8. Use the Fill feature to enter the employee numbers. Start with 1000 and increase by 100.

9. Recenter the title across the columns.

10. Use Save As to save the spreadsheet as WESTCOX6.

11. Print the spreadsheet.

JOB 67

Continued

3. Add the title "Southwestern Region."

4. If necessary, edit the legend. Do not use compact format. If needed, size and move the legend.

5. Save the document as SUNSET.

6. Select and print the map.

Modify and Sort a Database

Outstanding Video Network wants to keep a list of the number of packages it has available. Use the Data Fill function to number these items.

1. Open TAPES5.

2. The following items need to be deleted from the inventory: 595V, 015V, 993V, 266V, 145V, 113V, 111V, 118V, and 804V.

3. Add the following items.

995V	Inflation	3	Fritz Co.	39.95
996V	Utility Package	2	Hi Tec Co.	29.95

4. Center the column heading "Package" in cell G6 and "Number" in cell G7.

5. Move the cell pointer to cell G9 and key "1." Use the Fill feature to enter numbers 1–32 in cells G9..G40. Center column G.

6. Center the data in column C.

7. Add "Total" in cell A42.

8. Create a formula or use the Autosum feature to calculate the total cost per package in cell F42.

9. Format for commas with two decimal places. Adjust column width as necessary.

10. Sort the catalog numbers in column A in ascending order.

11. Use Save As to save the spreadsheet as TAPES6.

12. Print the spreadsheet.

JOB 68

Create a Map

1. Create the spreadsheet as shown below. Make the heading bold.

2. Select cells A6..C9, and create a map (if available with your software). Use the "Europe Countries" map.

3. Use the Zoom feature to gain a closer view of the countries. Place the map in cells A4..F19.

4. Add the title "Flights to Europe."

5. If necessary, edit the legend. Do not use compact format. Size and move the legend if needed.

6. Recenter the heading across the columns.

7. Save the document as FLIGHTS.

8. Print the full document centered horizontally and vertically on the page.

	A	B	C
1	WORLD FLIGHT AIRLINES		
2	Summer, 19--		
3			
4	Country		No. of Flights
5			
6	Germany		220
7	France		489
8	Italy		206
9	Switzerland		209

4. Determine the net amount due in column G. (The net amount is the amount of invoice minus the cash discount.)

5. Format the appropriate columns for commas with two decimal places. Center column D.

6. Save the spreadsheet as BUTLER.

7. Print the spreadsheet.

CHAPTER 10

Jobs 69–100
Create and Use
Database and Other
Miscellaneous Functions

Time Estimate: 15 hrs.

OBJECTIVES

In this chapter, students will:

1. Sort data

2. Use Spell Check and sort a database

3. Sort data and extract records

4. Create a template for a balance sheet

5. Use a template for a balance sheet

6. Create a template for a depreciation schedule

7. Use a template for a depreciation schedule

8. Create a template for an amortization table

9. Use a template for an amortization table

10. Create a template for an invoice

11. Use a template for an invoice

12. Use the IF function

13. Modify and sort a database

14. Use the Future Value function

15. Use Vertical Lookup

16. Use Horizontal Lookup

17. Integrate a spreadsheet and a word processing document

18. Integrate spreadsheet, word processing, and graphics

JOB 85

Use the IF Function

Create a report for Butler Manufacturing Company to determine which of their customers will receive a cash discount. Butler Manufacturing allows a 2% cash discount if the invoice is paid within 10 days.

1. Create the spreadsheet as shown below and center the column headings. Format columns B and C as shown below.

2. Prepare an IF statement in cell F7 to determine the cash discount. The customer receives a 2% cash discount if the invoice is paid within 10 days. If the invoice is paid after 10 days, a zero should appear.

3. Copy and paste the formula to complete column F.

	A	B	C	D	E	F	G
1			BUTLER MANUFACTURING				
2			INVOICE PAYMENT SCHEDULE				
3							
4	Account	Date of	Date of	Payment	Amount of	Cash	Net Amount
5	Number	Invoice	Payment	Period	Invoice	Discount	Due
6							
7	5676	1/4/96	1/14/97	10	985.45	*formula*	*formula*
8	7856	1/4/96	1/31/97	27	1222.55		
9	6545	1/7/96	1/10/97	3	456.98		
10	5267	1/7/96	1/28/97	21	2223.25		
11	6545	1/10/96	1/15/97	5	888.52		
12	4326	1/10/96	1/20/97	10	1222.36		
13	1239	1/11/96	1/28/97	17	989.52		
14	5678	1/11/96	1/26/97	15	1256.88		
15	4587	1/14/96	1/20/97	6	852.26		
16	2345	1/17/96	1/31/97	14	456.77		
17	6545	1/20/96	1/25/97	5	1886.67		
18	3478	1/24/96	1/31/97	7	978.88		
19	7788	1/28/96	2/4/97	7	2322.25		

Continued on Next Page

Sort Data

The Sports Grill would like the employees on the payroll listed in alphabetical order.

1. Open GRILL.

2. Insert two rows above row 19.

3. Add the new employee information as shown below in rows 19 and 20. To complete the payroll information for these employees, use the Copy and Paste functions to insert formulas in columns D–H.

4. Edit the formulas in rows 22–25 to include rows 19 and 20.

5. Use Save As to save the spreadsheet as GRILL2.

6. Sort the employee names in column A in alphabetical order (ascending).

7. Save and print the spreadsheet.

	A	B	C
19	Christopher, Jamie	5	20
20	Vance, William	5	20

JOB 84

Use the IF Function

Young's Video needs a report of accounts that are more than 30 days past due. If the account is more than 30 days past due, a 1.5% service charge is applied to the unpaid balance. Prepare a report to indicate which customers owe a service charge.

1. Create the spreadsheet as shown below. Center the column headings, and adjust column widths as necessary.

2. Prepare an IF statement in cell D7 to compute a 1.5% service charge on the account balance of all accounts that are more than 30 days past due. If the days overdue total less than 30 days, a zero should appear.

3. Copy and paste the formula to complete column D.

4. Format columns B and D for commas with two decimal places.

5. Save the spreadsheet as YOUNG.

6. Print the spreadsheet.

	A	B	C	D
1	Young's Video			
2	Schedule of Accounts Receivable			
3				
4		Account	Days	Service
5	Customer Name	Balance	Overdue	Charge
6				
7	Jacobs, Inc.	1452.25	31	*formula*
8	Creative Video	3235.26	10	
9	Horn and Company	999.65	35	
10	Medford Corporation	458.52	8	
11	Crestview, Inc.	1256.88	15	
12	Abbott and Associates	3256.85	10	
13	Taylor Interiors	1259.75	32	
14	King Storage	2352.25	60	
15	McPhee Enterprises	1235.45	33	

FINISH

Use Spell Check and Sort a Database

Outstanding Video Network would like an alphabetical list of the videos listed in its catalog.

1. Open TAPES3.

2. Use the Spell Check function.

3. Use the data range A9..F47, and sort the company (column D) in ascending order.

4. Use Save As to save the spreadsheet as TAPES4.

5. Print the spreadsheet.

6. When two or more records have the same entry in the first key, you need to choose a second key to decide the order of the matching records. Use column D (the company that developed the video) as the first key, and use column B (title of video) as the second key. Sort both columns in alphabetical (ascending) order.

7. Use Save As to save the spreadsheet as TAPES5.

8. Print the spreadsheet.

JOB 83

Use a Template

After Susan Hart has added her room, she still does not have enough living space, so she has decided to buy a new home. She has checked with Home Loan and Savings Company and has found that she can borrow money at an 8% rate for 20 years (240 months). After reviewing her budget, she decides that she can make a down payment of $10,000 and payments of $1,000 per month.

Use the spreadsheet named AMORT to determine the monthly payment for the houses listed below. The base month for the loan is May. Print spreadsheets (range A1..D10) for the homes she can afford. Key the address of the home in cell A2. Save the spreadsheets you print using the first six characters in the street name as your file name.

6001 N. Brookline	$ 89,500
8401 East Reno	165,000
1111 North Dewey	115,000
4821 Agnew	145,500
7102 N. Classen	159,000

JOB 71

Sort Data and Extract Records

Westcox, Inc. would like a list of its employees that includes the city of employment and the employee's department assignment. The list should also include current salary and the number of years each employee has worked for the company.

1. Key the spreadsheet as shown below. Make the title bold, and adjust the column widths as necessary.

	A	B	C	D	E
1	WESTCOX, INC.				
2	BRANCH OFFICES				
3	EMPLOYEE RECORDS				
4					
5	Employee	Office			Years of
6	Name	Location	Department	Salary	Experience
7	Aaron, Vicki S.	Dallas	Art	48000	15
8	Page, Ryan	Dallas	Production	32000	11
9	Carew, Barbara K.	Houston	Sales	66900	7
10	Lewis, Ken T.	Los Angeles	Administration	75800	12
11	Ryan, Janice P.	Los Angeles	Administration	75000	11
12	Ferguson, Tamika	Houston	Art	36000	5
13	Cranford, Taylor	Chicago	Sales	37200	3
14	Mayes, Mikella	Dallas	Sales	44100	2
15	Frye, Amy L.	Chicago	Administration	86200	15
16	Irwin, Glenda M.	Los Angeles	Sales	26000	0
17	Claxton, Bill F.	Dallas	Administration	84000	15
18	Nelson, Leon J.	Los Angeles	Art	28000	2
19	Meharg, Tommie	Los Angeles	Art	28200	2
20	Bender, Jeffrey G.	Chicago	Art	36000	6
21	Ward, Joel	Chicago	Administration	71400	5
22	Oakley, Stacy L.	Dallas	Sales	80800	12
23	Harless, Stephen	Houston	Administration	70000	4

Continued on Next Page

JOB 82

Continued

4. Create a second invoice for South-West Vending with the same template. Enter the information as shown below.

5. Save the spreadsheet as ARBUCK2.

6. Print the spreadsheet.

INVOICE NUMBER: M20651
INVOICE DATE: September 21, 19--
TERMS: Net 30
SALES REP.:   Katrina Morris
SHIPPED: Will Transit, Inc.
PREPAID OR COLLECT: Prepaid

QUANTITY:	DESCRIPTION	UNIT PRICE
6	Easy Reference CD-Rom (photographs)	99.95
4	The Gallery 2X (clipart images)	64.95
FREIGHT:	3.00	

2. Center and bold the column headings in rows 5 and 6. Format column D for commas with zero decimal places. Center the data in column E.

3. Save the spreadsheet as WESTCOX.

4. Sort the spreadsheet so that employee names in column A are in ascending order.

5. Save and print the spreadsheet.

6. Sort the spreadsheet so that the salaries in column D are in descending order (from highest to lowest).

7. Use Save As to save the spreadsheet as WESTCOX2.

8. Print the spreadsheet.

9. Use Autofilter (extract) to list all employees who work in the Dallas office.

10. Change cell A2 to "Dallas Offices."

11. Use Save As to save the spreadsheet as WESTCOX3.

12. Print the extracted records.

JOB 82

Use a Template for an Invoice

Arbuckle Sports Association needs invoices for merchandise sold to South-West Vending Sales.

1. Create an invoice with the invoice template you created in Job 81. Enter the information as shown below.

2. Save the spreadsheet as ARBUCK.

3. Print the spreadsheet.

SOLD TO:	South-West Vending Sales
	4430 Memorial
	Morgantown, IN 46160
SHIPPED TO:	South-West Vending Sales
	922 Sheridan
	Morgantown, IN 46160
INVOICE NUMBER:	M20642
INVOICE DATE:	September 9, 19--
TERMS:	Net 30
SALES REP.:	Katrina Morris
SHIPPED:	Will Transit, Inc.
PREPAID OR COLLECT:	Prepaid

QUANTITY	DESCRIPTION	UNIT PRICE
4	Laser Printer Labels (400 labels)	5.95
3	Disk Files (200 files)	10.99
10	3.5" Disks (HD, package of 10)	6.99
FREIGHT:	4.50	

Continued on Next Page

JOB 72

Extract Records

Westcox would like a list of all employees who work in the Art Department and another of all employees who work in the Administration Department and make less than $80,000.

1. Open WESTCOX2.

2. Use Autofilter (extract) to list all employees who work in the Art Department.

3. Use Save As to save the spreadsheet as WESTCOX4.

4. Use Page Setup to center the spreadsheet horizontally.

5. Print the extracted records with the header "EMPLOYEES - ART DEPARTMENT." Save the spreadsheet.

6. Open WESTCOX2.

7. Use Autofilter (extract) to list all employees in the Administration Department who make less than (<) $80,000.

8. Use Save As to save the spreadsheet as WESTCOX5.

9. Use Page Setup to center the spreadsheet horizontally.

10. Print the extracted records with the header "EMPLOYEES - ADMINISTRATION DEPARTMENT (salaries under $80,000)."

11. Save the spreadsheet.

	A	**B**	**C**	**D**
1				*INVOICE*
2				
3		**Arbuckle Sports Association**		
4	440 East Park Street		Inv. No.:	
5	Oklahoma City, OK 73122		Inv. Date:	
6	Tele.: 555-555-1212		Terms:	
7	Fax: 555-555-1200		Sales Rep.:	
8			Shipped:	
9	SOLD TO:		Prepaid or Collect:	
10				
11				
12				
13				
14	SHIPPED TO:			
15				
16				
17				
18				
19	QUANTITY	DESCRIPTION	UNIT PRICE	AMOUNT
20				*formula*
21				
22				
23				
24				
25			SUBTOTAL	*formula*
26			TAX	*formula*
27			FREIGHT	
28	Questions concerning this invoice? 555-555-5506		Pay this amount	*formula*
29				

FINISH

JOB 73

Sort Data and Extract Records

Create a spreadsheet showing alumni information for Eastlake Business College.

1. Create the spreadsheet as shown below. Make the title and column headings bold. Adjust the column widths as necessary.

2. Format column I for commas with zero decimal places.

3. Save the spreadsheet as ALUMNI.

4. Print the spreadsheet on one page.

5. Use Autofilter (extract) to list all accountants who live in Texas.

	A	B	C	D	E	F	G	H	I
1				EASTLAKE BUSINESS COLLEGE					
2				ALUMNI INFORMATION					
3									
4	Last	First	Sex	Address	City	State	Graduated	Profession	Salary
5	Short	Kari	F	105 W. Cottage	Albuquerque	NM	1992	Comptroller	25262
6	Svetgoff	Julia	F	232 Belmont	Amarillo	TX	1992	Accountant	26850
7	Vasquez	Shawn	M	104 S. Monroe	Abilene	TX	1993	Analyst	23256
8	Hamlett	Melissa	F	467 Stadium Dr.	Houston	TX	1992	Buyer	20255
9	Buxton	Katie	F	672 Kerr Lab Dr.	Dallas	TX	1989	Analyst	32555
10	Hoover	Angie	F	322 Sandy Creek Dr.	Carlsbad	NM	1992	Accountant	27555
11	Walbrick	T.K.	F	256 Highland	Childress	TX	1993	Sales	18958
12	Miller	Meagan	F	133 Gardina Dr.	Dallas	TX	1992	Marketing	21566
13	Boatwright	Brent	M	723 Broadway	El Paso	TX	1991	Accountant	16899
14	Smith	John	M	1416 Cherry Blvd.	Roswell	NM	1992	Secretary	16899
15	Odom	Brian	M	1433 Johnston Blvd.	Houston	TX	1993	Programmer	22567
16	Cowart	Carley	F	2335 Lakeview Dr.	Dallas	TX	1990	Secretary	23599
17	Glasgow	Courtney	F	233 Ridgeview Dr.	Oklahoma City	OK	1989	Sales	18555
18	Boatwright	Dale	M	236 Valley View Rd.	Shreveport	LA	1988	Accountant	33555
19	Choate	Lauren	F	233 Richard	Little Rock	AR	1992	Marketing	36325
20	Bodine	Sarah	F	1544 Fairview	Ft. Worth	TX	1990	Programmer	32547
21	Cowart	Andrew	M	2230 N. Monta Vista	Denton	TX	1990	Sales	28963
22	Smith	Reagan	F	456 Townsend	Arlington	TX	1991	Accountant	26588
23	Wolff	Rodney	M	1223 Augusta	Houston	TX	1991	Buyer	27850

Continued on Next Page

Create a Template for an Invoice

Create a template invoice for Arbuckle Sports Association.

1. Create the invoice template as shown on the next page. Change column widths as follows: column A = 10 spaces, column B = 30 spaces, and columns C and D = 15 spaces. Make adjustments to point size, style, and alignment as shown. Shade row 19 as shown on the next page.

2. Center "QUANTITY" and the cells under this heading (A19..A24).

3. Right align "UNIT PRICE" and the cells under this heading (C19..C24).

4. Right align "AMOUNT" and the cells under this heading (D19..D28).

5. Create a formula in cell D20 to multiply quantity by unit price. Copy and paste this formula to cells D21..D24.

6. Create a formula in cell D25 to add cells D20..D24.

7. Create a formula to multiply the subtotal (D25) by the tax rate (8%).

8. Create a formula in cell D28 to add cells D25..D27.

9. Format the numbers in columns C and D for commas with two decimal places.

10. Save the template as INVOICE.

11. Print the worksheet.

Continued on Next Page

6. Sort the extracted records so that last names are in alphabetical order.

7. Use Save As to save the spreadsheet as ALUMNI2.

8. Print the extracted records with the header "ACCOUNTANTS WHO LIVE IN TEXAS." Save the spreadsheet.

9. Use Autofilter (extract) to list *all* of the alumni who graduated after 1990 and live in Houston or Dallas. You may need to open ALUMNI first.

10. Sort the extracted data in ascending order by year graduated and alphabetically by last name.

11. Use Save As to save the spreadsheet as ALUMNI3.

12. Print the extracted data with the header "ALUMNI LIVING IN HOUSTON OR DALLAS (graduated after 1990)." Save the spreadsheet.

JOB 80

Use a Template for an Amortization Table

Susan Hart is adding a room to her house. She will borrow the money for this addition from the First State Bank.

1. Open AMORT.

2. Starting in cell D6, key the amounts below to create an amortization table for her loan.

Loan Principal Amount:	$20,500.00
Annual Interest Rate:	7%
Number of Monthly Payments:	24

3. Use Save As to save the spreadsheet as HART.

4. Print the spreadsheet.

Susan Hart has found another institution that will lend her the money for her new room at 5%. She would like to revise the amortization table and extend the loan for 30 months to get a lower payment.

5. Edit the amortization table, and enter the amounts as shown below.

Loan Principal Amount:	$20,500.00
Annual Interest Rate:	5%
Number of Monthly Payments:	30

6. Use Save As to save the spreadsheet as HART2.

7. Print the spreadsheet on one page.

JOB 74

Sort Data and Extract Records

Create a spreadsheet for Walker Real Estate's current listings. They need a current listing for all of the houses in the area that have more than 2,500 square feet and cost less than $190,000.

1. Create the spreadsheet as shown below. Center and bold the title and column headings. Adjust the column widths as necessary.

2. Format columns B and G for commas with zero decimal places.

3. Use Save As to save the spreadsheet as WALKER.

	A	B	C	D	E	F	G
1	WALKER REAL ESTATE						
2	CURRENT LISTINGS						
3							
4	Address	Sq. Ft.	Bedrooms	Baths	Heat	Age	Cost
5	723 Motiff Drive	2449	4	3	Gas	2	170500
6	283 N. Greenley Drive	1500	3	2	Electric	3	75000
7	251 18th Street	2550	3	2	Electric	5	162500
8	101 Prospect Ave.	3342	4	3	Electric	1	215500
9	145 Augusta Drive	2000	3	2	Electric	4	125500
10	400 E. Murfield Drive	2863	3	2	Gas	3	185500
11	98 Collins Blvd.	2931	3	2	Gas	2	190500
12	432 Blossom Circle	2211	3	3	Gas	5	140500
13	231 Sam Houston	2277	3	3	Electric	10	123500
14	281 Riverside Drive	2561	4	3	Gas	8	126465
15	182 Churchill Drive	3177	4	3	Gas	25	205000
16	252 Whispering Hills	1366	3	2	Electric	7	68790
17	115 Willowbrook	4025	5	4	Gas	15	240500
18	425 University Street	1800	3	2	Gas	22	92500
19	533 Banks Street	2210	4	2	Gas	18	123500
20	88 Melrose Drive	1698	3	2	Gas	4	100500

Continued on Next Page

6. Copy cell B18 and paste to cells B19..B41 for payments 2–24.

7. Move the cell pointer to cell C18, and create a formula to calculate the Interest for the first payment.

8. Move the cell pointer to cell D18, and create a formula to calculate the Principle Amortization for the first payment.

9. Move the cell pointer to cell E18, and create a formula to calculate the remaining balance after the first payment.

10. Copy cells C18..E18 and paste to cells C19..E41 to complete the amortization table.

11. Format cell D6 for currency with zero decimal places.

12. Format cell D7 for percent with zero decimal places.

13. Format cells B10..E41 for commas with two decimal places.

14. Save the template as AMORT.

15. Print the document.

4. Print the spreadsheet.

5. Extract the houses that have more than 2,500 square feet and cost less than $190,000.

6. Sort the extracted data in descending order by cost.

7. Use Save As to save the spreadsheet as WALKER2.

8. Print the extracted records with the header "OVER 2,500 SQ. FT. - UNDER $190,000." Save the spreadsheet.

9. Extract the houses that are ten years old or less, cost less than $125,000, and have three or more bedrooms.

10. Sort the extracted data in ascending order by cost.

11. Use Save As to save the spreadsheet as WALKER3.

12. Print the extracted data with the header "HOUSES UNDER $125,000 (not over 10 years old with at least three bedrooms)." Save the spreadsheet.

Create a Template for an Amortization Table

Create a template for an amortization table.

1. Create a 24-month amortization table by keying the information as shown below.

2. Move the cell pointer to cell D10, and calculate the monthly payment by creating a payment formula. When keying this formula, consider that the interest rate will be in cell D7, the number of payments in cell D8, and the principal in cell D6.

3. Move the cell pointer to cell E17, and key a reference for the principal (D6).

4. Use the Data Fill function to enter payment number 1–24 in cells A18..A41.

5. Move the cell pointer to cell B18, and key an absolute reference for the first payment.

	A	B	C	D	E
1	AMORTIZATION TABLE				
2					
3					
4					
5					
6	Loan Principal				
7	Annual Interest Rate				
8	Number of Monthly Payments				
9					
10	Monthly Payments Will Be			*formula*	
11					
12	Amortization Table				
13					
14					
15	Pmt.			Prin.	Prin.
16	No.	Pmt.	Int.	Amort.	Bal.

Continued on Next Page

Create a Template for a Balance Sheet

Cunningham Furniture prepares a balance sheet for each month of the year. Prepare a master spreadsheet showing the assets, liabilities, capital, and total liabilities and capital.

1. Create a template using the spreadsheet information as shown below.

2. Create a formula in cell E12 to compute the total assets.

	A	B	C	D	E
1			CUNNINGHAM FURNITURE		
2			BALANCE SHEET		
3			For the Month of		
4					
5	ASSETS:				
6	Cash				
7	Accounts Receivable				
8	Merchandise Inventory				
9	Supplies				
10	Prepaid Insurance				
11					
12	TOTAL ASSETS:				*formula*
13					
14	LIABILITIES:				
15	Accounts Payable				
16					
17	CAPITAL:				
18	Roger Cunningham, Capital				*formula*
19					
20	TOTAL LIABILITIES AND CAPITAL:				*formula*

Continued on Next Page

JOB 78

Use a Template for a Depreciation Schedule

Tipton Graphics purchased a new photocopy machine on January 4, 1996. Use the template you created in Job 77 to determine the annual depreciation.

1. Open DEPR.

2. In the cells indicated, enter the following information.

---

cell D4: Photocopy Machine
cell D5: 15500
cell D6: 1996
cell D8: 2500

---

3. Use Save As to save the spreadsheet as DEPR2.

4. Print the spreadsheet.

3. Create a formula in cell E18 to compute the capital (E12–E15).

4. Create a formula in cell E20 to compute the total liabilities and capital.

5. Place double underlines under cells E12 and E20.

6. Format column E for fixed with two decimal places and cells E12 and E20 for currency with two decimal places.

7. Save the spreadsheet as BALANCE.

8. Print the spreadsheet.

FINISH

6. Create a formula for the book value in cell D15 (D5-C15). Copy and paste the formula in cell D15 to cells D16..D19.

7. Create a formula to increase by one year in cell A16 (A15+1). Copy and paste the formula to cells A17..A19.

8. Create a formula for the accumulated depreciation in cell C16 (C15+B16). Copy and paste the formula to cells C17..C19.

9. Add double underlines above row 12 and below row 13.

10. Format cells D5, D8, and D9 for commas with zero decimal places.

11. Format cells B15..D19 for commas with zero decimal places.

12. Save the spreadsheet as DEPR.

13. Print the spreadsheet.

Use a Template for a Balance Sheet

1. Open BALANCE.

2. Prepare a balance sheet for Cunningham Furniture. Date the spreadsheet December, 19--.

3. Starting in cell E6, enter the amounts *only* under "Assets."

Cash	7650
Accounts Receivable	15777
Merchandise Inventory	82374
Supplies	840
Prepaid Insurance	525

4. In cell E15, enter the amount 15955 for accounts payable.

5. Adjust column widths as necessary.

6. Use Save As to save the spreadsheet as BALANCE2.

7. Print the spreadsheet.

8. Open BALANCE or edit BALANCE2.

9. Prepare a balance sheet for Cunningham Furniture. Date the spreadsheet January, 19--.

10. Starting in cell E6, enter the amounts *only* under "Assets."

Cash	10,878
Accounts Receivable	30,752
Merchandise Inventory	62,361
Supplies	750
Prepaid Insurance	425

11. The accounts payable balance is 15,055. Enter this value in column E.

12. Use Save As to save the spreadsheet as BALANCE3.

13. Print the spreadsheet.

Create a Template for a Depreciation Schedule

Tipton Graphics needs a depreciation schedule to determine the annual depreciation on equipment purchased if the useful life is five years.

1. Create a template with the spreadsheet information as shown below. Center the column headings in rows 12 and 13.

2. Create a formula in cell D9 for the annual depreciation (D5-D8/D7).

3. Enter a reference to cell D6 in cell A15.

4. Enter an absolute reference for cell D9 in cell B15 (D9). Copy and paste the absolute reference to cells B16..B19.

5. Enter a reference to cell B15 in cell C15.

	A	B	C	D
1	TIPTON GRAPHICS			
2	DEPRECIATION SCHEDULE			
3				
4	ASSET			
5	ORIGINAL COST			
6	YEAR ACQUIRED			
7	USEFUL LIFE			5
8	SALVAGE VALUE			
9	ANNUAL DEPRECIATION			*formula*
10				
11				
12		ANNUAL	ACCUM.	BOOK
13	YEAR	DEPR.	DEPR.	VALUE
14				
15	*reference*	*reference*	*reference*	*formula*
16	*formula*		*formula*	

Continued on Next Page

REFERENCE GUIDE

Letters

Block Style Letters

All letter parts begin at the left margin, and open or mixed punctuation may be used. See the following example of a block style letter.

Modified Block Style Letters

Dateline, complimentary close, signature line, and title begin at the center point. The paragraphs may be indented five spaces or blocked as shown in the example. Open or mixed punctuation may be used. See the following example of a modified block style letter.

Vertical Placement

Short or average letters (less than 200 words)	Centered on the page
Long letters (200 words or more)	2-inch top margins

Side Margins

Short letters (less than 100 words)	2-inch side margins
Average letters (100 to 200 words)	1.5-inch side margins
Long letters (more than 200 words)	1-inch side margins

Note: The margins may need to be adjusted if the letter has some unusual features such as additional lines in the address or the closing or tabulated material in the body of the letter.

Continued on Next Page

Block Style Letter with Open Punctuation

April 6, 19--   *(Press Enter 4 times)*

2S

Mr. Larry Hill
Douglas Business College
4409 Mississippi Avenue
El Cajon, CA 92021-4421
DS

Dear Mr. Hill
DS

Subject: Word Processing Positions
DS

I am happy to answer your request for information about the skills we require for word processing positions.
DS

Future applicants need the following skills: (1) the ability to type at least 50 words a minute, (2) the ability to proofread accurately, (3) the ability to spell, punctuate, divide words, and recognize proper sentence structure, and (4) the ability to key from handwritten rough drafts and edited typewritten copy.
DS

The best people for the jobs will be those who have excellent typing skills and who have experience in working with word processing equipment.
DS

I am enclosing an information sheet with skills needed for other positions with our company. If you have any further questions, please call me. My telephone number is 406-555-2244.
DS

Sincerely
2S

Connie Fleming
Personnel Manager
DS

kk
DS

Enclosure

Continued on Next Page

Continued

Modified Block Style Letter with Mixed Punctuation

(Start at center point)
April 6, 19--

DS

Mr. Larry Hill
Douglas Business College
4409 Mississippi Avenue
El Cajon, CA 92021-4421

DS

Dear Mr. Hill:

DS

Subject: Word Processing Positions

DS

I am happy to answer your request for information about the skills we require for word processing positions.

DS

Future applicants need the following skills: (1) the ability to type at least 50 words a minute, (2) the ability to proofread accurately, (3) the ability to spell, punctuate, divide words, and recognize proper sentence structure, and (4) the ability to key from handwritten rough drafts and edited typewritten copy.

DS

The best people for the jobs will be those who have excellent typing skills and who have experience in working with word processing equipment.

DS

I am enclosing an information sheet with skills needed for other positions with our company. If you have any further questions, please call me. My telephone number is 406-555-2244.

DS

(Start at center point)
Sincerely,

DS

FLEMING CORP.

DS

Connie Fleming
Personnel Manager

DS

kk

DS

Enclosure

Formatting guides for an *unbound report* are shown in the example on the following page.

For *leftbound report* format, change the left margin to 1.5 inches.

For *topbound report* format, change the top margin for page 1 to 2 inches and the top margin for all other pages to 1.5 inches. Center the page numbers at the bottom of each page.

Continued on Next Page

REFERENCE GUIDE

Continued

UNBOUND REPORT, pages 1 and 2

1.5-inch
top margin

WHAT A BUSINESS EXPECTS FROM PROSPECTIVE EMPLOYEES

28

Recommended Skills

28

Computer Skills. Today almost all companies use computers in one form or another. Employees must be computer literate to find a place in the business world (John Williams, 1992, 321). Any computer experience you have will be helpful to you when you apply for an office job.

Accounting Skills. A day seldom goes by in most companies when basic accounting skills are not used. Debits, credits, depreciation, and the general ledger are common business terms. As Susan Coleman (1991, 36) points out: "If you have at least a good basic understanding of accounting, you will have the edge on many of your fellow employees."

1-inch
side margin

Communication Skills. Businesses today require employees to possess both strong speaking and writing skills. Though often overlooked, listening is also an important communication skill.

You are encouraged to take as many "speech" classes as your schedule will allow. These classes help remove the natural fear of speaking before a group and teach you to write and speak clearly and to listen carefully.

Your ability to communicate well will set you apart from other job applicants or employees.

1-inch
side margin

At least 1-inch
bottom margin

1-inch top margin   2 *(page number)*
                                                          DS

Applying or Interviewing for Employment

In many places of business, the way you apply for a job is "graded" and has a lot to do with whether or not you get the job. Listed below are some guidelines to follow when interviewing for employment.

<table>
<tr><td>1.</td><td>Dress appropriately. Do not wear jeans or tennis shoes! Men are encouraged to wear slacks, a dress shirt, and dress shoes. Women are encouraged to wear a business suit with hose and shoes with low heels.</td></tr>
<tr><td>2.</td><td>Be prepared. Bring a pen and any other material you will need to complete the job application. Bring a list of questions you wish to ask the interviewer about the job.</td></tr>
<tr><td>3.</td><td>Be polite and courteous. The impression you make on the receptionist who gives you the application form may have as much to do with whether or not you get the job as your skills do.</td></tr>
<tr><td>4.</td><td>Fill out the application completely. It is very important to fill out each area completely. Write "N/A" in areas of the application which do not apply to you.</td></tr>
<tr><td>5.</td><td>Bring your reference list. Nearly every job application will have a place for you to list references.</td></tr>
</table>

1.5-inch indents for numerical items (left margin annotation)

1.5-inch indents for numerical items (right margin annotation)

2S

REFERENCES

2S
Coleman, Sarah. "Employment Strategies." *Business World Today*, (Fall 1991).
DS
Williams, John. *Employment.* 12th ed. Boston: Fillmore Publishing Company, 1992.

At least 1-inch bottom margin

Two styles of memorandums are commonly used—the *formal memorandum* and the *simplified memorandum*. The top margins should be 1 inch or 1.5 inches and the side margins should be 1 inch. All paragraphs begin at the left margin.

A memorandum may be printed on a full sheet or a half sheet of paper. Formal memorandums may be prepared on forms with special printed headings. When forms are not available, prepare formal memorandum in the style shown.

See the examples of memorandum styles on the following pages.

Formal Memorandum

1.5-inch
top margin

TO: *(Tab 2 times)* All Office Employees
SS
FROM: Katie Stephens, Personnel Director
SS
DATE: January 4, 19--
SS
SUBJECT: Reception for New Employees
SS

I am pleased to announce that we have several new employees to fill new positions created by growth in the firm. Please join me in welcoming them to the company.
SS

Kunio Akita, director of marketing, joins us from the west coast region. Kunio is from the Fox Corporation where he was assistant marketing director.
SS

Julie Anderson, office manager, comes from the Indianapolis area. Julie joins us from a local firm where she was in charge of office administration and payroll.
SS

Greg Patton will be director of security. Greg joins us from a local security firm.
SS

A reception will be held for our new employees in the employee dining room, Tuesday, January 8, 19--. All employees are invited.
SS

kk

At least 1-inch
bottom margin

1-inch side margin (left)   *1-inch side margin* (right)

Continued on Next Page

Simplified Memorandum

1-inch
top margin

November 9, 19--

2S

All Secretaries
DS
MANAGING YOUR TIME
DS
In even the busiest offices there are quiet days. Such days present opportunities to catch up on all kinds of matters that cannot be taken care of on busy days. This precious time should not be wasted. Below are some suggested things to do:
DS
1. One of the first jobs might be some housecleaning. Start with your desk, restocking it with supplies and discarding unneeded items.
    DS
2. Even the best-organized files need attention from time to time. Certain sections will need arranging. Some folders will need new labels.

1-inch   *DS*   *1-inch*

side margin   3 .   Records such as address lists, personal telephone lists, and special reference lists   *side margin*
                     need updating from time to time.
DS
You will be able to think of numerous other jobs that can be done during this time to make your job much easier during a busy time. Make a list and have it available for use.
2S

A. B. Phillips
DS
kk

At least 1-inch
bottom margin

FINISH

REFERENCE GUIDE

Proofreader's Marks

Capitalize Caps or ≡

Close up ◠

Delete ⌐

Insert ∧

Insert comma ⌄

Insert space # or |

Move right]

Move left [

Set in lowercase lc or /

Paragraph ¶

No new paragraph no new ¶

Let it stand; Ignore correction stet

Transpose ∪ or tr

Underline —————

Double-space for 1 blank line DS

Quadruple-space for 3 blank lines QS

Spell out ◯ sp